MW01234645

BIBLIOGRAPHIC RECORD TARGET

Graduate Library
University of Michigan

Preservation Office

Storage Number: _____

ABN2472
UL FMT B RT a BL m T/C DT 07/18/88 R/DT 07/18/88 CC STAT mm E/L 1
010: : |a   46033810//r85
035/1: : |a (RLIN)MIUG86-B41895
035/2: : |a (CaOTULAS)160031648
040: : |a DLC/ICU |c ICU |d MiU
050/1:0 : |a QA483 |b .E2
100:1 : |a Eagles, T. H. |q (Thomas Henry)
245:00: |a Constructive geometry of plane curves. |b With numerous examples, |c by T. H. Eagles.
260: : |a London, |b Macmillan & Co., |c 1885.
300/1: : |a xx, 374 p. |b illus. (diagrs.) |c 19 cm.
590/1: : |a engn: ENGIN copy imperfect: title page lacking, manucscript t.-p. inserted
650/1: 0: |a Geometry, Descriptive
998: : |c RSH |s 9120

CONSTRUCTIVE GEOMETRY

OF

PLANE CURVES.

CONSTRUCTIVE GEOMETRY

OF

PLANE CURVES

WITH NUMEROUS EXAMPLES

BY

T. H. EAGLES, M.A.

INSTRUCTOR IN GEOMETRICAL DRAWING AND LECTURER IN ARCHITECTURE
AT THE ROYAL INDIAN ENGINEERING COLLEGE, COOPERS HILL.

London:

MACMILLAN AND CO.

1885

Cambridge:

PRINTED BY J. J. CLAY, M.A. & SON,
AT THE UNIVERSITY PRESS.

PREFACE.

THE appearance of another text-book on Geometry may perhaps be considered to demand an apology, but I venture to hope that an examination of the following pages will shew them to differ considerably from any existing treatise. The extending use of graphic methods in the solution of many practical engineering problems has appeared to me to demand a corresponding extension in the practice of drawing the curves on which such solutions may frequently depend, and, though the properties of conic sections have been discussed thoroughly both geometrically and analytically, there is so far as I am aware no book treating of the actual delineation of the curves from given data to anything like the extent here attempted. Independently however of their applied use, the problems generally will, I think, be found useful merely as drawing exercises in science and other schools. A great deal of attention is devoted to the construction of regular polygons, circles packed into another circle and similar fancy figures, by methods which no practical draughtsman ever uses, while the construction of an ellipse is at the most limited to drawing it from the principal axes or from a pair of conjugate diameters; and the time spent on these and similar exercises might, I think,

E.   *b*

be more profitably devoted to work bringing out the nature
and properties of this and other curves.

I can say from experience that the practice of sketching
a curve freehand through a series of previously found points
is a most valuable element in teaching mechanical drawing,
while the finding the points furnishes abundant exercise in
handling square and compasses, and impresses on the student
in a very striking manner the necessity for neatness and
accuracy in their use.

Each problem may of course be drawn on paper without
reference to the proof of the principle on which its construction depends, but I consider that for the advanced
student at any rate it must be much more satisfactory to
work with as complete an insight as possible into the
methods he is using instead of groping along by mere rule
of thumb, so that in nearly all cases notes in proof of the
property made use of have been added, although such proofs
may be found in numerous published works, and are indeed
so completely common property that I have not thought it
necessary to give direct references to the pages from which
they have been taken.

I cannot however here omit to notice my indebtedness
to Dr Salmon's classical work on Conic Sections, or to
Chasles' *Géométrie Supérieure* for the chapter on Anharmonic Ratio and the Anharmonic Properties of Conics.
Chap. VIII. will, I hope, convince a draughtsman that he
can if he likes make use of an engine very little known in
England and of enormous power. The methods of Modern
Geometry deserve to be brought into much closer relation
with the drawing-board than has hitherto been the case.

The chapter on Plane Sections of the Cone and Cylinder
involves some elementary notions of Solid Geometry or
Orthographic Projection, but the explanations given will, I
hope, enable the average student to work through the chapter

without referring to any special treatise on Projection. The ordinary pseudo-perspective diagrams usually given in books on Conics are I think unsatisfactory, and the method of referring the solid to two rectangular planes seems to me in every way preferable. When the mental conception of a plan and elevation is once thoroughly realised the student is well repaid by the exactness with which he is able to lay down on paper any point or line on the surface of the cone.

The later chapters cannot be read without some knowledge of trigonometry, but the practice of translating a trigonometrical expression into something which can be represented to the eye is a valuable one, and the hints given in the chapter on the Graphic Solution of Equations will I trust be found useful.

My warmest thanks are due to my friend and colleague Professor Minchin for much valuable advice and assistance most freely and readily given: without his help the book would have been much less complete than it is, whatever its imperfections may be found to be.

It would be too much to hope that a work of this character should have been compiled and gone through the press without some errors creeping in. I hope they are not more numerous than from the nature of the case may be considered unavoidable, and I shall be thankful for any such being brought to my notice.

COOPERS HILL,
Oct. 1885.

TABLE OF CONTENTS.

CHAPTER I.

INTRODUCTORY.

CHAPTER II.

THE CIRCLE.

CHAPTER III.

THE PARABOLA.

CHAPTER IV.

THE ELLIPSE.

CHAPTER V.

THE HYPERBOLA.

CHAPTER VI.

THE RECTANGULAR HYPERBOLA.

CHAPTER VII.

RECIPROCAL POLARS.

CHAPTER VIII.

ANHARMONIC RATIO.

CHAPTER IX.

CONE AND CYLINDER.

CHAPTER X.

CYCLOIDAL CURVES.

CHAPTER XIII.

SOLUTION OF EQUATIONS.

CONSTRUCTIVE TREATISE ON PLANE CURVES.

CHAPTER I.

INTRODUCTORY.

THE Instruments required for the accurate representation on paper of almost all known curves are few in number and of simple construction. For accurate work however it is essential they should be of good quality, and be kept in good order. A limited number of good instruments is in every way to be preferred to a larger number of inferior articles, and where economy is an object therefore, in preference to the usual large and small single jointed compasses found in cheap boxes of mathematical instruments the author strongly recommends the purchase of one medium size, double jointed pair of compasses with pen and pencil points, which can be used for both large and small circles if care be taken to adjust the legs so that the lower portions of both may be perpendicular to the paper. This is a *sine quâ non* for good work and it is of course impossible with the ordinary single jointed instruments. In addition to the above a pair of dividers, a drawing pen for inking in straight lines, a protractor which should also contain a diagonal scale of half-inches, a couple of set squares (45° and 60°), pencil and paper may be considered a complete equipment for the work of the following pages.

More may be learnt as to the proper way of handling these tools by ten minutes' observation of a practised draughtsman than from pages of explanation, but failing the opportunity of this practical instruction, the following hints may be useful.

E.   1

Parallel lines should be drawn by means of the set squares; (they are far better than parallel rulers). The edge of one must be adjusted in the required direction and held firmly on the paper, the other should be placed in contact with a second edge of the first and held in that position, and the first may then be made to slide along the second till it comes into the position of the required parallel line. A line perpendicular to another and passing through a given point should be drawn by adjusting an edge containing the right angle of one of the squares to the given line, placing the second square in contact with the hypotenuse of the first and sliding the first along the second until its third side passes through the given point, when the required perpendicular can be drawn.

If a line is to be drawn through two given points, the point of the pencil should first be placed on one of the points, the square can then be brought up to the pencil and worked against it as a centre till it coincides with the other, when the line can be drawn, and care must be taken that the line passes accurately through both points, as owing to the thickness of the edge of the square it is quite possible to make a slight but quite appreciable error. This is particularly the case if the pencil is cut to a chisel edge instead of to a circular point, and the author would express his decided conviction as to the superiority of the circular point. It is of course quite impossible to draw accurately unless a good sharp point to the pencil be constantly maintained.

Lines whether straight or circular should be bisected, tri-sected, &c. by trial, mechanical methods however good in theory being unnecessary and indeed objectionable in practice. A very little practice in handling a pair of dividers will enable this to be done with great ease and with all attainable accuracy, if the amount by which the first shot exceeds or falls short of the desired result is noted and the legs of the dividers closed up or extended to the necessary estimated fraction of this amount. If the required number of parts admits of division, the line should first be divided in the smaller number of parts necessary, i.e. if it is to be divided into six parts, it should be first bisected, and then each half trisected; if into nine parts it should be first trisected, and so on. Care must be taken by a light handling of the instruments, not to damage the paper, until it is found that it can be marked with the points in the right places, and when a point is being marked on a line with the dividers, special care should be taken to press in the point *on* the line and not merely somewhere in its neighbourhood. In handling the instruments they should be constantly kept in as nearly vertical planes as possible. A point when found should be marked by a light pencil ring round it and not by a smudge made with a blunt pointed pencil, which entirely obscures the exact position of the point.

PROBLEM 1. (Figs. 1, 2.) *To draw a line bisecting the angle between two given lines.*

It is frequently necessary to do this when the lines are so nearly parallel or are otherwise so situated that their point of intersection does not fall within the limits of the sheet of paper, or drawing-board, and since the method of proceeding in this case includes the ordinary simple case, it is the one chosen as

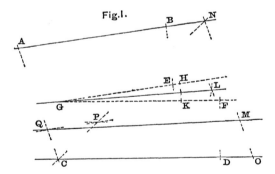

Fig.1.

an example. Let *AB, CD* (fig. 1) be the given lines. Draw *GH* parallel to *AB* at any convenient distance (*BE*) from it, and draw *GK* parallel to *CD* at a distance *DF* equal to *BE* from it. This can be done by drawing *BE* perpendicular to *AB* from any point *B* on it, and *DF* perpendicular to *CD* from any point *D* on it and making *BE* = *DF*, and then using two set squares in the

1—2

way referred to in the introduction.   The distance BE ? ___
be so chosen as to bring the point G about as in the figure,
i.e. BE should be somewhat greater than half the least distance
between the given lines.   If the angle EGF be now bisected,
its bisector will obviously also by symmetry bisect the angle
between AB and CD.   Take any equal distances GH, GK on GE,
GF respectively or, what comes to the same thing, with centre
G and any radius describe an arc HK, and with centres H and K,
and with any (the same) radius describe arcs intersecting in L.
Then GL will be the required bisector.   For the triangle GHL
is obviously equal and similar in all respects to the triangle GKL.

This method is scarcely satisfactory when the lines are nearly
parallel, on account of the smallness of the angle EGF and the
difficulty of determining accurately the point of intersection G
of two nearly coincident lines, and an alternative method evading
this difficulty is shewn in fig. 2.   As before, let AB, CD be the

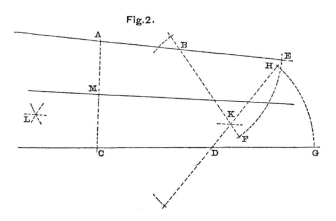

Fig.2.

two given lines.   At any point B of the one line draw a line as
BF, and at any point D of the other construct an angle GDH
equal to the angle EBF.   The exact size of this angle is im-
material but preferably it should not differ much from half a
right angle.   [An angle (GDH) can be constructed equal to a
given angle (EBF) by describing arcs EF, GH, with the angular
points B, D as centres and with any (equal) radius, and then

making the chord GH equal to the chord EF by means of a pair of dividers.]

Let BF and DH intersect in K. The bisector of the angle BKD will, by symmetry, *be parallel to* the required bisector, i.e. bisecting the angle BKD by the line KL, the *direction* of the required bisector is known. To find its position, draw any line AC perpendicular to KL meeting the given lines in A and C. The required bisector must evidently pass through M the centre point of AC. It can therefore be drawn through this point parallel to KL.

PROBLEM 2. (Fig. 3.) *To find a fourth proportional to three given lines* AB, CD, EF, *or to find a line of such length* (l) *that*

$$AB : CD :: EF : l,$$

or that the rectangle contained by the two lines AB and l shall be equal in area to the rectangle contained by CD and EF.

All questions involving proportionals depend on the construction of similar triangles. Draw any two lines OK, OL meeting

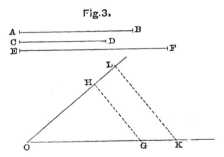

Fig.3.

in O and containing any angle. From O along one line set off $OG = AB$, the first term of the proportion, and $OK = EF$, the third term of the proportion. From O along the other line set off $OH = CD$, the second term of the proportion, then through K draw KL parallel to GH meeting OH in L. OL will be the required fourth term. For obviously by the similar triangles OGH, OKL,

$$OG : OH :: OK : OL,$$

i.e. $$AB : CD :: EF : OL.$$

A similar construction will obviously give a third proportional to two given lines AB, CD; i. e. a line of length (l) such that

$$AB : CD :: CD : l,$$

or that the rectangle contained by AB and l shall be equal in area to the square on CD; the only difference being that in this case the lengths OH and OK will be equal to each other.

PROBLEM 3. (Fig. 4.) *To divide a line of given length* (AB) *similarly to a given line CD divided in any manner as at E, F......* (*There may be any manner of points of division.*)

Draw any two lines as OG and OH. Make $OG = AB$, $OH = CD$, $OK = CE$, $OL = CF$... and draw KM, LN... parallel to HG. The

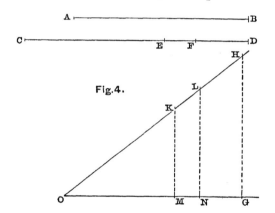

Fig.4.

line OG, i. e. AB will be divided in M, N... similarly to CD in E, F....

PROBLEM 4. (Fig. 1.) *To draw a line through a given point and through the intersection of two given lines.*

It is of course the simplest possible thing to do this when the actual point of intersection of the two lines is available. As in Problem 1 however it is frequently necessary to draw a line the direction of which depends on an inaccessible point. Let AB, CD be the two given lines and M the given point. (M may be between the lines as in fig. 1 or on the farther side of either with regard to the other.) Draw any line through M meeting the given lines in N and O, and at any convenient distance from M

draw a second line parallel to *NO* meeting the given lines as at
A and *C*. If we divide *AC*, as in *Q*, in similar segments to those
in which *M* divides *NO* (Problem 3) the line *QM* will be the
required line passing through the intersection of *AB* and *CD*.
The most convenient method for dividing *AC* is probably thus :
join *CN*, draw *PM* through *M* parallel to *CD* and meeting *CN* in
P, and through *P* draw *PQ* parallel to *AB* meeting *AC* in *Q*. *AC*
is obviously divided in *Q* similarly to *NC* in *P* and therefore
to *NO* in *M*.

PROBLEM 5. (Fig. 5.) *To find the geometric mean between two
given lines AB, CD, i.e. to find a line of length (l) such that*

$$AB : l :: l : CD,$$

or that the square on l shall be equal in area to the rectangle contained by AB and CD.

Draw any straight line *EOF* and set off on it on opposite
sides from *O*, *OE* = *AB*, *OF* = *CD*. On *EF* describe a semicircle

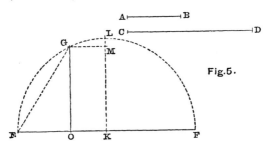

Fig.5.

and from *O* draw *OG* perpendicular to *EF* meeting the circumference in *G*. *OG* will be the required mean proportional or
geometric mean. For, since the angle in a semicircle is a right-angle (Euclid III. 31), ∴ the angles *OEG*, *EGO* are together equal
to the angles *EGO*, *OGF*, and ∴ the angle *OEG* = the angle *OGF*,
∴ the right-angled triangles *OEG*, *OGF* are similar and

$$\therefore EO : OG :: OG : OF,$$

i. e. $$AB : OG :: OG : CD.$$

PROBLEM 6. *To divide a given line so that the rectangle contained by its segments is equal to the square on a given line which must obviously be not greater than half the line to be divided* (fig. 5).

This is the converse of the last problem. Let *EF* be the given line, on it describe a semicircle. Draw the radius *KL* perpendicular to *EF* and on it make *KM* equal to the side of the required square. Through *M* draw a parallel to *EF* meeting the circle in *G* and from *G* drop a perpendicular on *EF* meeting it in *O*, *O* will be the required point of division.

The construction is obvious from the last problem.

PROBLEM 7.   (Fig. 6.)   *To divide a line medially, or in extreme and mean proportion, i.e. to find a point (F) in a line AB such that*

the whole line AB : the greater segment (BF)

:: BF : the lesser segment (AF),

or that the rectangle contained by the whole line and the lesser segment is equal in area to the square on the greater segment.

Bisect *AB* in *C*, from *A* draw *AD* perpendicular to *AB* and make $AD = AC = \frac{1}{2}AB$. Join *BD* and on it from *D* cut off

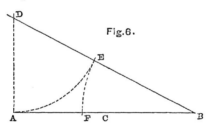

Fig.6.

$DE = DA$; from *B* on *BA* cut off $BF = BE$. *F* will be the required point. This construction is simplified from Euclid II. 11, the proof may be shewn thus.

The sq. on *BD* = sq. on *AB* + sq. on *AD* (Euclid I. 47).

Also   „   = sq. on *EB* + sq. on *ED* + 2 rect. *EB* . *ED*,

but   *ED* = *AD* and *EB* = *FB*,   (Euclid II. 4),

∴ sq. on *AB* = sq. on *FB* + 2 rect. *FB* . *AD*.

Again sq. on *AB* = sq. on *FB* + sq. on *AF* + 2 rect. *AF* . *FB*

(Euclid II. 4),

= sq. on *FB* + rect. *AF* (*AF* + *FB*)

+ rect. *AF* . *FB*.

$\therefore$ 2 rect. $FB . AD$ = rect. $AF . AB$ + rect. $AF . FB$,

i. e. rect. $FB \{2AD - AF\}$ = rect. $AF . AB$,

but $\qquad 2AD = AB$ and $AB - AF = FB$,

$\therefore$ finally sq. on FB = rect. $AF . AB$.

PROBLEM 8. (Fig. 7.) *To find graphically a series of terms in geometrical progression, being given either two successive terms or one term and the common ratio.*

Draw two lines Oe, OF meeting in O at any convenient angle. On one mark off the 1st given term as OA, and on the other the

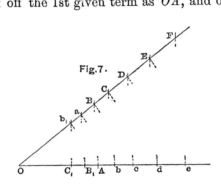

Fig.7.

2nd given term as OB, or if the common ratio be given a length OB = 1st term multiplied by the common ratio.

[In the figure OA the first term $= 2$, and $OB = 2 \cdot 4$; the common ratio therefore is $1 \cdot 2$, the unit being $3''/8$.]

With centre O and radius OB describe an arc cutting OA in b ; through b draw bC parallel to AB cutting OB in C. OC will be the required third term of the series. Similarly make Oc on OA $= OC$ and through c draw cD parallel to AB cutting OB in D, OD will be the required fourth term, and so on in succession. Terms on the other side of OA can also be determined as shown at OB_1, OC_1, &c.

The construction evidently depends on the similarity of the triangles OAB, ObC, &c.

by which $\qquad OC : OB :: Ob : OA$,

i. e. since $\qquad Ob = OB$, $OB^2 = OA . OC$,

or each term is a mean proportional between the two on opposite sides of it, in other words the series is in geometrical progression.

Since $OB = r \cdot OA$, the above expression for OB^2 becomes

$$r^2 \cdot OA = OC,$$

and so also $\quad\quad r^3 \cdot OA = OD$ and so on.

Very careful drawing is required to ensure accuracy, and the scale should be as large as possible, as otherwise, since errors are cumulative, the lengths obtained for the fourth or fifth and succeeding terms may differ considerably from their true values.

PROBLEM 9. *Given two ratios $\dfrac{a}{b}$ and $\dfrac{l}{m}$ to determine the ratio $\dfrac{al}{bm}$, or to divide a given line so that the ratio of its segments shall equal the product of two given ratios* (Fig. 8).

Draw any line AB and on it make $AD = a$, $DB = b$. With centre B and radius $l + m$ describe an arc, and with centre

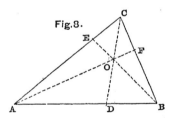

Fig. 8.

A and radius AC the length of the given line to be divided describe an arc intersecting the former in C. Make BF on $BC = l$ so that $FC = m$. Draw AF, CD intersecting in O and draw BO meeting AC in E. E will be the required point of division:

i.e. $\quad\quad \dfrac{AE}{EC} = \dfrac{AD}{DB} \cdot \dfrac{BF}{FC} = \dfrac{a}{b} \cdot \dfrac{l}{m}$,

for $\quad\quad \dfrac{AD}{OD} = \dfrac{\sin AOD}{\sin ODA}$ and $\dfrac{DB}{OD} = \dfrac{\sin BOD}{\sin ODB}$,

$\therefore \quad\quad \dfrac{AD}{DB} = \dfrac{\sin AOD}{\sin BOD}$, similarly $$\frac{BF}{FC} = \frac{\sin BOF}{\sin COF} = \frac{\sin BOF}{\sin AOD},$$

and $$\frac{AE}{EC} = \frac{\sin AOE}{\sin EOC} = \frac{\sin BOF}{\sin BOD} = \frac{AD}{BD} \cdot \frac{BF}{FC}.$$

It follows of course that in any triangle if lines be drawn from the vertices ABC meeting the opposite sides in F, E, D and all passing through the same point O, $AD \cdot BF \cdot CE = DB \cdot FC \cdot EA$, i.e. that the continued products of the alternate segments taken in order are equal.

PROBLEM 10. *To determine graphically the square root of any number (n), i.e. to determine a line the length of which : length of a line containing n units measured on any scale :: $1 : \sqrt{n}$.*

This is sometimes, though misleadingly, called determining the square root of a given line. The fact is that the expression the square root of a given line has no meaning unless we take the line to represent, by the number of units it contains, a given area; and then the line to be found is the side of a square, the number of square units in which is equal to the number of units contained in the line—the same scale of course being used for each. If a triangle ABC be drawn, right angled at A and having the sides AB, AC each one inch long, the side BC is the side of a square of two square inches area, and in this sense BC may be said to be the square root of a line two inches long, or of the number 2, the unit being one inch, but if the unit be half-an-inch the same line BC represents the square root of 8, since (Euc. I. 46) $BC^2 = AB^2 + AC^2 = 2^2 + 2^2 = 8$.

If we use a diagonal scale of half-inches, the length BC may be read on it to two places of decimals, and the number so obtained is the square root of 8 to two decimal places. Any question relating to the square root of a number, must therefore always be taken as involving the application of some particular scale. The square root of any proposed number can be found by splitting the number up so as to make it equal to the sum or difference of two or more squares, and then constructing right-angled triangles having sides equal to the sides of these squares. Thus $\sqrt{3} - \sqrt{4-1}, = \sqrt{2^2 - 1^2}$ so that if a right-angled triangle ABC be drawn, right angled at C and having $AB = 2$ inches, and $AC = 1$ inch, BC represents $\sqrt{3}$, an inch being the unit. (The triangle may be constructed by drawing a semicircle on AB as diameter and making AC in it $= 1$ inch.) If the unit is half-an-inch BC represents $\sqrt{AB^2 - AC^2}$, i.e. $\sqrt{4^2 - 2^2}$ or $\sqrt{12}$.

$\sqrt{5} = \sqrt{3^2 - 2^2}$, i.e. is the perpendicular of a right-angled triangle the hypotenuse of which is 3 and the base of which is 2, or it may be determined as the hypotenuse of a right-angled triangle one side of which is 2 and the other 1, since $\sqrt{5} = \sqrt{2^2 + 1^2}$. If we halve the unit the same line would represent $\sqrt{20}$.

$\sqrt{6} = \sqrt{2^2 + \sqrt{2}^2}$, i.e. if $\sqrt{2}$ be first determined, $\sqrt{6}$ is the hypotenuse of a right-angled triangle the sides of which are 2 and $\sqrt{2}$, or it may be determined from $\sqrt{6} = \sqrt{3^2 - \sqrt{3}^2}$.

$\sqrt{7} = \sqrt{2^2 + \sqrt{3}^2}$, and can be determined if $\sqrt{3}$ is known.

$\sqrt{8}$ has already been given.

$\sqrt{10} = \sqrt{3^2 + 1^2}$.

$\sqrt{11} = \sqrt{4^2 - \sqrt{5}^2}$, and can be determined if $\sqrt{5}$ is known.

$\sqrt{12}$ has been given above; and the method is probably sufficiently exemplified by the above, but we will take two examples of larger numbers

$\sqrt{47} = \sqrt{6^2 + \sqrt{11}^2}$, thus being made to depend on $\sqrt{11}$.

$\sqrt{179} = \sqrt{13^2 + \sqrt{10}^2}$ thus being made to depend on $\sqrt{10}$, it might also be written $= \sqrt{11^2 + \sqrt{47}^2}$ or could be determined in other ways. No definite instructions can be given as to the best mode of working in any particular case, but as a rule triangles having sides of nearly equal magnitude should be selected, since the intersections of lines cutting at very acute angles cannot be accurately determined.

DEFINITION. Three magnitudes are said to be in harmonic progression when the first is to the third as the difference between the first and second is to the difference between the second and third : and the second magnitude is said to be an harmonic mean between the first and third.

Thus if the magnitudes represented by the lengths of three lines (as AB, AC, AD, fig. 9) are in harmonic progression and the lines be superimposed with a common extremity as in that fig.:—
then $\qquad AB : AD :: BC : CD.$

The reciprocals of magnitudes in harmonic progression are in arithmetic progression and conversely :—for, if AB, AC, AD are in harmonic progression then by definition

$$AB : AD :: BC : CD, \text{ or } \frac{BC}{AB} = \frac{CD}{AD},$$

and if $\dfrac{1}{AB}$, $\dfrac{1}{AC}$, $\dfrac{1}{AD}$ are in arithmetic progression then by

definition, $\qquad \dfrac{1}{AB} + \dfrac{1}{AD} = \dfrac{2}{AC},$

but this may be written

$$\frac{1}{AB} - \frac{1}{AC} = \frac{1}{AC} - \frac{1}{AD},$$

or $\qquad \dfrac{AC - AB}{AB \cdot AC} = \dfrac{AD - AC}{AC \cdot AD},$

or $\qquad \dfrac{BC}{AB} = \dfrac{CD}{AD},$

an identical expression with the above.

PROBLEM 11. (Fig. 9.) *To find the harmonic mean between two given lines AB, AD, i.e. to find a line of length l such that*
$AB : AD ::$ *the difference between AB and l*
$\qquad\qquad : $ *the difference between AD and l.*

Set off the given lengths from the same point (A) on any line and in the same direction along it, as AB, AD. Take any point E outside AD and join AE, DE. Through B draw FBG parallel to *DE* meeting *AE* in *F* and make *BG = BF*. Join *EG* cutting *AD* in *C* and *AC* will be the required harmonic mean. For by the

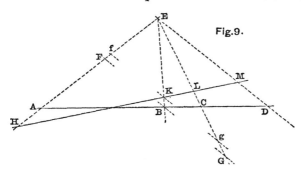

Fig.9.

similar triangles *ABF, ADE,*

$$AB : AD :: BF : DE.$$

Also by the similar triangles *CBG, CDE,*

$$BC : CD :: BG : DE,$$

and $$BG = BF,$$

$$\therefore \quad AB : AD :: BC : CD,$$
$$:: AC - AB : AD - AC.$$

PROBLEM 12.   (Fig. 9.)   *To find the third term of a harmonic progression, the first two terms being given.*

The above construction may be adapted to find the third term of a harmonic progression the first two terms being given. Suppose *AB* and *AC* given. Superpose them with a common extremity as in the fig. 9. Take any point *F* outside *AC*. Join *FB* and produce it to *G* making *BG = BF*. Join *AF* and *GC* producing them to meet in *E* and draw *ED* through *E* parallel to *FB* meeting *AC* (produced if necessary) in *D*. *AD* will be the required third term.

DEF.   When four points in a straight line as *ABCD* in fig. 9 fulfil the condition

$$AB : AD :: BC : CD,$$

they constitute *a Harmonic Range*, and if through any point *E* outside the line the four straight lines *EA, EB, EC, ED* be drawn these four lines constitute *a Harmonic Pencil*, which is denoted by *E{ABCD}*. Any straight line drawn across the pencil is called a

Transversal, and every transversal of a harmonic pencil is divided harmonically in the points in which it intersects the lines of the pencil : i. e. the four points of intersection constitute *a Harmonic Range.* For in fig. 9 draw any transversal as *HKLM,* and through *K* draw *fKg* parallel to *ED* and therefore to *FG,* meeting *EA, EC* in *f* and *g.* Obviously since $BF = BG$, $\therefore Kf = Kg$.

By similar triangles *HKf, HME*

$$HK \ : \ HM \ :: \ fK \ : \ EM,$$

and by similar triangles *KLg, MLE*

$$KL \ : \ LM \ :: \ gK \ : \ EM,$$

but $\qquad\qquad Kf = Kg,$

$$\therefore \ HK \ : \ HM \ :: \ KL \ : \ LM,$$

or *HKLM* constitute a Harmonic Range.

A particular case of a Harmonic Pencil is furnished by the pencil formed of two straight lines and the bisectors of the angles between them, as shewn in fig. 10, where *AD* bisects the angle

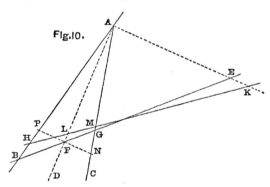

Fig.10.

BAC and *AE* is drawn perpendicular to *AD,* and therefore bisecting the exterior angle between *AC* and *BA* produced. For draw any transversal as *BFGE,* and through *F* draw *PFN* parallel to *AE* and meeting *AB, AC* in *P* and *N.*

Then $PF = FN$ and

$BF \ : \ BE \ :: \ PF \ : \ AE,$ by similar triangles *BPF, BAE,*

$FG \ : \ GE \ :: \ FN \ : \ AE,$ by similar triangles *FGN, EGA,*

$$\therefore \ BF \ : \ BE \ :: \ FG \ : \ GE,$$

or the pencil is harmonic.

A line of given length may obviously be divided harmonically in an infinite number of ways, since a line of length $HK = BE$ can be drawn from any point H on AB to terminate on AE and

$$HL : HK :: LM : MK.$$

Harmonic Properties of a complete Quadrilateral.

If $FBeA$, FDe_1C be harmonic ranges (fig. 11), the straight lines AC, ee_1, BD meet in a point, as also AD, BC and ee_1.

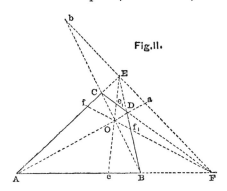

Fig. 11.

For if BD, AC meet in E, draw Ee; then the pencil $E(AeBF)$ is harmonic and FC is a transversal, so that e_1 must lie on Ee.

Similarly if AD and BC meet in O, the pencil $O(AeBF)$ is harmonic and FC a transversal, so that e_1 must lie on Oe.

If $ABCD$ is any quadrilateral, E the intersection of the sides AC and BD, F of the sides AB and CD, O the intersection of the diagonals AD and BC; it follows conversely that EA, EO, EB, EF form a harmonic pencil, as also FE, FC, FO and FA. If EO meet AB in e and CD in e_1, $AeBF$ and Ce_1DF are therefore harmonic ranges, and if FO meet AC in f and BD in f_1, $AfCE$ and Bf_1DE are both harmonic ranges.

Further if AD meet FE in a and BC meet it in b, $BOCb$ is a harmonic range since it is a transversal of the pencil $F(ECfA)$, therefore AF, Aa, AE and Ab form a harmonic pencil, and therefore $FaEb$ is a harmonic range, i.e. FE is divided harmonically in a and b.

DEF. A system of pairs of points Aa, Bb, &c. on a straight line such that $XA \cdot Xa = XB \cdot Xb = \ldots = XP^2 = XQ^2$ is called a system in Involution, the point X being called the *centre*, P and Q the *foci* of the system, and any two corresponding points A, a, *conjugate points*.

PROBLEM 13. *Two pairs of conjugate points A, a and B, b, being given, to find the centre and foci of the involution.*

The existence of a focus is only possible when both points of a pair are on the same side of the centre, and hence two cases arise, 1st, in which one pair of points lies within the other, and 2nd in which each pair lies wholly outside the other.

Case 1. (Fig. 12.) Let ab be less than AB. Through a the extreme point of the range draw any line ac, and through B the

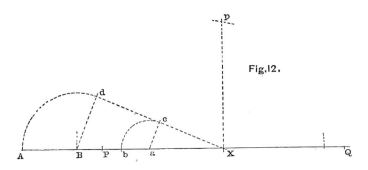

Fig. 12.

more distant from a of the second pair of points draw a parallel line Bd. Make $ac = ab$, $Bd = BA$, then dc will intersect $ABba$ in X the required centre—for

$$Xa : ac :: XB : Bd,$$
$$\therefore \quad Xa : ab :: XB : BA,$$
$$\therefore \quad Xa + ab : Xa :: XB + BA : XB,$$
$$\text{i. e.} \quad Xb : Xa :: XA : XB,$$

therefore by definition X is the centre of the system.

Take a mean proportional between either XA and Xa or XB and Xb, which determines the distance XP and XQ from X of the foci.

E.

2

Case 2.   (Fig. 13.)   Through the extreme points of the system draw any two parallel lines as bc, Ad.   Make $bc = ba$ the distance

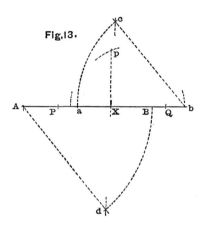

Fig.13.

from b of the nearer point of the opposite pair and make $Ad = AB$ the distance from A of the similar point, then cd will cut Ab in X the required centre—for

$$XA \; : \; Ad \; :: \; Xb \; : \; bc,$$
$$\text{i.e.} \quad XA \; : \; AB \; :: \; Xb \; : \; ab,$$
$$\therefore \quad XA \; : \; AB - XA \; :: \; Xb \; : \; ab - Xb,$$
or $$XA \; : \; XB \; :: \; Xb \; : \; Xa.$$

The foci must be determined as in Case 1.

Since $$XA \; : \; XP \; :: \; XP \; : \; Xa,$$
$$\therefore \quad XA - XP \; : \; XA + XP \; :: \; XP - Xa \; : \; XP + Xa,$$
$$\text{i.e.} \quad AP \; : \; AQ \; :: \; Pa \; : \; aQ,$$

or each pair of conjugate points forms, with the foci of the system, a harmonic range.

It follows of course that if $APaQ$ be an harmonic range and X the centre point of PQ,

$$XA \, . \, Xa = XP^2 = XQ^2.$$

The following relations between two pairs of conjugate points Aa and Bb, and their centre X and foci P and Q are sometimes useful.

Since $\qquad XA : Xb :: XB : Xa,$

$\therefore\quad XA : Ab :: XB : aB,$

or $\qquad XA : XB :: Ab : aB$.....................(1),

and since $\qquad Xb : Xa :: XA : XB,$

$\therefore\quad Xb : ab :: XA : AB,$

or $\qquad Xb : XA :: ab : AB$.....................(2);

therefore, multiplying (1) and (2),

$$Xb : XB :: Ab . ba : AB . Ba.$$

Again, since $QbPB$ is harmonic,

$$\therefore\quad Qb : QB :: Pb : PB,$$

or $\qquad Qb : Pb :: QB : PB,$

$$\therefore\quad Qb \pm Pb : Pb :: QB \pm PB : PB,$$

or $\qquad 2XP : Pb :: 2XB : PB,$

$$\therefore\quad Pb^2 : PB^2 :: XP^2 : XB^2$$

$$:: Xb : XB$$

$$:: Ab . ba : AB . Ba.$$

This determines the ratio in which Bb is divided by P.

PROBLEM 14. (Fig. 14.) *Through a given point P to draw a line meeting two given lines AB and CD in B and D so that $PB = PD$.*

Through P draw any line meeting one of the given lines as at A. On AP produced make $Pa = PA$ and draw aD parallel to BA

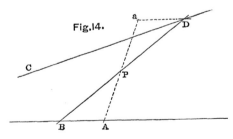

Fig. 14.

meeting the other given line in D. The line DPB will be the line required, i.e. $PB = PD$ (by the similar and equal triangles APB, aPD).

PROBLEM 15. *To draw a triangle with its sides passing through three given points A, B, C, and with its vertices on three given concurrent lines OD, OE, OF* (Fig. 15).

Take any point (as *E*) on any one of the given lines and from it draw lines to any two of the given points (as *EA*, *EB*) meeting

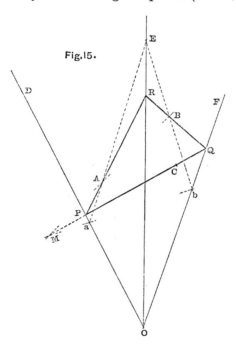

Fig. 15.

the other lines in *a* and *b*.   Let the lines *AB* and *ab* meet in *M*. Through *M* draw a line *MC* passing through the remaining point (*C*) and meeting the lines *Oa* and *Ob* in *P* and *Q*. *PQ* will be one side of the required triangle which can be completed by drawing the lines *PA*, *QB* which will intersect in *R* on the third given line.

There are generally six solutions as lines can be drawn through each point terminated by either pair of lines.

PROBLEM 16. *To draw a triangle with its vertices on three given lines AP, BQ, CQP, and with its sides passing through three given points A, B, C one on each line* (fig. 16).

Let two of the given lines (as *AP*, *BQ*) meet in *O* ; the third line meets the others in P and Q. Draw the lines AQ and BP intersecting in D, and draw OD intersecting PQ in E. Take a mean

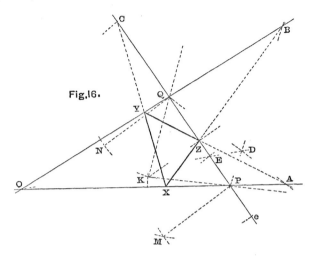

Fig,16.

proportional PM between CP and PE (Problem 5), and a mean proportional QN between CQ and QE. With centres P and Q and radii respectively equal to PM and QN describe arcs intersecting in K. Draw a line bisecting the angle PKQ, intersecting PQ in Z. Z will be one of the vertices of the required triangle which can be completed by drawing BZ intersecting AP in X and AZ intersecting BQ in Y. X and Y are the other vertices and XY will pass through C.

PROBLEM 17. *To determine the locus* of the vertex of a triangle on a given base AB and with sides BP, AP in a given ratio a : b.* (Fig. 17.)

On the given base AB describe any one triangle with sides
$$BP \ : \ AP \ :: \ a \ : \ b.$$

Bisect the angle APB by PD meeting AB in D and draw PC perpendicular to PD meeting AB in C.

On DC as diameter describe a circle, which will be the required locus of the vertex.

---

* For definition of locus, see p. 29 *post*.

Proof. Take any point Q on the circle, and draw QA, QD, QB, QE. Since PD bisects the angle APB

$$\therefore\ BD : AD :: a : b \qquad \text{(Euc. vi. 3),}$$

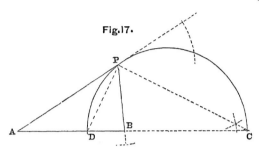

Fig. 17.

and since DPC is a right angle and PD bisects the angle APB
$\therefore\ P(ADBC)$ is a harmonic pencil (p. 15),

$\therefore$ also $Q(ADBC)$ is a harmonic pencil, and consequently since DQC is a right angle, QD bisects the angle AQB,

$$\therefore\ BQ : AQ :: BD : AD :: a : b. \qquad \text{(Euc. vi. 3.)}$$

PROBLEM 18. *To construct a rectangle equal in area to the sum or difference of two given rectangles ABCD, DEFG (fig. 18).*

Apply the smaller rectangle to the side of the larger as in the figure. Complete the rectangle $ABHE$. Draw DH cutting FG

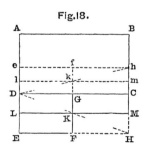

Fig. 18.

in K. Through K draw LM parallel to AB and the rectangle $ABML$ will be equal in area to the sum of the two given rectangles. (Euc. i. 43.)

The dotted lines and the small letters in the fig. shew the construction for the difference of two rectangles.

PROBLEM 19. *From a given point P in a given straight line PM to draw lines making equal angles with PM and cutting a second given line CM at equal distances CD, CE from a given point C* (fig. 19).

From P and C draw PN, CF perpendicular to CM. Make the angle MPF equal to the angle MPN and let PF meet CF in

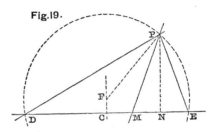

Fig.19.

F. With centre F and radius FP describe a circle cutting CM in D and E which will be the required points.

Proof. $CD = CE$ since CF is perpendicular to DE.

The angle DFP is double the angle DEP. (Euc. III. 20.)

Half the angle DFP together with the angle $FPD = $ a right angle.

The angle DEP together with the angle $EPN = $ a right angle.

∴ the angle $FPD = $ the angle EPN,

and ∴ the angle $MPD = $ the angle MPE.

The point C must evidently lie on the opposite side of M to N.

This is also a solution of the problem to construct a triangle, given the vertex, the bisector of the vertical angle, and the difference of the segments of the base made by that bisector: for

$$DM - ME = 2CM.$$

Examples on Chapter I.

1. Draw a circle of radius 2·87. In it place a chord AB of length 4·8, and draw BC making 60° with AB. If C is on the circle shew that the side AC of the triangle is approximately 4·96.

Shew that the geometrical mean between 3·76 and 2·43 is ·02 approximately.

2. Inscribe a square in a given triangle ABC.

(Through A draw a parallel AD to BC; make AD equal in length to the perpendicular from A to BC, and join D to the end of the base BC that will enable it to cut one of the sides AB or AC in E. E is one of the angular points of the required square, the base of which will coincide in direction with BC.)

3. Bisect a given triangle ABC by a straight line drawn through a given point D in AC. $AD < DC$.

(Bisect BC in E and through A draw AF parallel to DE meeting BC in F. DF will be the required line.)

4. Given the middle points P, Q, R of the sides of a triangle, construct the triangle.

(The side through P is parallel to QR, and so for the others. Take $PQ = 2$, $QR = 1·8$, $RP = 1·3$.)

5. Construct a triangle having given the base AB, the vertical angle C, and the difference of the sides AC, CB.

(Construct a triangle ADB having the angle $ADB = 90° + \dfrac{C}{2}$, $DA =$ the given difference and AB the given base. Produce AD to C, and make the angle $DBC =$ the angle BDC.)

6. Construct a triangle, being given the base AB the difference of the base angles, and the difference of the sides AC, and BC.

(Make a triangle DBA, with angle $DBA = \frac{1}{2}$ the given difference. BA = the given base and AD the given difference of sides: produce AD to C and make the angle DBC = angle BDC.)

7.   Construct a triangle, being given the base AB, the vertical angle C and the sum of the sides AC and BC.

(Make an angle $ADB = \dfrac{C}{2}$, make $DA = AC + BC$, and AB = the given base; make the angle $DBC = \dfrac{C}{2}$, and so that BC cuts AD in C between A and D.)

8.   Let ABC be any triangle, CD a perpendicular from C on AB and E a point on AB such that $DE = DB$. AE is the difference of the segments of base made by the perpendicular, then given AE and any one of the following pairs of data, construct the triangle.

α.   Sum of sides $(AC + BC)$ and difference of base angles.

(We are given in the triangle ACE, $AC + CE$, AE and vertical angle ACE, i. e. base, vertical angle and sum of sides. The triangle can therefore be constructed (last example) and from it the required triangle ABC.)

β.   Difference of sides and difference of base angles.

(Make an angle ADE containing $90^{\circ} + \dfrac{a}{2}$ where a is given difference. Make DA = the given difference of sides, and AE the given difference of segments; produce AD to C and make $DEC = EDC$; produce AE to B and make $CB = CD = CE$. ABC will be the required triangle.)

γ.   Sum of sides and vertical angle.

(Construct a triangle AEC on the given difference of segments AE as base, with $AC + CE$ = given sum of sides and the given vertical angle as difference of base angles (a above), produce AE to B and make $CB = CE$).

δ.   Difference of sides and vertical angle.

(Make an angle AEF = half the given angle, make AF = the given difference of sides, produce AF to C and make the angle $FEC = EFC$, produce AE to B and make $CB = CE = CF$.)

9. Given the lengths AD, BE, CF of the bisectors of the sides of a triangle ABC, to construct the triangle.

(Construct a triangle FOG making $FG = \frac{1}{3}AD$, $GO = \frac{1}{3}BE$, $FO = \frac{1}{3}FC$; produce FO to C and make $OC = 2 \cdot OF$ so that FC is the given length; produce GO both ways to B and E and make $BG = OE = GO$ so that BE is the given length. Join BC and draw BF, CE, producing them to meet in A. ABC will be the required triangle.)

10. Given the lengths AD, BE, CF of the perpendiculars on the sides from the opposite angles of a triangle ABC, to construct the triangle.

(Determine a length Mb such that $CF : BE :: AD : Mb$, and on it construct a triangle Mbc, making $bc = BE$ and $Mc = AD$. From M drop a perpendicular on bc and on it make $Md = AD$. Through d draw BdC parallel to b, meeting Mb, Mc in B and C. MBC will be the required triangle.)

11. Given three points D, E, F, to construct a triangle of which these points shall be the feet of the perpendiculars on the sides from the opposite angles.

(The sides are perpendicular to the bisectors of the angles of the triangle DEF.)

12. Divide a given straight line AB into two parts AC, CB, such that the difference of the squares on the parts may be equal to the square on a given line $DE < AB$.

(Take a third proportional FG to AB and DE. FG will be the difference between the required parts, and AB is their sum, so that AC, and CB are known.)

13. Divide a given line AB into two parts AC, CB, such that the square on AC may be double the square on CB.

(Take $AC : CB :: \sqrt{2} : 1$.)

14. Divide a given straight line AB into two parts AC, CB, such that the sum of their squares shall be equal to the square on a given line DE.

$$DE > \frac{AB}{\sqrt{2}} < AB.$$

(Construct a rectangle equal in area to $\overline{2DE}|^2 - AB^2$ (Prob. 18). Take a mean proportional between its sides which will be the difference between AC and CB; the sum and difference of the parts being known, the parts are known.)

15. Divide a given straight line AB into two parts AC, CB, such that $AB^2 + CB^2 = 2 . AC^2$.

(Take $AC : CB :: 1 + \sqrt{3} : 1$.)

16. Draw any triangle ABC, bisect AB in D, join CD, and through C draw CE parallel to AB; shew by drawing a transversal, that the rays CA, CD, CB, CE form a harmonic pencil.

17. Given the directions of one pair of opposite sides of a quadrilateral AB and CD, and the point (F) of intersection of the other pair, shew that the locus of the intersection of the diagonals is a straight line.

(If AB, CD intersect in F, and G is the intersection of the diagonals, the pencil $E(AGCF)$ is harmonic.)

18. Find the geometric mean (BD) between two given lines $(AB$ and $BC)$ and shew by construction that the harmonic mean between $AB + BD$, and $BC + BD$ is $2BD$.

19. A line AB is divided harmonically in C and D, and a part CB of the line which contains two terms CD and DB is bisected in E. Shew that EC is the geometric mean of EA and ED.

20. Divide a given straight line AB medially in the point C, and produce the line so that the part produced is equal to AC the smaller segment; shew by construction that the rectangle contained by AC and the whole line thus produced, together with the square on AB is equal to four times the square on CB.

CHAPTER II.

THE CIRCLE.

Euclid's well known definition is "A circle is a plane figure contained by one line, which is called the circumference, and is such, that all straight lines drawn from a certain point within the figure to the circumference are equal to one another : and this point is called the centre of the circle". A radius of a circle is a straight line drawn from the centre to the circumference, and therefore by the above definition all radii of a circle are equal.

Hence a circle is completely determined if we know its centre and the length of its radius, and it might seem at first sight that *two* geometrical conditions would be sufficient to determine it. The position of the centre however must be counted as two conditions, and a circle can generally be drawn to satisfy *three* geometrical conditions, and three are in general necessary and sufficient for its determination. Thus an infinite number of circles can be drawn to pass through two points, or to touch two lines, and some other condition, such as the position of a third point through which it must pass or of a line which it must touch in the first case, or of a third line which it must touch or of a point through which it must pass in the second, or such as the length of the radius in either, must be given to make the exact solution of the problem possible.

The above limitation "in general" is necessary because it is possible to give certain special positions to the lines and points which would render the problem impossible : thus e.g. in the first case a circle cannot be drawn through three points in the same straight line, or at least no circle of finite radius, or if the given conditions are ."to pass through two given points and touch a given line" the line must obviously lie outside the points, i. e. it must not pass between them, and similarly if the conditions are "to touch three given lines" one at least of the lines must not be parallel to the other two, but notwithstanding these special cases it is generally true that a circle can be drawn to satisfy any *three* geometrical conditions.

DEFINITION. When a point is restricted by conditions of any kind, to occupy any of a particular series of positions, that series of positions is called the *locus of the point*.

PROBLEM 20. (Fig. 20.) *To describe a circle through three given points A, B, C, not in the same straight line.*

If the line joining A, B is bisected in D and DO is drawn perpendicular to AB, DO will obviously be the locus of the centres of

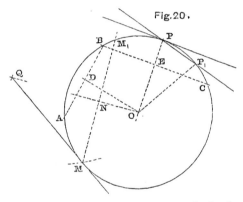

Fig. 20.

all circles passing through A and B, i. e. any circle through A and B must have its centre on DO, since in the equal right-angled triangles ADO, BDO, AO is equal to BO. Similarly, bisecting BC in E and drawing EO perpendicular to BC, EO is the locus of centres of circles passing through B and C. Hence the centre of the circle passing through A, B and C must lie simultaneously on both these loci, i. e. must be at their intersection, and the distance from this point to either A, B or C will be the radius of the required circle.

Euclid in definition 2 of Book III. defines a tangent to a circle in these words. "A straight line is said to touch a circle when it meets the circle, and being produced does not cut it," and shews in Corollary to Prop. 16, Bk. III. that the line drawn perpendicular to a radius at its extremity fulfils the condition of this definition. This is the most convenient way in which to draw the tangent at any point on the circumference, and the tangent so drawn can easily be shewn to agree with the general definition of a tangent usually given as applicable to all curves, which is as follows :—

DEFINITION. If two points be taken on a curve and a chord drawn through them ; then, if the first point remains fixed while the second, moving along the curve, approaches indefinitely near to the first, the chord in its limiting position is called the tangent to the curve at the first point.

To shew that such chord in its limiting position will in the circle be perpendicular to the radius at the point, take two points P, P_1, (fig. 20) on the curve, and draw PP_1, then since $OP = OP_1$ the angles OPP_1 and OP_1P are equal and will remain equal however close P_1 may be taken to P. But when P_1 coincides with P each of these angles becomes a right angle, i.e. the tangent at P will be perpendicular to OP.

To draw a tangent to the given circle from an external point Q. Join OQ and on it as diameter describe a circle cutting the given circle in M and M_1. (It will necessarily do so in two points on opposite sides of its diameter.)

Then QM, QM_1 will be tangents to the circle since QMO is a right angle being in a semicircle. (Euclid, Prop. 31, Bk. III.) It is always possible to draw two tangents to a circle from any external point.

POLE AND POLAR.   (Fig. 20.)

The line MM_1 is evidently perpendicular to OQ for the triangles QOM, QOM_1 are equal in all respects, i.e. the angle MOQ = the angle M_1OQ; then if MM_1 meets OQ in N we have in the two triangles NOM, NOM_1, $OM = OM_1$, ON common and the angle, NOM = the angle NOM_1, ∴ the angle ONM = the angle ONM_1, and ∴ each is a right angle.

The triangle MON is $\therefore$ similar to the triangle QOM and

$$\therefore ON : OM :: OM : OQ,$$

or $$ON \cdot OQ = r^2,$$

where r is the radius of the circle.

Now whether the point Q be taken inside or outside the circle, it is always possible to find on the line OQ a point N fulfilling the above condition, and a line MNM_1 drawn perpendicular to OQ through the point N so determined is called the *polar* of Q with respect to the circle, while the point Q is called the *pole* of MM_1 with respect to the circle.

To draw the *polar* of any point Q with respect to a given circle.

If the given point be without the circle the polar is, by the previous definition, the *chord of contact* of the tangents drawn from Q to the given circle. If the given point be within the circle, draw OQ and produce it, and through Q draw MQM_1 perpendicular to OQ, and meeting the circle in M and M_1 and at either M or M_1 draw MN or M_1N a tangent to the circle, meeting OQ produced in N, then a line through N perpendicular to OQ will be the required *polar*.

Cor. 1. If the given point be *on* the circle its polar is the tangent at the point, i.e. the *polar* passes through the *pole*.

Cor. 2. If a point A lie on the polar of Q then Q lies on the polar of A. For draw OA and on it drop a perpendicular Qq from Q meeting it in q and the circle in m and m_1 : then the triangles OQq, OAN are similar and

$$\therefore Oq : OQ :: ON : OA, \text{ i.e. } Oq \cdot OA = OQ \cdot ON = r^2,$$

by definition, r being the radius of the circle, i.e. mQm_1 is the polar of A which consequently passes through Q.

Cor. 3. The pairs of tangents drawn at the extremities of *any chord* through Q intersect in the straight line AB the polar of Q. Hence the *polar* may be defined as the locus of the points of intersection of tangents at the extremities of chords through a fixed point.

Given a circle and a triangle ABC, if we take the polars with respect to the circle, of A, B, C, we form a new triangle $A'B'C'$ called the *conjugate* triangle, A' being the pole of BC, B' of CA, and C' of AB.   In the particular case where the polars of A, B, C respectively are BC, CA, AB, the second triangle coincides with the first, and the triangle is called a *self-conjugate* triangle.

PROBLEM 21. (Fig. 21.) *To describe a circle to pass through two given points and touch a given straight line, lying outside the points.*

Let A and B be the given points and DD_1 the given straight line.   It will be observed that the point of contact of the line is

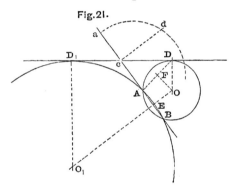

Fig.21.

not given—this would be a fourth geometrical condition and therefore if a circle is required to *touch a given line at a given point*, it can only in general fulfil one other condition as e.g. pass through one point outside the line.   See next problem.

Join AB and produce it to cut DD_1 in C and indefinitely beyond as to a.   It is a known proposition (Euclid 36, Book III.), that "if from any point without a circle two straight lines be drawn, one of which cuts the circle, and the other touches it; the rectangle contained by the whole line which cuts the circle and the part of it without the circle, shall be equal to the square on the line which touches it."

If therefore a mean proportional cd be taken between CA and CB, and its length be set off from C along DD_1 as CD, then obviously a perpendicular to DD_1 through D will be the locus of the centres of circles touching the given line in D.   If AB be bisected in E, and EO be drawn perpendicular to AB, EO will be the locus of centres of circles through A and B. The required centre will therefore be at O, the intersection of these loci and the distance to A, B, or D will be the required radius. Since the length CD may be set off on either side of C there are obviously two solutions as shewn.

If the line joining A and B be parallel to the given line, this solution fails, but the point of contact can be at once determined, since by symmetry it is obviously where EO cuts the given line, and a third point through which the circle must pass being thus obtained the solution can be completed by Problem 20.

PROBLEM 22. (Fig. 21.) *To describe a circle to pass through a given point A and to touch a given straight line DD_1 in a given point D.*

The straight line DO through D perpendicular to DD_1 is obviously the locus of centres of all circles touching the straight line in D, and the straight line FO through F the centre point of AD, perpendicular to AD is the locus of centres of all circles through A and D. The centre of required circle is therefore at O, the intersection of these loci, and the distance from O to A or D will be the required radius.

PROBLEM 23. (Fig. 22.) *To describe a circle to touch two straight lines AB, CD, one of them in a given point A.*

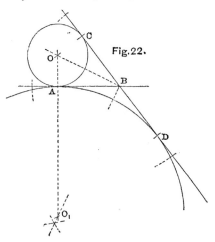

Fig. 22.

A locus of the centre is of course the line AO perpendicular to AB. A second locus will obviously be the line BO bisecting the angle ABC, and the required centre will therefore be at O. If at O a perpendicular OC be drawn to BC, the triangles OBA and OBC are equal in all respects and therefore $OA = OC =$ the required radius. The given lines make with each other the angle ABD as well as the angle ABC, and therefore bisecting the angle ABD, the centre O_1 of a second circle is obtained touching the other side of AB.

PROBLEM 24. (Fig. 23.) *To describe a circle to pass through a given point G and to touch two given lines AC, DF.*

The centre must obviously lie on the line KH bisecting the angle between the given lines in which the given point lies.

Fig.23.

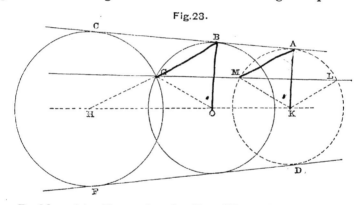

(See Problem 1.) Draw also the line GL passing through G and the intersection of the given lines (Problem 6). Take any point K on HK as centre, and describe a circle touching AC and DF, and cutting GL in M and L. This is always possible, since KH is the bisector of the angle between these lines. Draw GO parallel to MK and GH parallel to KL, O and H will be centres of circles fulfilling the required conditions: for if A is the point of contact of the trial circle, KA will be perpendicular to AC, and if OB, HC be drawn perpendicular to AC, KA, OB and HC will all be parallel, and therefore the triangle GOB will be similar to MKA and GHC to LKA, but the triangles MKA, LKA are isosceles, therefore also OG must be equal to OB and HG to HC.

PROBLEM 25. (Fig. 24.) *To describe a circle to touch three given lines AB, BC, CA, not more than two of which are parallel.*

The line AO bisecting the angle BAC will be the locus of centres of circles touching BA and CA, the line CO bisecting the

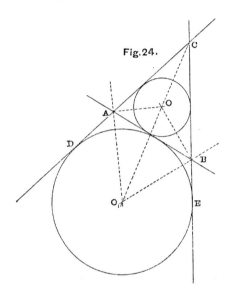

Fig. 24.

angle BCA will be the corresponding locus for BC and CA. Hence O will be a centre for a circle touching all three lines. Since BA makes with BC and CA not only the angles ABC, BAC respectively, but also the angles ABE, BAD, a second solution is obviously obtained by bisecting the exterior angle BAD as shewn by AO_1, and similarly for the remaining sides. Hence four circles can be drawn touching three straight lines. The exterior circles are said to be *escribed* to the triangle ABC.

PROBLEM 26. (Fig. 25.) *To describe a circle to touch a given circle (centre C, radius CD) and a given straight line AB in a given point A.*

The line AO drawn through A perpendicular to AB is a locus of the required centre. Draw a diameter DD_1 of the circle parallel to AO. Join AD cutting the given circle in E, and join

3—2

CE producing it to cut *AO* in *O*, *O* will be the centre of a circle fulfilling the given condition. A second solution is possible, since

Fig. 25.

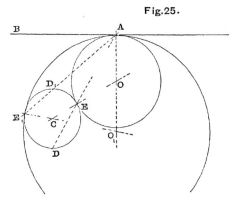

A may be joined to either extremity of DD_1. O_1 is the centre of a second circle.

Proof.   The angle *OAE* = angle *CDE*,   (Euc. I. 29.)

,,   *CED* =   ,,   *CDE*,   (Euc. I. 5.)

,,   *CED* =   ,,   *OEA*,   (Euc. I. 15.)

∴ ,,   *OAE* =   ,,   *OEA*,

and   ∴   *OE = OA*.   (Euc. I. 6.)

Hence a circle through *A* from centre *O* will pass through *E* and will there touch the given circle, since they will have a common tangent perpendicular to *CO*.

PROBLEM 27.   (Fig. 26.)   *To describe a circle to touch a given circle (centre A, radius AD) and pass through two given points B, C, which must be either both inside, or both outside the circle.*

Draw a line through *BC*; bisect *BC* in *E* and draw *EO* perpendicular to *BC*.   *EO* is the locus of centres of circles through *B* and *C*.   Take any point *O* such that a circle described with centre *O* and radius *OB*, or *OC* will cut the given circle as in *MN*.   Draw a line through *MN* cutting *BC* in *T*, and from *T* draw tangents *TD*, TD_1 to the given circle (Prob. 20).   Lines joining *AD*, AD_1 will cut *EO* in points O_1, O_2 which will be the centres of circles fulfilling the required conditions.

Two circles can generally be drawn. If the line joining the given points lie wholly without the given circle, one circle will

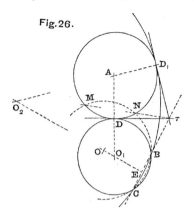

Fig. 26.

touch the given circle externally and one internally (as in the fig.); if the line joining the points cut the given circle, and both points lie on the same side of the circle, both circles will touch the given circle externally, and if the points lie on opposite sides of the circle both will touch it internally. If the line joining the given points touch the given circle one circle only can be drawn.

Proof. The rectangle $TM . TN =$ rect. $TB . TC$ (Euc. III. 36, Cor.),

,, ,, $=$ sq. on TD. (Euc. III. 36).

$\therefore$ sq. on $TD =$ rect. $TB . TC$

$\therefore TD$ is a tangent to the circle going through B, D, C.

PROBLEM 28. (Fig. 27.) *To describe a circle to touch a given circle (centre A, radius AR) and two given straight lines BC, DE.*

There are several solutions depending on the relative positions of the lines and circle. If the lines are parallel the problem is impossible unless some part of the circle lies between the lines. In this case the line drawn midway between the lines parallel to either of them is evidently a locus of the required centre; a second locus will be the circle described with centre A and radius equal to the sum of AR and half the distance between the lines, and since these loci intersect in two points, either may be taken as the centre of the required circle. If the given lines are not parallel and the given circle cuts one of them, as in the fig., then by

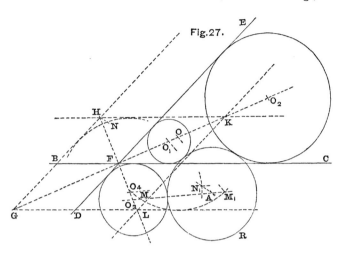

Fig. 27.

drawing lines parallel to the given lines at a distance from them equal to the radius of the given circle, the problem may be reduced to describing a circle to touch these lines (in pairs) and to pass through the centre of the given circle, i.e. may be reduced to Problem 24.   Let the given lines intersect in F and consider first the circles which can be drawn in the angle EFC.   Draw GH, LK parallel to FE at a distance from it equal to AR and similarly HK and GL parallel to FC. FK will bisect the angle CFE and will be the locus of the required centres.   Take any point O on it as centre and describe a circle to touch GH and GL cutting GA in M, M_1.   Then AO_1 drawn parallel to M_1O to cut FK in O_1 determines O_1 a required centre and AO_2 parallel to MO determines O_2 a second required centre.   Similarly for the circles lying in the angle DFC.   Any point O_4 on FL being taken as centre and a circle described to touch GH and HK cutting HA in N and N_1; AO_3 parallel to N_1O_4 determines O_3, the centre of a third circle fulfilling the required conditions and a line through A parallel to NO_4 would determine a fourth centre.   It is of course accidental that in the figure O_3 falls nearly on GA.

If the given circle did not cut either of the given lines, it would still be possible to draw four circles touching the lines and the circle, but two of them would have internal contact with the given circle, instead of all touching it externally as in the figure.

If the given circle cut *both* lines there would be six possible solutions.

PROBLEM 29. (Fig. 28.) *To describe a circle to touch a given circle (centre A, radius AF) to touch a given line BC and to pass through a given point D.*

If the given point be within the circle, the given line must not be wholly outside the circle.

From A draw AC perpendicular to the given line and meeting the circle in E and F. First join ED and on it determine a point

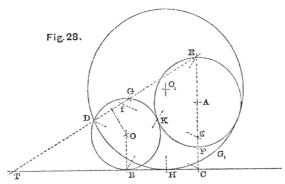

Fig. 28.

G such that the rect. $ED \cdot EG = \text{rect. } EC \cdot EF$, i.e. take EG a fourth proportional to ED, EC, EF. [Making Ef (on ED) $= EF$, draw fg parallel to DC meeting EC in g and make $EG = Eg$.] Then a circle through D and G and touching the given line will also touch the given circle and the problem is reduced to Problem 21. If ED, BC intersect in T, a mean proportional (TB) must be taken between TG and TD so determining the point of contact. TB may be set off along BC on either side of T and hence there are two solutions giving external contact. Second.—Join FD and on it determine a point G_1 such that rect. $FD \cdot FG_1 = \text{rect. on } FC$, FE. i.e. take a fourth proportional to FD, FC, FE. G_1 must be taken on the opposite side of F to D because C and E are on opposite sides of F. Then circles through D and G_1 touching the given line

will also touch the given circle, and this case also reduces to
Problem 21. There are again two possible circles because if
DF and BC intersect in T_1 the mean proportional (T_1H) between
T_1D and T_1G_1 may be set off on either side of T_1.

Proof. Join B the point of contact of circle through D and G
to E meeting the given circle in K and join FK. Then the triangles EKF and ECB are similar

$$\therefore EC : EB :: EK : EF,$$

or $\qquad\qquad$ rect. $EC . EF =$ rect. $EB . EK,$

but $\qquad\qquad\qquad$,, $\quad=$ rect. $ED . EG$ (const.).

$$\therefore \text{rect. } ED . EG = \text{rect. } EB . EK.$$

$\therefore K$ must be on circumference of circle through BDG. (Euc.
II. 36 Cor.)

Join OK, then angle $OBK =$ angle OKB (Euc. I. 5),

$\qquad\qquad$,, $\quad AKE = \quad$,, $\quad AEK ($ $\quad$,, $\quad),$

$\qquad\qquad$,, $\quad AEK = \quad$,, $\quad OKB$ (Euc. I. 29),

$$\therefore \text{,, } \quad AKE = \text{ ,, } \quad OBK,$$

and therefore OKA is a straight line, i.e. the two circles will
touch at K.

PROBLEM 30. *On a given straight line AB to describe a segment
of a circle which shall contain a given angle* (Fig. 29).

Bisect AB in C and through C draw CO perpendicular to AB.
CO is of course a locus of the centre.) Make the angle OCD

Fig.29.

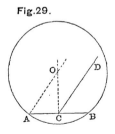

qual to the given angle (p. 4) and through A draw AO parallel
to CD meeting CO in O. O will be the centre of the required
ircle. (Euc. III. 20.)

PROBLEM 31. (Fig. 30.) *To draw a line touching two given circles, neither of which lies wholly inside the other.*

A and AB are the centre and radius of the larger circle and C and CD those of the smaller circle.

Join AC, cutting larger circle in B.

From B on AC make $BM = BN = CD$, and with A as centre describe circle MM_1M_2. From C draw tangents CM_1, CM_2 to

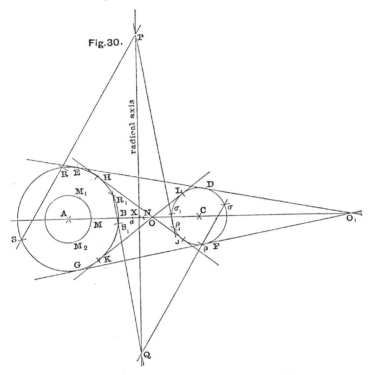

Fig. 30.

touch this circle (Prob. 20). Produce AM_1, AM_2 to meet the circle in E and G, and lines ED, GF through E and G parallel to CM_1, CM_2 will be tangents to both circles. These tangents meet in (O_1) a point lying on AC produced, and are the only pair that can be drawn if the given circles intersect. If the smaller circle lies wholly outside the larger, as in fig. 30, a second pair can be drawn by describing a circle through N with A as centre, drawing tangents CN_1, CN_2 to it, and drawing HJ, KL parallel to these lines respectively, which will intersect in (O) a point on AC between the given circles. The construction is obvious, since $EM_1 = BM = CD.$

Common tangents to two circles may be drawn practically with all attainable accuracy by adjusting a set square to touch the circles, and drawing a line by its edge; but the points of contact should always be determined by drawing the radii perpendicular to the tangent.

Properties of a system of Two or more circles.

The points O, O_1 in which common tangents to two circles intersect are called the centres of similitude of the two circles. As is easily seen, they are the points where the line joining the centres is cut externally and internally in the ratio of the radii: and in this sense both exist when the circles cut each other, in which case of course only one pair of common tangents can be drawn, and even when one circle lies wholly inside the other, so that it is impossible to draw any common tangent.

If through a centre of similitude we draw any two lines meeting the first circle in the points R, R_1, S, S_1, and the second in the points ρ, ρ_1, σ, σ_1, then the chords RS, $\rho\sigma$ will be parallel, as also the chords R_1S_1 and $\rho_1\sigma_1$; and the chords RS and $\rho_1\sigma_1$, R_1S_1 and $\rho\sigma$ will intersect respectively in points P and Q on a line perpendicular to the line joining the centres of the circles.

This line is called the *radical axis* of the two circles.

The rectangle $OR \,.\, OR_1$ is constant, since it equals the square on OH the tangent from O (Euc. III. 36), i.e.

$$OR \,.\, OR_1 = OS \,.\, OS_1$$

and $\qquad OP \,.\, O\rho_1 = O\sigma \,.\, O\sigma_1.$

Proof. In the triangles OAR, $OC\rho$, the angle $AOR =$ the angle $CO\rho$ and $OA : OC :: AR : C\rho$,

$\therefore$ also $\qquad OR : O\rho :: AR : C\rho$ (Euc. VI. 7),

i.e. the ratio $\dfrac{OR}{O\rho}$ is constant and equal to the ratio of the radii of the circles wherever the line $OR\rho$ be drawn,

$$\therefore \quad OR : OS :: O\rho : O\sigma$$

and the angle $ROS =$ the angle $\rho O \sigma$;

$\therefore$ the triangles ROS, $\rho O \sigma$ are similar in all respects, so that the angle $ORS =$ the angle $O \rho \sigma$ and $\rho \sigma$ is parallel to RS.

Similarly $R_1 S_1$ is parallel to $\rho_1 \sigma_1$, which proves the first part of the proposition.

Again, since SRR_1S_1 is inscribed in a circle, the angle $PRO =$ the angle $SS_1R_1 =$ the angle $S\sigma_1P$. The triangles $PR\rho_1$ and $P\sigma_1S$ are therefore similar, since the angle $RP\rho_1$ is common to both.

$$\therefore \quad PR : P\rho_1 :: P\sigma_1 : PS,$$

i. e. $$PR \cdot PS = P\rho_1 \cdot P\sigma_1,$$

but $\quad PR \cdot PS =$ square of tangent from P to circle A,

and $\quad P\rho_1 \cdot P\sigma_1 = \quad$,, $\qquad$,, $\qquad\qquad$,, $\quad C$;

$\therefore$ the tangents from P to the two circles are equal, and

$$\therefore \quad \overline{PA}|^2 - \overline{AB}|^2 = \overline{PC}|^2 - \overline{CD}|^2 ;$$

similarly tangents from Q to the two circles are equal.

But the locus of the intersection of equal tangents to two circles is a straight line perpendicular to the line joining their centres, and dividing the distance between them so that the difference of the squares of the parts is equal to the difference of the squares of the radii: for if X be such a point and PX perpendicular to AC, at every point on it we shall have

$$PA^2 - AX^2 = PX^2 = \overline{PC}_{|}{}^2 - CX^2,$$

$$\therefore \quad \overline{PA}|^2 - \overline{PC}|^2 = AX^2 - CX^2 ;$$

and as above $\quad PA^2 - PC^2 = AB^2 - CD^2 = AX^2 - CX^2.$

Hence the line PQ in the figure must be such locus which proves the second part of the proposition.

DEFINITION. A line drawn perpendicular to AC, the line joining the centres of two given circles, through a point X on it, such that the difference of the squares of AX and CX is equal to the difference of the squares of the radii of the two circles is called the *radical axis* of the two circles.

As already shewn, it is the locus of the intersection of equal tangents to the two circles.

It may be constructed as in the last proposition or immediately from the definition by bisecting AC in a (fig. 30), and making aX towards C, the centre of the smaller circle, a fourth proportional to $2AC$, $AB + CD$, and $AB - CD$,

i.e. by making $aX : R - r :: R + r : 2AC$,

where R and r are the radii of the circle, and drawing a line through X perpendicular to AC; for in this case

$$AC \times 2aX = R^2 - r^2 \text{ but } AC = AX + XC \text{ and } 2aX = AX - CX$$
$$\therefore (AX + CX)(AX - CX) = R^2 - r^2 = AX^2 - CX^2.$$

The radical axis bisects the distance between the polars with respect to the two circles, of either centre of similitude, which furnishes another method of constructing it.

Given three circles (centres C, C_1, C_2, radii r, r_1, r_2); the line joining a centre of similitude of C and C_1 to a centre of similitude of C and C_2 will pass through a centre of similitude of C_1 and C_2. Let S_2 and S_2' (fig. 31) be the centres of similitude of

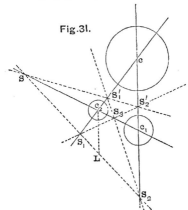

Fig.31.

C and C_1, and S_1 a centre of similitude of C and C_2, and let $S_2 S_1$, $C_1 C_2$ meet in S, S will be a centre of similitude of C_1 and C_2.

For since $\qquad CS_2' : C_1 S_2' :: r : r_1 :: CS_2 : C_1 S_2$,

$$\therefore \quad CS_2' : CS_2 :: C_1 S_2' : C_1 S_2,$$

or $CS_2' C_1 S_2$ is a harmonic range; therefore $S(CS_2' C_1 S_2)$ is a harmonic pencil, and therefore if CC_2 cuts SS_2' in S_1',

$CS_1' C_2 S_1$ is a harmonic range, and since S_1 is a centre of similitude of C and C_2, S_1' must be the other.

Through C_2 draw C_2L parallel to CS_2 and meeting SS_2 in L.
Then by similar triangles

$$C_2S : C_1S :: C_2L : C_1S_2,$$

and $\qquad C_2L : C_2S_1 :: CS_2 : CS_1,\ \text{or}\ C_2L = \dfrac{C_2S_1 . CS_2}{CS_1},$

$$\therefore\ C_2S : C_1S :: \frac{C_2S_1 . CS_2}{CS_1} : C_1S_2,$$

or $\qquad \dfrac{C_2S}{C_1S} = \dfrac{C_2S_1}{CS_1} . \dfrac{CS_2}{C_1S_2} = \dfrac{r_2}{r} . \dfrac{r}{r_1}$

$$= \frac{r_2}{r_1},$$

or S is a centre of similitude of C_1 and C_2.

Since for each pair of circles there are two centres of similitude, there will be in all *six* for the three circles, and these will be distributed along *four* axes of similitude, as represented in the figure.

Corollary. If a circle (centre A) touch two others (centres C and C_1) the line joining the points of contact will pass through a centre of similitude of C and C_1. For when two circles touch, one of their centres of similitude will coincide with the point of contact. If A touch C and C_1 either both externally or both internally, the line joining the points of contact will pass through the *external* centre of similitude of C and C_1. If A touch one externally and the other internally, the line joining the points of contact will pass through the *internal* centre of similitude*.

Given any three circles, if we take the radical axis of each pair of circles, these three lines will meet in a point, which is called the *radical centre* of the three circles.

For let the radical axes of A and C and of B and C intersect in R (fig. 34), then the tangents from R to A and C are equal, as also the tangents from R to B and C; therefore the tangent from R to A must be equal to the tangent from R to B, i.e. R must be a point on the radical of A and B, which proves the proposition.

If two circles have a common radical axis, and points L and L_1 be taken on the line joining their centres at a distance from its

* Salmon's *Conic Sections.*

intersection (X) with the radical axis equal to the tangent which can be drawn from X to either circle, these points are called the *limiting* points of the entire system of circles which have the same (common) radical axis. They "have many remarkable properties in the theory of these circles, and are such that the polar of either of them, with regard to any of the circles, is a line drawn through the other perpendicular to the line of centres. These points are real when the circles of the system have common two imaginary points, and are imaginary when they have real points common*."

When they are real it is evidently impossible for the centre of any circle of the system to lie between them, and the more nearly the centre approaches to either of them the smaller must the corresponding radius be. The *limiting* points themselves may therefore be considered as circles of the system of infinitely small radius.

If a system of circles have a common radical axis, and from any point on it tangents be drawn to all the circles, the locus of the points of contact must be a circle, since all these tangents are equal; and it is evident that this circle cuts any of the given system at right angles, since its radii are tangents to the given system. It is the circle passing through the *limiting points* of the system.

Conversely all circles which cut the given system at right angles pass through the limiting points of the system.

PROBLEM 32. (Fig. 32.) *To describe a circle to touch two given circles (centres A and B, radii AD, BE respectively) and to pass through a given point C.*

Take S a centre of similitude (p. 42) of A and B; draw CS and find the poles P and P_1 of this line with respect to each circle, (i.e. draw AP, BP_1 perpendicular to CS and intersecting the chords of contact of tangents from S in P and P_1). Draw XR the radical axis of the given circles (p. 44): draw AC, bisect it in m and make mM on it towards C of length such that

$$AC : AD :: AD : 2mM;$$

* Salmon's *Conic Sections.*

draw MR perpendicular to AC meeting the radical axis in R. The lines RP, RP_1 will cut the circles in the points of contact a, b; a_1 b_1 of the required circles and their centres can be at once found by producing Aa, Ba_1 &c. to meet in O and O_1.

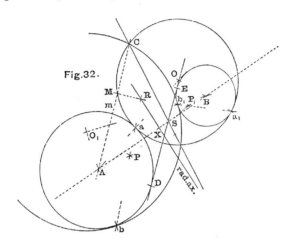

Fig.32.

In the figure the circles touch one of the given circles internally and one externally because S is the internal centre of similitude. If the external one be taken two more circles can be drawn, one touching both externally, the other both internally.

PROBLEM 33. *To describe a circle to touch two given circles (centres A and B, radii AC, BD respectively) and a given straight line EF* (fig. 33).

Draw the radical axis of the given circles, meeting EF in R, p. 44. From A and B drop perpendiculars on the given line meeting it in E and F and the circles in C, C_1, D and D_1 respectively. Join $C_1 D_1$ cutting AB in S a centre of similitude of A and B. Find P and P_1 the poles of this line with respect to the circles (p. 31). Draw RP, RP_1 cutting the circles in ab, $a_1 b_1$. Then aa_1, bb_1 are the points of contact of circles fulfilling the required conditions, and the intersections of Aa, Ba_1 and of Ab, Bb_1 give the corresponding centres. The above circles each touch both of the given circles externally or both internally since S is the external centre of similitude of A and B (p. 45). If C_1 be joined to D or C to D_1 cutting AB in the internal centre of similitude, the poles of these lines give the points of contact of circles touching one of the given circles internally and the other externally—

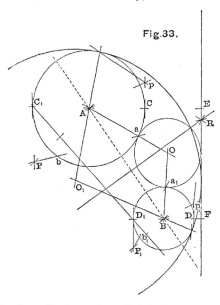

Fig.33.

and if C be joined to D the poles of this line give another pair of circles touching both externally or both internally. One of these latter is shewn in the fig.   There are altogether 8 solutions.

Second Solution.   This problem may also be solved by dropping perpendiculars from A and B on the given line as AE, BF, bisecting the parts lying between the circles and the lines as CE, DF, in G and H and describing parabolas having A and B as foci and G and H as vertices respectively (Prob. 36). The first will necessarily be the locus of the centres of circles touching the line and the circle A externally, and the second will be the locus of the centres of circles touching the given line and the circle B externally, and hence their intersection (O) will determine the centre of a circle touching both circles externally and the given line.   Similarly if C_1E be bisected in G_1 and D_1F in H_1 and parabolas be described having A and B as foci and G_1, H_1, as vertices respectively, each of these curves will be the locus of centres of circles touching the line and the corresponding given circle *internally*. Hence the points of intersection of these four parabolas determine the centres of circles fulfilling the conditions of the problem.

O_1 gives internal contact with both circles,

O_2 gives internal with A external with B,

O_3 gives external or internal „ „

and so on.

The proof of the construction is obvious from the definition of a parabola subsequently given.

PROBLEM 34.   *To describe a circle to touch three given circles (centres ABC, radii AD, BE, CG respectively) (Fig. 34).*

If the circle be required to touch the three either all externally or all internally draw the external axis of similitude SS_1 p. 45,

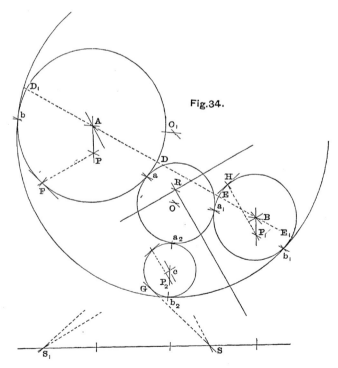

Fig.34.

and take the poles PP_1P_2 of this line with respect to each circle, p. 31.

Find the radical centre R of the three circles (p. 45). Then the lines RP, RP_1, RP_2 cut the circles in the points ab, a_1b_1, a_2b_2, in which the required circles must touch them : and the centre of the circle touching all three externally is given by the intersection of Aa, Ba_1, Ca_2, which three lines will meet in a point, and the centre of the circle touching all three internally is given by the intersection of Ab, Bb_1, Cb_2.

A similar construction with the remaining three axes of similitude, will determine the circles touching one internally and the remaining two externally and vice versâ.

There are altogether eight solutions.

Second solution.   Join AB cutting the circles in D, D_1, E and E_1.   Bisect DE in K and D_1E_1 in K_1. BK will necessarily be equal to AK_1.   With B and A as foci, and K, K_1 as vertices describe an hyperbola (Prob. 89), the branch of which through K will be the locus of the centres of circles touching circles A and B *externally*, and the branch of which through K_1 will be the locus of centres of circles touching these circles *internally*.   Similarly, join BC cutting the corresponding circles in F_1, F, G, G_1.   Bisect FG in L, and F_1G_1 in L_1 and with C and B as foci, and L, L_1 as vertices, describe an hyperbola, the two branches of which will be the loci of centres of circles touching circles B and C externally and internally.   The intersection of corresponding branches of the two hyperbolas will therefore determine O_1, O_2, the centres of circles touching the three given circles all externally or all internally.

Again bisecting DE_1 in M and D_1E in M_1 and taking B, A as foci and M, M_1 as vertices, an hyperbola can be described the branches of which will be the loci of centres of circles touching circles A and B, the one internally and the other externally, and the intersections of this hyperbola with that through L and L_2 in O_3, O_4 will give centres of two more circles fulfilling the given conditions.   The hyperbola through N and N_1, points corresponding to

M, M_1, will determine O_5 and O_6, two additional centres corresponding to O_3, O_4 and lastly, by its intersection with the two branches through M and M_1 will determine O_7 and O_8.

The construction is obvious from the definition of the hyperbola subsequently given.

PROBLEM 35. (Fig. 35.) *To draw a circular arc through three given points A, B, C without using the centre.*

Let AB be greater than either AC or BC. With centre A and radius AB describe an arc BD meeting AC in D, and with

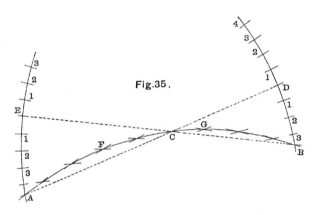

Fig. 35.

centre B and the same radius describe an arc AE meeting BC in E. From D on each side of it set off on the arc any equal distances $D1$, and set off the same distances from E on the arc EA, similarly make $D2 = E2$, and so on. The line joining A to any point *above* D will intersect the line joining B to the corresponding point *below* E and vice versâ in points (as F, G) on the required arc.

Proof. It is easily seen that the angle AFB = angle ACB = the angle AGB, &c., and therefore $AFCGB$ all lie on a circular arc.

EXAMPLES ON CHAPTER II.

1.   Describe a circle to pass through two given points, P and P_1, and to bisect the circumference of a given circle (centre C, radius CA).

(Draw PC and produce it to D so that $PC . CD = AC^2$.   The circle through P, D, P_1 fulfils required condition.)

2.   Draw two circles cutting orthogonally, and shew by construction that any line through the centre of either cutting both circles is divided harmonically at the points of intersection.

3.   Given the base AB of a triangle and the sum of the squares of the sides $AC^2 + BC^2$, draw the locus of the vertex.

(A circle, centre at E the middle point of AB, and radius $= \sqrt{\dfrac{AC^2 + BC^2}{2} - \overline{AE}|^2}.$)

4.   Draw two circles (centres A and B) cutting orthogonally, and draw their common chord meeting AB in C.   Draw DE a chord of the first circle passing through B, and shew that a circle can be described through $ADEC$.

5.   The centre A of a circle lies on another circle which cuts the former in B, C; AD is a chord of the latter circle meeting BC in E, shew that the polar of D with respect to the first circle passes through E.

6.   At two fixed points A, B are drawn AC, BD at right angles to AB and on the same side of it, and of such magnitude that the rectangle AC, BD is equal to the square on AB: prove that the circles whose diameters are AC, BD will touch each other, and that their point of contact will lie on a fixed circle.

(The circle on AB as diameter.)

7.   With three given points A, B, C not lying in one straight line as centres describe three circles which shall have three common tangents.

(Bisect the angle BAC by AD meeting BC in D,
   „   „ CBA by BE „ CA in E,
   „   „ ACB by CF „ AB in F,
then ED, DF, FE will be the required common tangents.)

The question is obviously, given the centres of the escribed circles of a triangle, to draw the triangle.

8. A and B are two given points on the same side of a given straight line CD, which AB meets in C. Determine the points on CD on each side of C at which AB subtends a greater angle than at any other point on the same side.

(The points of contact of circles through A and B, and touching CD. Prob. 21.)

9. A and B are two given points within a circle; and AB is drawn and produced both ways so as to divide the whole circumference into two arcs. Determine the point in each of these arcs at which AB subtends the greatest angle.

(The points of contact of circles through A and B touching the given circle. Prob. 27.)

10. Shew by construction that the circle which passes through the middle points of the sides of any triangle ABC will pass through the feet of the perpendiculars from A, B, C on the opposite sides, and if O be the intersection of these perpendiculars, will also pass through the middle points of OA, OB, OC. Shew also that it will touch the inscribed and escribed circles of the triangle, and that its radius is half that of the circumscribing circle.

(The circle is called the nine point circle.)

11. Given four points $ABCD$ in a straight line taken in order. Shew that the locus of the point P moving so that the angle $APB =$ the angle CPD, is a circle which may be constructed in the following manner. Let AB be less than CD, and take b between C and D so that $bD = AB$. The centre is on the given straight line at a distance from A, such that

$$AO \, : \, AC \, :: \, AB \, : \, Cb,$$

and the radius (r) is such that

$$r^2 = OB, \; OC = OA, \; OD.$$

12. Find the locus of a point such that the area of the triangle whose angular points are the feet of the perpendiculars from it on the three sides of a given triangle, has a constant area.

[It is a circle of radius ρ, concentric with the circle circumscribing the given triangle; and ρ is determined from the equation

$$\rho^2 = R^2\left(\frac{4k}{\Delta} - 1\right),$$

where R is the radius of circumscribing circle, k is the given constant area and Δ is the area of the given triangle. If $4k < \Delta$, ρ is given by the equation

$$\rho^2 = R^2\left(1 - \frac{4k}{\Delta}\right).$$

(Salmon's *Conic Sections*, Chap. IX.)]

As a numerical example, draw any triangle ABC, and take

$$\rho : R :: \sqrt{7} : 1,$$

shew that in this case $k = \dfrac{\Delta}{2}$.

13.　Given on a straight line four points in the order P, A, B, Q; describe a circle passing through A and B such that tangents drawn to it from P and Q may be parallel.

[With centres P and Q and radii $\sqrt{PA, PB}$, $\sqrt{QA, QB}$ respectively describe two circles. A circle passing through A and B, and through the points of contact of a common tangent to these circles will be the one required.]

14.　Given a fixed circle and an external point O. Draw the tangent at any point P of the circle and complete the rectangle which has OP for side and the tangent for diagonal. Shew that the angular point opposite O will lie on the polar of O.

15.　From the obtuse angle A of a triangle ABC draw a line meeting the base in D so that AD shall be a mean proportional between the segments of the base.

[Find O the centre of the circle circumscribing ABC. On AO as diameter describe a circle cutting the base in D, the required point.]

16.　Find on a given line AB a point A such that its polar with respect to a given circle shall pass through a given point C.

[Find P the pole of AB, then the pole of CP will lie on AB i.e. will be the required point A.]

17.   Given a point A, a line through it AB, and a circle centre C ; draw a triangle APB which shall be *self-conjugate* with respect to the circle (p. 32).

Take P the pole of the given line and from C draw CB perpendicular to AP meeting AB in B, APB will be the required triangle ; for since B is on the polar of P the polar of B will pass through P, and is perpendicular to CB, i.e. is the line AP.

18.   Given a triangle APB obtuse-angled at P, to draw the circle with respect to which the triangle shall be self-conjugate.

The centre (C) of the circle must evidently be the intersection of the perpendiculars from the angular points on the opposite sides.   Let the perpendicular from P on AB meet it in D.   The radius of the circle will be a mean proportional between CP and CD.

19.   Given a circle, describe a triangle which shall be self-conjugate with respect thereto, and with its sides parallel to those of a given triangle abp, obtuse-angled at p.

Through C the centre of the given circle draw CA perpendicular to bp, CB perpendicular to ap and CM perpendicular to ab. The vertices of the required triangle will lie, one on each of these lines.   Through any point m on CM draw dme perpendicular to CM meeting CA in d and CB in e, and through d draw df perpendicular to CB and Bf perpendicular to CA ; f will necessarily lie on CM.

If D is the point on Cm through which the side of the required triangle perpendicular to Cm passes :—

$$\overline{CD}|^2 = r^2 \frac{Cm}{Cf},$$

where r is the radius of the given circle, i.e. CD is a mean proportional between r and a length l determined by taking a fourth proportional to Cf, Cm, and r ; for if

$$Cf : Cm :: r : l,$$
$$l = r\frac{Cm}{Cf}, \text{ and } \therefore \overline{CD}|^2 = lr.$$

CHAPTER III.

THE PARABOLA.

If a line be drawn through the centre of a given circle perpendicular to the plane of the circle, the surface generated by a straight line which passes through a fixed point on the first line and moves round the circumference of the circle is called a right circular cone. It will be shewn in Chap. IX. that the intersection of this surface with any plane must be one or other of the following:—a point, a pair of straight lines, a circle, a parabola, an ellipse or an hyperbola. The construction of these last three curves from their definition as the sections of a cone seems *à priori* to be the natural way of treating the subject; but the fact is they are more easily constructed from some of their known plane properties, and therefore, deferring the consideration of them as lying on the surface of a solid, each will at first be defined as the locus of a point moving in a plane so that its distance from a fixed point is always in a constant ratio to its distance from a fixed line, both point and line being in the plane of motion.

The fixed point is called the focus, and the fixed line the directrix.

In the parabola the ratio is one of equality, i.e. the distance from the fixed point is always equal to the distance from the fixed line.

In the ellipse the ratio is one of less inequality, i.e. the distance from the fixed point is always less than the distance from the fixed line.

In the hyperbola the ratio is one of greater inequality, i.e. the distance from the fixed point is always greater than the distance from the fixed line.

The eccentricity of a conic is the numerical value of this ratio.

A parabola can generally be drawn to satisfy four geometrical conditions, and four conditions are in general necessary and sufficient to determine the curve. Thus an infinite number of parabolas can be drawn to pass through three given points or to touch three given lines, or to pass through two points and touch a given line, or to fulfil any three similar conditions, and in each case a fourth condition must be added to make the exact solution possible. At the same time four conditions may sometimes lead to more than one solution, just as, more circles than one can frequently be drawn satisfying three given conditions; and occasionally some limitation as to the position of the points or lines given as data of the problem, is necessary to enable a real curve to be drawn.

If the focus is given in any particular problem, this is equivalent to two geometrical conditions, and therefore in general only two others can be fulfilled, i.e. given the focus and two points through which the curve is to pass, the problem is completely determinate and a parabola cannot be drawn to have a given point as focus and to pass through any *three* random points. The directrix being given is also equivalent to two geometrical conditions, and therefore along with it, only two others can be fulfilled, such as, e.g. to pass through a given point and touch a given line, or to touch two given lines, or to touch a given line at a given point, &c.

PROBLEM 36. (Fig. 36.) *To draw a parabola the focus F and the directrix MX being given.*

Draw FX from F perpendicular to MX. Bisect FX in A and A will be a point in the curve. With F as centre and any radius greater than FA (as $F\,3$) draw a circular arc $D3D_1$ set off from A towards F a distance $A3'$ equal to $A3$, and at $3'$ erect a perpendicular to FX meeting the circular arc in DD_1. These will be points in the curve, and similarly drawing any number of arcs with F as centre and setting off from A towards F, distances equal to the distances of the arcs beyond A, and erecting per-

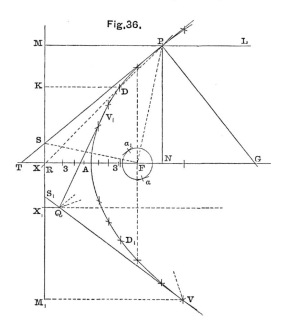

Fig.36.

pendiculars to FX at these points meeting the corresponding arcs, any number of points on the curve may be determined and the curve drawn through the points thus obtained.

The construction is obvious: at any point as P draw PN perpendicular to AX meeting it in N; then the distance FP from the focus is to be equal to PM the perpendicular distance from the directrix. But $FP = FA +$ the distance of the arc beyond A; and $PM = XN = XA +$ the same distance.

$$\therefore FP = PM \text{ since } FA = AX.$$

(See also the next problem.)

DEF. From the construction the curve is evidently symmetrical about FX which is called *the axis*. The point A where the curve cuts the axis is called *the vertex*, and any line parallel to the axis is called *a diameter* of the curve.

The parabola consists of one infinite branch. Like the focus and the directrix, the vertex and axis are each equivalent to two conditions in the construction, but it should be noticed that certain pairs of these lines and points given together are equivalent not to four but only to three conditions. This apparent anomaly may be thus explained. Suppose directrix and axis are given, these are two lines at right angles to each other and hence the direction of either is implicitly involved in that of the other, and thus instead of the two conditions of *position* and *direction* being given independently along with the second line, one only, namely position, is really given, and the two lines together are therefore equivalent to *three* conditions only. Similarly focus and axis, or vertex and axis make only three conditions since the position of the axis is partly involved in that of the focus or of the vertex.

To draw a tangent at any point.

P and D (fig. 36) being any two points on the curve, if the line through PD meet the directrix in R and DK is parallel to PM, then

$$FP : FD :: PM : DK$$
$$:: PR : DR$$

by similar triangles, and ∴ FR bisects the exterior angle between FP and FD (Euc. vi. Prop. A). Hence if the point D move up to and coincide with P so that the chord PD becomes the tangent at P (Def. p. 30), in which case FD of course coincides with FP, the line FS drawn from the focus to the point in which the tangent at P meets the directrix, must be perpendicular to FP. The triangle SFP is therefore equal and similar to the triangle SMP. Hence *the tangent at any point P of a parabola bisects the angle between the focal distance FP and the perpendicular PM from P on the directrix.* It can therefore be drawn either by bisecting the angle FPM or by making FT on the axis equal to FP, and joining PT; for in this case the angle FPT = angle FTP, which is equal to the alternate angle TPM, PM, FT being parallel.

DEF. The perpendicular PN from P on the axis is called the *ordinate* of P. The double ordinate through the focus is called the *latus-rectum* of the curve, and its length is always equal to $4AF$. It is sometimes called the *principal parameter* of the curve. Since

$$FP = PM = XN = FT \text{ and } FA = AX,$$
$$XN - AX = FT - FA,$$
$$\text{i. e. } AT = AN \text{ or } NT = 2, AN.$$

DEF.   The line NT is called *the sub-tangent* at the point P.

The line PG perpendicular to the tangent at P is called *the normal* at P.

It has been shewn that the tangent bisects the angle FPM, ∴ PG bisects the angle FPL where L is a point on MP produced,

i. e. the angle $FPG = $ angle $LPG = $ angle PGF,

and ∴ $FG = FP = PM = XN$,

∴ $FG - FN = XN - FN$,

i. e. $NG = FX = 2AF$.

DEF.   The line NG is called the *sub-normal* of the point P.

The tangent at the vertex is perpendicular to the axis, as is obvious from the symmetry of the curve, and a perpendicular from the focus on any tangent intersects it and the tangent at the vertex in the same point.

The focus and directrix being given, tangents to the curve can be drawn from an external point Q thus (fig. 36). With centre F and radius equal to the distance of Q from the directrix describe a circle; draw tangents to it from Q, and join F to the points of contact a, a_1, producing the lines to meet the curve in VV_1. QV, QV_1 will be tangents, for, if VM_1 be the perpendicular on the directrix, and the diameter at Q meet the directrix in X_1 and VQ meet it in S_1,

$$VM_1 : QX_1 :: VS_1 : Q_1S_1,$$
$$\text{or } FV : Fa :: VS_1 : Q_1S_1,$$

∴ FS_1 is parallel to aQ, but aQ is perpendicular to FV, ∴ FS_1 is perpendicular to FV, and ∴ VS_1 or VQ is a tangent through the point Q; similarly for V_1Q.

A tangent to a parabola parallel to a given line may be drawn by constructing the angle $GFP =$ twice the angle which the line makes with the axis, so determining the point of contact P.

PROBLEM 37. (Fig. 37.) *To draw a parabola, the vertex A, the axis AN and a point P on the curve being given.*

This might be solved by first finding the focus and proceeding as in the last problem. It can however be solved independently

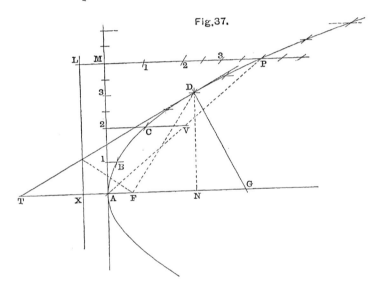

Fig. 37.

without using circular arcs, and the method is evidently applicable to the last problem after any one point on the curve has been found.

Draw the tangent at the vertex and a diameter through P meeting it in M. Divide MP into any number of equal parts (say four), and AM into the same number. Then diameters through the several points on AM will meet lines joining A to the corresponding points on MP (counting from A in the first case and from M in the second) in points of the curve as B, C, D. As the curve recedes from the axis the points found get more and more distant from each other (compare C to D and D to P), but, if desirable, points can be interpolated between any two points already found by subdividing the corresponding spaces on MP and

AM. In the figure points are thus interpolated between *C* and *D* and between *D* and *P*. The curve can be carried beyond *P* by carrying on the divisions on the two lines as in the figure.

The other half of the curve can be put in by symmetry.

The tangent at any point *D* can be drawn by drawing the ordinate *DN*, and making *AT* on the axis equal to *AN*, on the other side of the vertex; *DT* will be the tangent at *B*, as has already been shewn.

The focus *F* is found by drawing the normal at any point *D*, bisecting the sub-normal *NG* and setting off $AF = \frac{1}{2}NG$.

The construction for the curve depends on the fact that if a diameter be drawn through the centre point of any chord, the tangents at the extremities of the chord intersect on the diameter, and the curve cuts the diameter at the centre point between the chord and the intersection of the tangents. Thus *AP* is a chord, the diameter through 2 (on *AM*) will intersect it in its centre point *V*, *A*2 is the tangent at *A* and therefore the tangent at *P* will also pass through 2, and *C*, which bisects *V*2 since

$$C2 \,:\, CV \,::\, M2 \,:\, P2$$

will be a point on the curve.

Similarly *B* may be shewn to be on the curve, since it bisects the diameter between 1 and the centre point of the chord *AC*, and *D* may be shewn to be on the curve as bisecting the diameter between *C*3 the tangent at *C*, and the centre point of the chord *CP*.

PROBLEM 38. (Fig. 37.) *To draw a parabola the focus F, the axis FN, and a point P on the curve being given.*

The directrix and consequently the vertex can at once be determined by drawing *PM* parallel to the given axis, measuring along it a length *PL* equal to *FP* and from *L* dropping a perpendicular on the axis intersecting it in *X*. This perpendicular is, of course, the directrix, and the vertex bisects *FX*. The curve can then be drawn by either of the preceding methods.

PROBLEM 39. (Fig. 38.) *To draw a curve formed of circular arcs approximating to a parabola the focus F, and vertex A being given.*

The following method depends on the fact that in the parabola the sub-normal is constant and equal to twice AF.

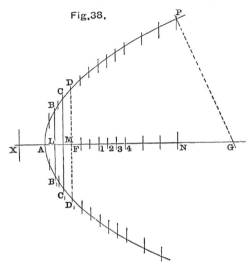

Fig. 38.

Draw the axis AFN and on it take $F1$ equal to FA, and draw any ordinates as BB_1, CC_1, DD_1, &c. With 1 as centre describe an arc through A, extending as far as the centre ordinate between A and BB_1, from L the foot of ordinate BB_1 make $L2$ equal to twice AF, and with centre 2 and radius to the point where arc through A meets the centre ordinate between A and B describe an arc extending to half-way between B and C; from M the foot of ordinate CC_1 make $M3$ equal to twice AF and with centre 3 and radius to the point where arc through B has been stopped describe an arc extending to half way between C and D. Similarly from the foot of the ordinate DD_1 measure a distance on the axis equal to twice AF so determining the centre (4) for an arc through D, and continue the process for any number of successive ordinates. It will be seen that the centres are determined by measuring a constant distance from the foot of the successive ordinates equal to the known constant length of the sub-normal in the parabola (p. 60), but that the radius of each arc depends entirely on the arc previously drawn, so that the curve must be commenced from the vertex. Each successive arc extends some distance on each side of the ordinate from which its centre is determined. It is convenient, though not essential, to commence with ordinates dividing AF into equal parts, and tolerably close together, and as the curve recedes from the vertex and cuts the ordinates more nearly at right angles the distance between them may be increased. Carefully drawn, the method gives a remarkably close approximation to the real form of the curve, as may be seen by comparing the distance of the point P in the figure from F with the distance NX, its perpendicular distance from the directrix. The half distance between the ordinates to which each successive arc has to extend, and which furnishes the starting point for the next arc can generally be estimated with quite sufficient accuracy by the eye.

PROBLEM 40. (Fig. 39.) *To draw a parabola, the focus F, and two points A and B on the curve being given.*

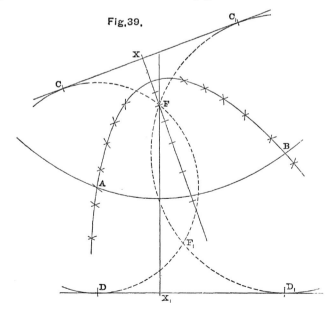

Fig. 39.

With centre A and radius AF describe a circle CFD, and with centre B and radius BF describe a circle C_1FD_1. Draw common tangents CC_1 and DD_1 to the two circles. (Prob. 31.) These will be the directrices of two parabolas fulfilling the given conditions, and the curves may be drawn by any of the preceding methods.

The construction is obvious.

PROBLEM 41. (Fig. 40.) *To draw a parabola, the focus F, a point A on the curve, and a tangent YT being given.*

The *point of contact* of the tangent is not given, as this would be a fifth condition. With centre A and radius AF

Fig. 40.

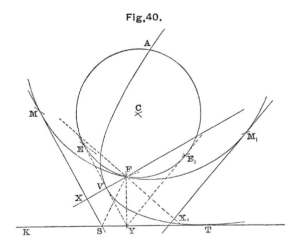

describe a circle FM, and on FA as diameter describe a circle EFE_1, the centre being C. From F drop a perpendicular FY on the given tangent, and from Y draw tangents YE, YE_1 to the given circle. Join FE, FE_1 and produce them to meet the larger circle in M, M_1, then MX, M_1X_1 drawn parallel to YE, YE_1 respectively will be the directrices of two parabolas fulfilling the given conditions.

Proof. It is known that the perpendicular from the focus on a tangent passes through the point of intersection of that

E. 5

tangent and the tangent at the vertex, hence Y is a point on the tangent at the vertex.

The directrix must evidently touch the circle MFM_1 and must meet the perpendicular on it from the focus at a point double the distance from F that it is from the tangent at the vertex.

In the triangles AEF, AEM, $AF = AM$, AE is common and the angles AEF, AEM are equal, each being a right angle;

$\therefore FE = EM$ and $\therefore AM$ is parallel to EC, since $FC = CA$; but EC is perpendicular to YE, and therefore MX which is parallel to YE is perpendicular to MA, and therefore touches the circle MFM_1.

Draw FX perpendicular to MX and let YE meet it in V,

then $FV : FX :: FE : FM$;

$\therefore FX = 2FV$,   since $FM = 2FE$.

Hence two parallel lines have been found, one of which touches the circle MFM_1, while the other passes through Y and bisects the distance between F and the first.

PROBLEM 42. (Fig. 41.) *To draw a parabola, the focus F and two tangents RT, RT_1 being given.*

(The problem is impossible if the given lines are parallel, i.e. they must always intersect in some point R; and F must not lie on either of them.)

Join RF, and at F on each side of RF construct an angle RFT, RFT_1 equal to T_1RS, the angle between the given lines alternate with that in which F is situated. T and T_1 will be the *points of contact* of the given tangents and the problem is reduced to Problem 40. As in that problem two lines can be drawn touching circles with centres T, T_1 and radii TF, T_1F respectively, which will be the directrices of parabolas having F as focus and passing through T and T_1, but only one of these will in addition touch the given lines at those points.

Proof. The construction depends on the well-known property of the parabola, that *the exterior angle between any two tangents is*

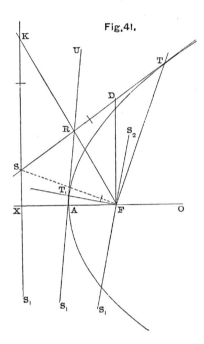

Fig. 41.

equal to the angle subtended at the focus, by the segment of either between the point of intersection and the point of contact. For if O be any point in AF produced, the angle $TFO =$ twice angle FTR, since (Prob. 36) the angle $FTR =$ angle which TR makes with the axis. Similarly angle $T_1FO =$ twice angle FT_1S_1;

∴ angle $T_1FO -$ angle $TFO =$ twice (angle $FT_1S_1 -$ angle FTR),

i.e. $TFT_1 =$ twice angle $URT =$ twice angle $T_1RS.$

Through F draw FD parallel to the directrix meeting TS in D, then $FD = FS$, since TS bisects the angle between FS and the directrix. Let FR meet the directrix in K.

By similar triangles

$$KS : FD :: KR : FR,$$
$$KS : KR :: FS : FR;$$

and similarly, if S_1 denote the intersection of RT_1 with directrix,

$$KS_1 : KR :: FS_1 : FR,$$

$$\therefore KS : KS_1 :: FS : FS_1.$$

Hence the angles KFS, KFS_1 are either equal or supplementary. In the figure they are supplementary, i.e. angle KFS = angle RFS_2.

But angle RFT is the complement of angle KFS

and   „ RFT_1 „   „   „ KFS_2,

$$\therefore \text{ angle } RFT = \text{angle } RFT_1,$$

and $\therefore$ each of them $= \frac{1}{2}$ angle TFT_1 = angle T_1RS,

which proves the property above referred to.

Second Solution.

The problem may also be solved by dropping perpendiculars from the focus on the given tangents, their points of intersection determining the tangent at the vertex.

PROBLEM 43. (Fig. 39.) *To draw a parabola, the directrix CC_1 and two points A and B on the curve being given.*

This is merely the converse of Prob. 40. With the given points as centres and with radii equal to the distance of each from the given directrix describe arcs intersecting in F and F_1, either of which may be taken as the focus.

PROBLEM 44. (Fig. 40.) *To draw a parabola, the directrix MX, a point A on the curve and a tangent YT being given.*

With centre A describe a circle MFM_1 touching MX. This will of course be a locus of the focus. At S, the point of intersection of the given tangent and directrix, construct an angle TSF equal to the angle between MS and TS produced, i.e. = the angle MSK. SF will be another locus, i.e. the focus will be at F, the intersection of the line and circle. The line SF will evidently meet the circle again beyond A and this point of intersection will be the focus of a second parabola fulfilling the given conditions, the point of contact of tangent and the point A being on the same side of the axis.

Proof. That the circle is a locus of the focus needs no demonstration: that the line is a locus of the focus is proved, since it has been shewn (Prob. 36) that FS is always perpendicular to the line joining F to the point of contact of the tangent through S, and that therefore the two triangles FST, LST, where TL is perpendicular to MS, are equal and similar in all respects; and that therefore angle $FST =$ angle $LST =$ angle MSK.

PROBLEM 45. (Fig. 41.) *To draw a parabola, the directrix KX and two tangents RT, RT₁ being given.*

At S, the point of intersection of RT with KX, construct an angle TSF equal to the angle TSK. As in the last problem SF

Fig.4la.

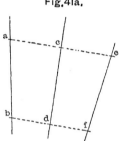

will be a locus of the focus. Similarly, if RT_1 meet the directrix in S_1, construct an angle $T_1 S_1 F$ equal to the angle $T_1 S_1 X$, and $S_1 F$ will be a second locus, therefore the intersection of these lines determines F, the focus. In the figure the directrix and the tangent RT_1 do not intersect within any reasonable distance, but the line through their intersection making the same angle with the tangent as the tangent does with the directrix can easily be drawn, as shewn in fig. 41*a*. Let *ab*, *cd* be any two converging lines; from any two points (*a*, *b*) on the one, drop perpendiculars *ac*, *bd* on the other and produce them: make $ce = ca$, $df = db$, then obviously *ab* and *ef* will pass through the same point on *cd* and will be equally inclined thereto.

PROBLEM 46. (Fig. 42.) *To draw a parabola, the axis AN and two points P, Q on the curve being given.*

[The two points must not be at equal distances from the axis whether on the same or on opposite sides of it, nor must they be on the same perpendicular to the axis.]

Draw the ordinates PN, QN_1, of which let PN be the greater; the vertex will then obviously lie on the same side of N as N_1

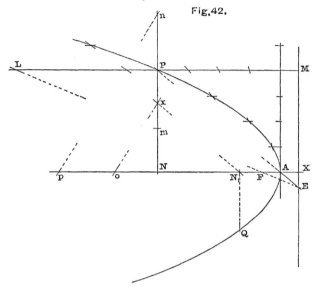

Fig. 42.

and beyond it. On NP produced make Pn equal to QN_1, and on PN make Pm also equal to QN_1. Then Nm is evidently equal to $PN-QN_1$. On the axis make $No=Nm$ and on the same side of N make $Np=NP$. Through o draw ox parallel to pn meeting PN in x, and through P draw PA parallel to N_1x meeting the axis in A. A will be the vertex of the required parabola and the problem is reduced to Prob. 37.

Proof.   It is a well-known property in the parabola that $\overline{PN}\,|^2 = 4AF \cdot AN$ where F is the focus, PN an ordinate and A the vertex.

$$\therefore \quad \overline{PN}\,|^2 : \overline{QN_1}\,|^2 :: AN : AN_1,$$

or $$\overline{PN}\,|^2 - \overline{QN_1}\,|^2 : \overline{PN}\,|^2 :: AN - AN_1 : AN,$$

i.e. $$(PN+QN_1)(PN-QN_1) : \overline{PN}\,|^2 :: NN_1 : AN,$$

or $$\frac{AN}{NN_1} = \frac{PN}{(PN+QN_1)(PN-QN_1)} PN.$$

If a fourth proportional be taken to
$$PN, \quad PN + QN_1, \quad \text{and} \quad PN - QN_1;$$
i. e. if a length l be determined such that
$$PN \; : \; PN + QN_1 \; :: \; PN - QN_1 \; : \; l,$$
the above equation may be written
$$\frac{AN}{NN_1} = \frac{PN}{l},$$
i. e. AN is a fourth proportional to such length l, NN_1 and PN. But this is really what has been done, for
$$Np \; : \; Nn \; :: \; No \; : \; Nx,$$
i. e. $\qquad PN \; : \; PN + QN_1 \; :: \; PN - QN_1 \; : \; Nx,$

i. e. $\qquad Nx$ is the required length l,

and $\qquad Nx \; : \; NN_1 \; :: \; PN \; : \; AN.$

That $\overline{PN}|^2 = 4AF \cdot AN$ may be shewn thus: Join PA and let it meet the directrix in E. Join EF (F being the focus) and produce it to meet the diameter through P in L, while the diameter meets the directrix in M. Then since $FA = AX$, $PL = PM = PF$, for ML is parallel to FX, therefore the circle on ML as diameter goes through F, and therefore the angles MFL, MFE are both right angles and
$$EX \cdot XM = \overline{FX}|^2 = 4\overline{AF}|^2,$$
also $\qquad AN \; : \; AX \; :: \; PN \; : \; EX$ by similar triangles,
$$:: \; \overline{PN}|^2 \; : \; EX \cdot MX$$
$$:: \; \overline{PN}|^2 \; : \; 4\overline{AF}|^2,$$
$$\therefore \quad \overline{PN}|^2 = 4AF \cdot AN, \text{ since } AF = AX.$$

PROBLEM 47. (Fig. 43.) *To draw a parabola, the axis AN, a point P on the curve and a tangent OT being given.*

[The tangent must not be parallel to the axis, and the point must lie within the angle formed by the tangent and a symmetrical line on the other side of the axis.]

Draw the ordinate PN and let it meet the given tangent in O. Make NP_1 on the other side of the axis equal to PN, and P_1 will

by symmetry be a point on the curve.   Find a mean proportional
between OP and OP_1 (Prob. 5) and set off its length OE on OP

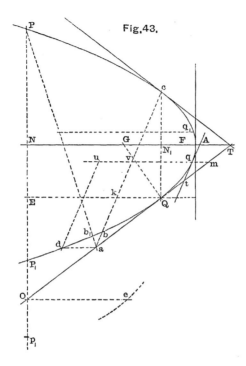

Fig.43.

from O towards the axis.   Draw through E a parallel to the axis
meeting the tangent in Q. Q is the *point of contact* of such
tangent.   Draw QN_1, the ordinate of Q, and the vertex, A, will
bisect N_1T, the subtangent of Q (Prob. 36).   The problem is therefore again reduced to Prob. 37.

Proof.   That the diameter through Q, the point of contact of
the given tangent, meets OP in E such that $OE^2 = OP \cdot OP_1$, may
be shewn thus.   Let PAP_1 be a parabola and OQ a tangent at Q.
Take any point a on the given tangent, and draw any two chords
as abc, $ab'P$, and let q and q_1 be the vertices of the corresponding
diameters, and let the diameter through q meet bc in v: through
a draw ad parallel to qv meeting the parabola in d, and draw du
parallel to bc meeting its diameter in u.

Then $\quad ab . ac = \overline{av}|^2 - \overline{bv}|^2 \quad$ (Euc. II. 6)

$$= 4Fq . (qu - qv) \text{ (p. 71) if } F \text{ is the focus,}$$

$$= 4Fq . ad,$$

and similarly $\qquad ab' . aP = 4Fq_1 . ad,$

$$\therefore \quad ab . ac : ab' . aP :: Fq : Fq_1,$$

i.e. the ratio of the rectangles depends only on the positions of q and q_1, and is independent of the position of the point a.

If the lines abc, $ab'P$ move parallel to themselves until they become the tangents at q and q_1, we shall then obtain, if these tangents intersect in t_1,

$$\overline{t_1 q}|^2 : \overline{t_1 q_1}|^2 : Fq : Fq_1,$$

and $\qquad \therefore \quad ab . ac : ab' . aP :: \overline{t_1 q}|^2 : \overline{t_1 q_1}|^2,$

but the tangent aQ may be regarded as a chord cutting the parabola in two coincident points, and therefore if the tangent at q meet aQ in t and vq meet it in m

$$ab . ac : \overline{aQ}|^2 :: \overline{qt}|^2 : \overline{tQ}|^2$$

$$:: \overline{qt}|^2 : \overline{tm}|^2.$$

Also if Qk is the diameter at Q meeting ac in k, by similar triangles

$$qt : tm :: ak : aQ,$$

$$\therefore \quad ab . ac : \overline{aQ}|^2 :: \overline{ak}|^2 : \overline{aQ}|^2,$$

or $\qquad\qquad ab . ac = \overline{ak}|^2,$

which justifies the construction.

PROBLEM 48. (Fig. 44.) *To draw a parabola, the axis UN and two tangents PT, QT being given.*

[The point T must not be on the axis.]

If from the point U in which either of the tangents (as QT) cuts the axis, a line UR be drawn making the same angle with the axis as QT but on the opposite side of it, this will, by symmetry, be a third tangent to the curve. Let it meet the other tangent (PT) in V. Describe a circle through the three points T, U, V (Prob. 20), cutting the axis in F. F will be the focus of

the required parabola, and *FU* will be the distance from *F* of
the point of contact of either of the tangents *QU, RU*. With

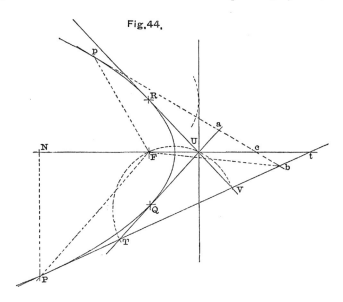

Fig. 44.

centre *F* and radius *FU* describe an arc cutting *UR* in *R*, with
centre *R* and the same radius describe a circle, and the directrix
will touch this circle and is of course perpendicular to the axis.
The problem is therefore reduced to Prob. 36.

Proof. The fact that the circle through the points of intersection of three tangents is a locus of the focus is generally true,
and is not confined to the case of two tangents meeting on the
axis. For draw any tangent *pab* meeting the parabola in *p*, the
two given tangents in *a* and *b* and the axis in *c*, and let *Tb* meet
the axis in *t*. It has been shewn (Prob. 42) that the angle *abt*
is equal to either of the angles *pFb, PFb*, also the angle *Fpc* = the
angle *Fcp* = the angle *bct*,

∴ the remaining angle *Fba* of the triangle *Fpb*,

= ,,   ,,   *btc*   ,,   *bct*,

i. e. *if two tangents intersect in b the angle which either makes with
Fb is equal to the angle which the other makes with the axis.*

Similarly, since QT, PT intersect in T, the angle FTa is equal to the angle Ftb, i.e. btc,

$$\therefore \text{ angle } Fba = \text{angle } FTa,$$

or a circle goes round aFTb.   (Euc. III. 27.)

PROBLEM 49. (Fig. 45.) *To draw a parabola, two tangents AT, BT, and their points of contact A and B being given.*

First method.   Divide AT, BT into any (the same) number of equal parts; the lines joining opposite points on the two tan-

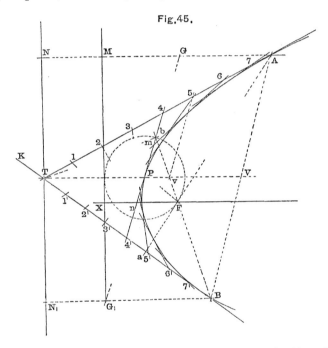

Fig. 45.

gents, (i. e. supposing each divided into 8 parts, the lines joining 1 on AT to $7'$ on BT, 2 on AT to $6'$ on BT, and so on,) will be tangents to the curve, which can easily be drawn to touch them all.   Or *points* on the curve may be found successively thus. Bisect AT, BT in the points 4, $4'$.   The line joining these points is a tangent to the curve at its centre point, i. e. bisect 4, $4'$ in P and P is a point on the curve.   Similarly the line joining the point of bisection (6) of $4A$ and the point of bisection of (m) $4P$

will be a tangent to the curve at *its* centre point, and the line joining the point of bisection (6) of $4'B$ and the point of bisection (n) of $4'P$ will be a tangent to the curve at *its* centre point, and the method of bisecting the tangents successively may be continued. It is obvious that the point m found by bisecting $4P$ is identical with the point of intersection of the line $44'$ and the line joining 6 on A to $2'$ on B. The focus may be found as the intersection of the circle circumscribing the triangle formed by any three tangents with that circumscribing the triangle formed by any other three, as e.g. the triangles $4T4'$ and $5T3'$, and the directrix may then be determined by Prob. 40.

Second method. The focus may be determined independently, without drawing additional tangents, thus. Join AB, bisect it in V and join VT. VT will be *a diameter* of the curve, and the curve will pass through P the centre point of VT. Bisect VT in P. Find a third proportional to VT, AV (Prob. 5), the length of which will be equal to $2FP$ if F is the focus. [This may conveniently be done by making Tv on TV equal to AV and drawing a line through v parallel to AV to meet AT. The length (l) of this line will be the required third proportional, since $TV : VA :: Tv$ or $VA : l$.]

Describe a circle with centre P and radius equal to $\frac{1}{2}l$ which will be a locus of the focus, and the directrix will be a tangent MX to this circle perpendicular to the diameter TV. Then F may be determined as the intersection of a circle, with centre A and radius AM, the distance of A from the directrix, and the previously drawn circle.

Third method. It has been shewn (Prob. 41) that *the exterior angle between any two tangents is equal to the angle which either subtends at the focus.* Therefore if on AT as chord a segment of a circle be described on the side towards B, containing an angle AFT equal to the angle ATK (Prob. 30), where K is on BT produced, this segment will be a locus of the focus. Similarly if a segment containing the same angle be described on BT towards A, it will be a second locus and the focus will be at the intersection of the two, and the directrix may be determined by Prob. 40.

Proof. That the line joining the intersection of tangents to a parabola to the point of bisection of the chord joining their points of contact, is a diameter may be shewn thus. Let AB be two points on a parabola, AT, BT tangents at the points, F the focus and AN, BN_1 perpendiculars on the directrix meeting NTN_1 parallel to the directrix in N and N_1. Join FA, FB and draw Ta perpendicular to FA and Tb perpendicular to FB. Then the angle TAa = angle TAN,

$$\therefore TN = Ta, \text{ and similarly } TN_1 = Tb.$$

But $Ta = Tb$, since it has been shewn that angle TFA = angle TFB. (Prob. 42.)

$$\therefore TN = TN_1.$$

If TV be drawn parallel to AN or BN_1, i.e. to the axis, meeting AB in V, it will make $AV : VB :: TN : TN_1$, i.e. $AV = VB_1$, or the diameter through T bisects AB. Since $TN = TN_1$ it follows that any straight line through T terminated by the diameters A and B is bisected in T and more generally that *every line through the point of intersection of two tangents terminated by diameters through the extremities of the corresponding chord of contact, is bisected by such point of intersection.*

That P, the point in which the curve meets TV, bisects TV and that the tangent at P is parallel to AB may be shewn thus:— Since AN, TV and BN_1 are parallel lines, it follows that every line meeting the three is bisected by TV; and therefore if the tangent at the point P be drawn meeting AN in G and BN_1 in G_1, $PG = PG_1$; but if it meets AT, BT in 4 and 4′, it follows as above that $P4 = 4G$, $P4' = 4'G_1$, and therefore $G4$, $4P$, $P4'$ and $4'G_1$ are all equal, which is only possible if GPG_1 bisects TV and is parallel to AB.

Hence $T4 = 4A$, $T4' = 4'B$ and $44' = \frac{1}{2}AB$.

To shew that AV is a mean proportional between VT (or $2PV$) and $2FP$, draw FU parallel to AB or to $44'$, meeting PV in U, hen the angle FUT = angle $4PU$,

$$= \text{angle } F4T, \quad \text{(Prob. 48),}$$

.nd therefore the circle which it is known can be drawn (Prob. 8) through $F4T4'$, will pass through U.

Hence, AV being twice $P4$,

$$\overline{AV}|^2 = 4\overline{P4}|^2 = 4PU \cdot PT. \quad \text{(Euc. III. 35.)}$$

But the angle UFP = angle $FP4'$, since FU is parallel to $P4'$,

$$= \text{angle } 4'PT = \text{angle } FUP,$$

.nd therefore $FP = PU$; also $PT = PV$,

herefore $\overline{AV}|^2 = 4FP \cdot PV.$

DEFINITION. A chord through the focus parallel to the tan-gent at P is called *the parameter* of the diameter through P, and t follows from the above that its length is always equal to $4FP$. See definition of latus-rectum, p. 60.)

PROBLEM 50. (Fig. 46.) *To draw a parabola, three tangents,* *TU, TV, UV and the point of contact P of one of them TU being* .iven.

Describe a circle through TUV (Prob. 20), then F the focus

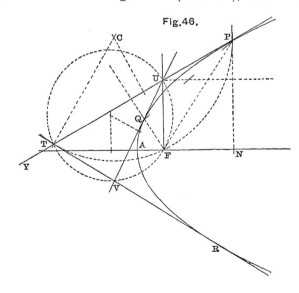

Fig.46.

lies on this circle (Prob. 48). On PT describe a segment of a circle containing an angle equal to the exterior angle between the tangents meeting in T, i.e. the angle VTY. (Prob. 30.) This segment will be a second locus of the focus (Prob. 42), which will therefore be at the intersection of the segment with the previously drawn circle.

If P (as in the figure) lies beyond U the segment must be described on the side of TP towards V: but if P lies between T and U, the segment must be described on the other side of TP, since the focus can never lie inside the triangle TUV and the angle it contains must be the angle UTV, since that would then be the exterior angle between the tangents.

[The centre for the segment may conveniently be found by drawing TC perpendicular to VT to meet the perpendicular bisector of PT in C.]

Construct the angle UFQ equal to the angle PFU. Q will be the point of contact of UV, and the direction of the axis is determined since it is parallel to the diameter joining U to the centre point of PQ. (Prob. 49.) It can then of course be drawn through F.

Lastly, the vertex may be found since it is the centre point between N the foot of the ordinate from P and the point in which PT cuts the axis (p. 60.)

The point of contact R, of TV, may of course be determined without drawing the curve by making the angle TFR=angle TFP.

The construction is evident from preceding problems.

PROBLEM 51. (Fig. 47.) *To draw a parabola, three points A, B, C, on the curve, and the direction of the axis, as BD, being given.*

Draw lines through AB, BC, CA, and let BD parallel to the given direction of axis meet AC in D. Bisect AC in E and draw EL parallel to BD to meet BC in L. Draw LG parallel to AC to meet BD in G. Join AG and it will cut EL in H, the vertex of the diameter through E.

If $HK = HE$, AK will be the tangent at A and the focus may be found by taking HU such that $\overline{AE}|^2 = 4HE \cdot HU$, i.e. taking

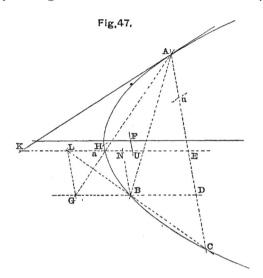

Fig, 47.

$2HU$ a third proportional to $2HE$, AE; drawing UF parallel to AC and making $HF = HU$. [If we take a third proportional to EK, AE it will be $2HU$. This may conveniently be done by making $Ea = EA$ and drawing au parallel to AK. Eu will be the required third proportional. The problem reduces to Prob. 40.]

Proof. To shew that H is the vertex of the diameter through E. Draw BN parallel to AC meeting EH in N. $BN = ED$, and

$$DA \cdot DC = \overline{AE}|^2 - ED^2 = AE^2 - BN^2 \text{ (Euc. II. 5)} ;$$

but in any parabola

$$AE^2 = 4 \cdot FH \cdot HE,$$

and

$$BN^2 = 4 \cdot FH \cdot HN,$$

$$\therefore \ AE^2 - BN^2 = 4FH \cdot EN = 4FH \cdot BD,$$

$$\therefore \ DA \cdot DC : AE^2 :: BD : HE ;$$

but in the figure

$$BD : EL :: DC : CE \text{ or } EL = \frac{BD \cdot AE}{DC},$$

and $AE : EH :: AD : DG,$

$$:: AD : EL,$$

$$:: AD : \frac{BD \cdot AE}{DC},$$

i.e. $DA \cdot DC : AE^2 :: BD : HE,$

or HE has been determined of the proper length.

PROBLEM 52. (Fig. 48.) *To draw a parabola, three tangents* UT, TV, VU *and the direction of the axis, as* AN, *being given.*

Through T draw MTM_1 perpendicular to the given direction of the axis. It is a known property of the parabola that if the

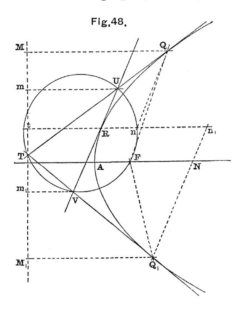

Fig.48.

portion of any tangent UV intercepted between two others UT, TV be *projected* on any line parallel to the directrix as on MM_1 by lines Um, Vm_1 perpendicular to MM_1, then any other tangent to the curve between the points of contact of TU, TV will have the same projected length mm_1 on the axis. If therefore TM, TM_1 be each made equal to mm_1, lines through M and M_1 perpendicular to MM_1 will intersect TU, TV respectively in Q and Q_1,

E.

6

the points of contact of TU and TV. The problem is therefore reduced to Prob. 49, or it may be completed by utilising other known properties of the curve already demonstrated, e. g.—making the angle TQF equal to angle TQM, QF is a locus of the focus; similarly Q_1F (the angle TQ_1F being made equal to angle TQ_1M_1) is a second locus, and F, the focus, is therefore the intersection of QF, Q_1F.

Again, the circle round UT, TV, VU is known to be a locus of the focus (Prob. 48), and the angle UFQ is known to be equal to the angle TUV. Prob. 42. Therefore, if on UQ a segment of a circle be described containing an angle equal to the angle TUV (Prob. 30), the intersection of this segment with the above circle will determine F. Any number of tangents to the curve between Q and Q_1 can be at once drawn without previously determining the focus by measuring the length mm_1 *anywhere* on MM_1 between M and M_1 and from the extremities drawing perpendiculars to MM_1 to meet TQ, TQ_1. Any pair of such points being joined will of course give a tangent to the curve.

Proof. That the projected length on MM_1 of the portion of any tangent intercepted between TQ, TQ_1 is constant may be shewn thus. Let R be the point of contact of UV and let the diameter through R meet MM_1 in t. Draw Qn, Q_1n_1 parallel to UV meeting tR in n and n_1. Then $UR = \frac{1}{2}Qn$ (Prob. 49) and therefore $tm = \frac{1}{2}tM$. Similarly $tm_1 = \frac{1}{2}tM_1$.

Therefore $mm_1 = \frac{1}{2}MM_1 = $ constant, since MM_1 is the projection of the chord of contact of two fixed tangents.

PROBLEM 53. (Fig. 49.) *To draw a parabola, two points A, B on the curve and two tangents TL, TM being given.*

[The tangents must not be parallel and the points must not be on opposite sides of either tangent.]

Draw a line through A and B meeting the given tangents in L and M. Take LC on LM a mean proportional between LA and LB (Prob. 5), and MD on ML a mean proportional between MB and MA. Bisect CD in E. TE will be the direction of the axis of a parabola fulfilling the required conditions and CQ, DQ_1 drawn parallel to TE to meet the given tangents will determine Q and Q_1,

Fig.49.

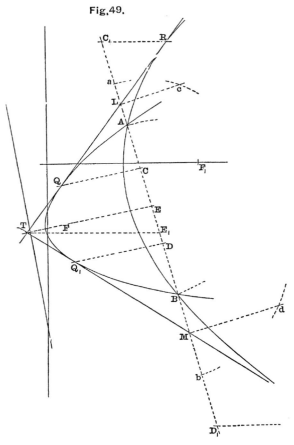

their points of contact. The problem therefore reduces to Prob. 49, or may be completed similarly to the preceding. Since LC and MD may be set off on either side of L and M, as LC_1, MD_1 in the figure, the point of bisection E_1 of C_1D_1 determines TE_1 the direction of the axis of a second parabola fulfilling the required conditions. Further, either C_1D or CD_1 may also be taken as the segment to be bisected, and there are consequently *four* solutions.

The proof depends entirely on the property of the parabola already referred to in Prob. 47.

PROBLEM 54. (Fig. 50.) *To draw a parabola, three points A, B,*
C, and a tangent LM being given.

[The points must all be on the same side of the tangent.]

Join two pairs of the given points as AB, BC and let the joining
lines cut the given tangent in L and M. On LB take LD a mean

Fig.50.

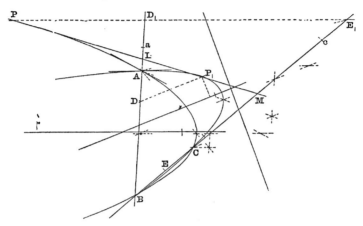

proportional between LA and LB (Prob. 5), and on MB take ME
a mean proportional between MC and MB. Then by the property
of the parabola already referred to (Prob. 47) a line through D
parallel to the axis of a parabola through A and B and touching
LM, will pass through the point of contact of LM with such
parabola ; and a line through E parallel to the axis of a parabola
through B and C and touching LM will pass through the point of
contact of LM with such parabola.   Hence the line joining DE
will be parallel to the axis of a parabola which can be described
through AB and C to touch the given line, and its intersection
with LM will determine the point of contact of such parabola.

Since LD, ME can be set off on either side of L and M (as
LD_1, ME_1), similarly the line joining D_1 and E_1 will be parallel to
the axis of a second parabola fulfilling the conditions of the
problem ; its point of contact being P : and similarly DE_1 and
D_1E will determine the direction of the axes of two more such
parabolas.   The line DE_1 determines P_1 as the point of contact.

Hence there are four solutions, and the problem in either case is reduced to Prob. 51. In the fig. two of the four parabolas are drawn, viz. those whose axes are parallel to D_1E_1 and DE_1 respectively; the necessary construction in each case being indicated.

It might be considered at first sight that if a mean proportional were taken between the segments NA, NC of the line joining AC, the third pair of the given points, cutting the given tangent in N, two additional points would be obtained which, being joined to either D, D_1, E or E_1, would give the directions of axes of additional parabolas. This however is not so, since it will be found that the points thus obtained coincide with the intersections of ED, E_1D_1, and of DE_1, ED_1 respectively, and therefore no more solutions than the four already mentioned are obtainable.

PROBLEM 55. (Fig. 51.) *To draw a parabola, a point A on the curve and three tangents BC, CD, DB being given.*

[No two of the tangents must be parallel, and the given point must not lie within the triangle formed by the tangents, nor so that any one tangent lies between it and either of the remaining tangents.]

Let C be the vertex of the triangle formed by the tangents, which cannot be reached from the given point without crossing BD. Through B draw BE parallel to CD and through D draw DE parallel to CB, meeting BE in E. Through C draw CK parallel to BD and join EA meeting CK in K, CB in L, and BD in M.

First let A lie between E and K; complete the harmonic range $KAEA_1$, i.e. find a point A_1 beyond E on KL such that

$$KA : KA_1 :: AE : EA_1 \qquad \text{(Prob. 12.)}$$

[Through A, K draw Aa, Ka any two lines intersecting in a, produce aA to a_1 making $Aa_1 = Aa$. Join a_1E and produce it to meet Ka in b. Draw bA_1 parallel to aA and it will intersect KA in the required point.]

Then A_1 will be a point on the curve and the problem reduces to Prob. 53.

Second, let the given point lie beyond E as A_1, then, completing the harmonic range A_1EAK (Prob. 11), A will be a

second point on the curve and the problem again reduces to
Prob. 53.

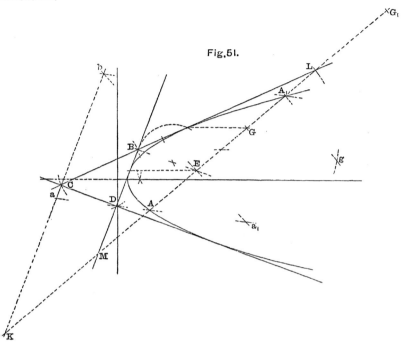

Fig. 51.

In completing the figure, one of the tangents employed should
be the one situated as BD in the figure, because it is necessary to
take a mean proportional between the segments of the chord AA_1
included between the tangent and the curve, i.e. to take a mean
proportional between MA and MA_1: but it will be found that
ME, MK are each equal to such mean proportional, and therefore
E and K can be at once used without any further construction.
If CB is the second tangent made use of, a mean proportional LG
or LG_1 must be determined between LA, LA_1 (Prob. 5), and
two of the four parabolas which can be constructed by means of pairs
of the points K, E, G, G_1 to pass through A and A_1 and to touch
BL, BD will also touch CD.   There is an ambiguity as to which
particular pairs of points must be selected, but this can easily
be settled by trial in any given case.   In the fig. it will be found
that the pairs E, G and E, G_1 are those required, and that

the pairs K, G and K, G_1 give parabolas which while touching BC, DB, do not touch CD.

There are in general *two* solutions.

Proof. It is shewn at the end of Chap. IV. among the harmonic properties of conics, that the three diagonals of a complete quadrilateral circumscribing a conic form a self-conjugate triangle. It is easily proved analytically that every parabola touches the line at infinity, i.e. has one tangent situated at an altogether infinite distance. Now BE and DE meet CD, CB respectively in infinitely distant points, pass, that is, through the points in which this infinitely distant tangent meets CB and CD, they are therefore diagonals of the circumscribing quadrilateral formed by the three given and the infinitely distant tangent, and its third diagonal must be the line CK since this meets BD in infinitely distant points. E is therefore the pole of the line CK, and conversely the polar of K passes through E.

But a straight line drawn through any point is divided harmonically by the point, the curve and the polar of the point (see end of Chap. IV.), therefore A_1 must be a point on the curve.

PROBLEM 56. (Fig. 52.) *To draw a parabola to pass through four given points A, B, C, D.*

[The points must not lie at the angles of a parallelogram, and must be so situated, that being joined in pairs, the two points of each pair are both on the same side, or on opposite sides of the point of intersection of the joining line*.]

Join BC, AD to meet in E. Through C draw CK parallel to AB meeting AD in K. Take a mean proportional EG between ED and EK (Prob. 5) and CG will be the direction of the axis of the required parabola. The Problem is therefore reduced to Prob. 51.

Since the distance EG may be set off on either side of E as EG_1, the line CG_1 will be the direction of the axis of a second parabola fulfilling the given conditions.

* Puckle's *Conic Sections.* Fourth Edition, Art. 313, Ex. 1.

Proof. From the construction

$$EB : EA :: EC : EK,$$

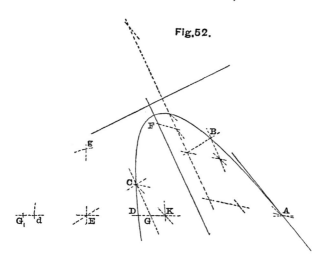

Fig.52.

and $$EK : EG :: EG : ED;$$

$$\therefore \ EB : EA :: EC : \frac{EG^2}{ED},$$

or $$EG^2 : EC :: ED.EA : EB,$$

which may be written

$$EG^2 : EC^2 :: ED.EA : EC.EB,$$

a relation which is known to hold in the parabola.   (Besant's *Geom. Conics*, 3rd Ed., Art. 213.)

PROBLEM 57. (Fig. 53.) *To draw a parabola to touch four given lines AB, BC, CD, DA, no two of which are parallel.*

Let *CD* meet *AB* in *E* and *AD* meet *BC* in *G*.

The circle circumscribing the triangle formed by any three of the lines will be a locus of the focus (Prob. 48), which may therefore be determined as the intersection of the circles circumscribing any two of such triangles. In the figure, the circles circumscribing *BCE* and *ABG* are drawn. They intersect in *F*, the focus. The tangent at the vertex can be at once determined, by dropping perpendiculars from F on any two of the given

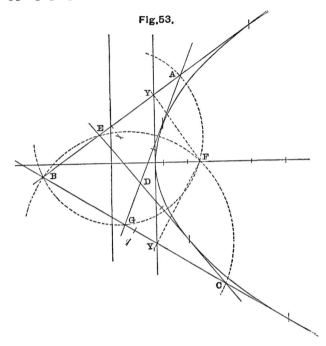

Fig.53.

tangents as FY, FY_1 perpendiculars on AB, BC ; Y and Y_1 are points on the tangent at the vertex. (Notes to Problem 36.)

PROBLEM 58. (Fig. 54.) *To determine the* centre of curvature *at any point P of a given parabola.*

[A circle can be drawn through any three points of a curve, but cannot in general be drawn through a greater number taken arbitrarily. If a circle be drawn through three points of a curve and the outside points be conceived to gradually move up to the centre one, the circle in the limiting position it assumes when the points approach indefinitely near to each other so as ultimately to coincide, is called the *circle of curvature* at the point, and its centre is called the *centre of curvature*. The circle is said to pass through three consecutive points of the curve, and obviously has closer contact with it at the point than any other circle can have, since it is not possible to draw a circle through *four* consecutive points. The centre of curvature will necessarily lie on the normal at the given point, and any circle having its centre on the normal and passing through the point really passes through two consecutive points of the curve, since curve and circle have a common tangent.]

F is the focus, *PT* the tangent, and *PG* the normal at the point *P* of the given parabola.

Join *PF* and produce it to *K*, making *FK* equal to *FP*. Draw *KO* perpendicular to *PK* to intersect the normal at *P* in *O*. *O* will be the *centre of curvature* at *P*.

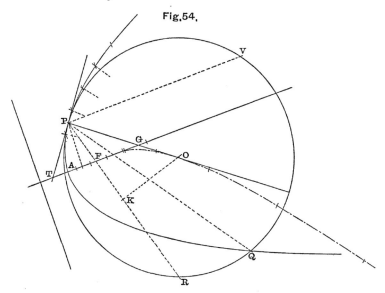

Fig,54.

If the circle of curvature cuts the parabola again in *Q*, it will be found that *PQ*, the common chord, makes the same angle with the axis as *PT*, the tangent, does, and that

$$PQ = 4PT.$$

The focal chord *FR* of the circle of curvature is known to be in length equal to $4FP$, and it is on this known value of the focal chord that the construction depends.

The chord (PV) of the circle of curvature through *P* parallel to the axis is also equal to $4FP$, since this chord and PR are equally inclined to the tangent at P.

The length PO of the radius of curvature may also be determined by taking a fourth proportional to FY, FP and $2FP$, where FY is the perpendicular from F on the tangent at P.

The locus of the centre of curvature of any curve is called the *Evolute* of that curve; and the original curve, when considered with respect to its evolute, is called an *Involute*. The chain-dotted curve in Fig. 54 is the evolute of the portion of the parabola lying above the axis.

Normals to the curve are tangents to the evolute; and since the focal radius of curvature at the vertex $= 2 . AF$, the evolute must touch the axis at a point $= 2 . AF$ from A.

If the ordinate of the point of intersection of the curve and evolute be drawn meeting the axis in N, it will be found that

$$AN = 8 . AF = \text{twice the latus rectum.}$$

The evolute of the parabola is a curve known as the semi-cubical parabola.

PROBLEM 59.   *To draw a parabola to touch two given circles, the axis being the line joining the centres.*

Let C be the centre of the larger circle, c that of the smaller, R and r their radii. Determine a fourth proportional to $2Cc$, $R + r$, and $R - r$. From C towards c set off on Cc a length CN equal to this fourth proportional, i.e. a length such that

$$CN : R - r :: R + r : 2Cc.$$

Draw NP perpendicular to Cc meeting the circle in P, and P will be the required point of contact of the curve. The problem therefore reduces to Prob. 47, the given point being also the point of contact of the given tangent.

Examples on Chapter III.

1.   Draw a parabola, the focus F, the position of the axis (FT) and a tangent (PT) being given.

(From F draw FY perpendicular to PT meeting it in Y, and from Y draw YA perpendicular to FT meeting it in A. A will be the vertex of the required parabola.)

2.   Draw a parabola, the focus F, a tangent PT and the length of the latus rectum being given.

(With centre F and radius equal to one-fourth of the given latus rectum, describe a circle ; from F draw FY perpendicular to the given tangent meeting it in Y, and from Y draw tangents to the circle.   Either point of contact will be the vertex of the required parabola (two solutions).   The given tangent must not cut the circle.)

3.   Draw a parabola, two points (P, Q), the tangent at one of them (PT), and the direction of the axis being given.

(Bisect PQ in V, draw VT parallel to given direction of axis meeting the given tangent in T ; QT is the tangent at Q, and problem reduces to Prob. 49.)

4.   Draw a parabola, the vertex (P) of a diameter, and a corresponding double ordinate QQ_1 being given.

(Bisect QQ_1 in V. PV will be a diameter ; on VP produced make $PT = PV$. TQ and TQ_1 are the tangents at Q and Q_1, and problem reduces to Prob. 49.)

5.   Draw the locus of the foci of the parabolas which have a common vertex (A) and a common tangent PT.

(The parabola which has A for vertex, the perpendicular on PT as axis, and the distance of PT from A as latus rectum.)

6.   Inscribe in a given parabola a triangle having its sides parallel to three given straight lines AB, BC, CA.

(Draw BD parallel to the axis of the parabola meeting AC in

D and CE parallel to the axis meeting AB in E. Draw a tangent to the parabola parallel to DE (p. 61) and from P its point of contact draw PQ, PR parallel to AB, AC meeting the parabola again in Q, R. PQR will be the required triangle.)

7. Draw a parabola with a given focus, and to touch a given circle at a given point.

[Let F be the focus, P the point on the circle, draw PT the tangent, and construct an angle $TPM =$ the angle FPT. The axis of the required parabola will be parallel to PM.]

8. Shew that if tangents be drawn to a parabola from any point O, and a circle be described with the focus as centre, passing through O and cutting the tangents in P and Q, PQ will be perpendicular to the axis, and its distance from O is twice its distance from the vertex.

9. Draw a circle to touch a parabola in P, and to pass through the focus. Let it meet the parabola again in Q and Q_1: draw a focal chord parallel to the tangent at P, and shew that the circle on this chord as diameter will pass through Q, Q_1, and that the focal chord and QQ_1 will intersect on the directrix.

10. Draw any right-angled triangle DEF (E being the right angle). Describe a parabola with focus F and to touch ED at D, and shew that if any circle be described to pass through D and F and cutting ED produced in P, the tangent to it at P will also be a tangent to the parabola.

11. Given two lines PR, QR, and a point P on one of them, shew that any point on the circumference of the circle passing through P and R and touching QR may be taken as the focus of a parabola passing through P and to which the given lines shall be tangents.

12. AB is the diameter of a circle; with A as focus and any point on the semi-circumference of which A is the centre as foot of directrix describe a parabola, and shew that it will touch the diameter perpendicular to AB.

13. If APC be a sector of a circle of which the radius CA is fixed, and a circle be described touching the radii CA, CP and the arc AP, shew that the locus of the centre of this circle is a parabola and describe it.

14. Given a segment of a circle, describe the parabola which is the locus of the centres of the circles inscribed in it.

15. If from a point P of a circle PC be drawn to the centre, and R be the middle point of the chord PQ drawn parallel to a fixed diameter ACB, describe the locus of the intersection of CP, AR, and shew that it is a parabola.

16. Describe a parabola with latus rectum $= 2 \cdot 7$ units, and in it draw a series of parallel chords inclined at 60^0 to the axis. Shew that the locus of the point which divides each chord into segments containing a constant rectangle $= 4$ sq. units in area, is a parabola, the axis of which coincides with the axis of the original parabola and with the latus rectum $= 2 \cdot 1$ units.

17. Draw a parabola to touch the three sides of a given triangle, one of them at its middle point; and shew that the perpendiculars drawn from the angles of the triangle upon any tangent to the parabola are in harmonical progression.

18. Given two unequal circles (centres G and g, radii R and r) touching each other externally, from G the centre of the larger circle make GN on Gg towards $g = \dfrac{R - r}{2}$. Draw NP perpendicular to Gg meeting the circle in P and describe a parabola with Gg as axis and to touch the circle in P (Prob. 47), and shew that it will also touch the smaller circle.

19. Given a point F and two straight lines intersecting in O; describe a parabola with F as focus and to touch the given lines (Prob. 42); and shew that if any circle be described passing through O and F and meeting the lines in P and Q, PQ will be a tangent to the parabola.

20. Draw the parabola which is the locus of the centre of a circle passing through a given point and cutting off a constant intercept on a given straight line.

(The point is the focus and a perpendicular to the line the axis.)

21. Given four tangents to a parabola, shew that the directrix is the radical axis of the system of circles described on the diagonals of the quadrilateral as diameters.

22. Given the focus F, a point P on the curve and a point L on the directrix, describe the parabola.

[Tangents from L to the circle described with centre P and radius PF are the directrices of two parabolas fulfilling required conditions.]

23. Given a focus F, a tangent PT, and a point L on the directrix, describe the parabola.

[From F draw a perpendicular FY to PT meeting it in Y; produce FY to f and make $Yf = FY$: f is a second point on the directrix.]

24. Given three tangents to a parabola and a point on the directrix, draw the curve.

[The ortho-centre of the triangle formed by the tangents is a second point on the directrix.]

CHAPTER IV.

THE ELLIPSE.

The ellipse has already been defined (p. 56) as the locus of a point which moves in a plane so that its distance from a fixed point in the plane is always in a constant ratio, less than unity, to its distance from a fixed line in the plane. The corresponding definition in the case of the parabola furnishes immediately the best condition for the geometrical construction of that curve, but this is not so with the ellipse. The ellipse can be more easily constructed geometrically from a property which will be shewn immediately to be involved in the above definition, and in virtue of which the curve may be defined as follows :—

Def. The ellipse is the locus of a fixed point on a line of constant length moving so that its extremities are always on two fixed straight lines perpendicular to each other.

In Fig. 55 let ACA_1, BCB_1 be two straight lines intersecting each other at right angles in C. If a length (as ab) be marked off on the smooth edge of a slip of paper, and the slip be moved round so that the point a is always on the line BCB_1 and the point b on ACA_1, then any point as P on the edge of the paper will trace out an ellipse. When the edge of the slip coincides with ACA_1 the tracing point will evidently be at a distance CA from C equal to aP, and when it coincides with BCB_1 the tracing point will be at a distance CB from C equal to bP. By this method of construction the curve is evidently symmetrical about both the lines ACA_1 and BCB_1, i.e. if CA_1 be made equal to CA, A_1 will be a point on the curve, and if CB_1 be made equal to CB, B_1 will be a point on the curve. It is moreover obvious that ACA_1 is the longest and BCB_1 the shortest line which can be drawn through C and terminated by the curve.

DEF. The line ACA_1 is called the *major axis*, the line BCB_1 the *minor axis*, the point C the *centre*, and the points A, A_1 *vertices* of the curve.

From B, the extremity of the minor axis, as centre with radius CA (the semi-major axis), describe arcs cutting the major axis in F and F_1; through B draw BM parallel to CA, from F draw FM perpendicular to BF meeting BM in M, and draw MX perpendicular to CA meeting it in X.

F will be the *focus* and MX the *directrix* (see definition, page 56).

From the similar triangles FBM, CFB,

$$FB : BM :: CF : CA :: CA : CX,$$

since $$FB = CA \text{ and } BM = CX;$$

$$\therefore \ CF : CA - CF :: CA : CX - CA,$$

i.e. $$CF : FA :: CA : AX,$$

or $$FA : AX :: CF : CA :: FB : BM;$$

also since $$CF : CA :: CA : CX,$$

$$\therefore \ CA - CF : CF + CA :: CX - CA : CA + CX,$$

or $$FA : FA_1 :: AX : A_1X,$$

i.e. $$FA : AX :: FA_1 : A_1X ;$$

therefore A, B and A_1 are points satisfying the original definition.

DEF. A circle described on the major axis as diameter is called the *auxiliary circle*.

Through any point P on the ellipse draw the ordinate PN (perpendicular to major axis) meeting the axis in N and the auxiliary circle in Q. Since QN is parallel to BC and $CQ = aP$,

$$\therefore \ aP \text{ is parallel to } CQ,$$

$$\therefore \ PN : QN :: Pb : QC$$

$$:: BC : AC,$$

or $$\overline{PN}|^2 : \overline{QN}|^2 :: \overline{BC}|^2 : \overline{AC}|^2;$$

but it is known that in the circle

$$\overline{QN}|^2 = AN \cdot NA_1,$$

$$\therefore \quad \overline{PN}|^2 : AN \cdot NA_1 :: \overline{BC}|^2 : \overline{AC}|^2.$$

This is a very important property of the ellipse and will now be shewn to result from assuming the ratio $FP : NX$ to be constant.

Through P draw PA, PA_1 meeting the directrix in E and H. Join FH and draw PLK perpendicular to the directrix meeting FH in L and the directrix in K.

Since PK is parallel to A_1X,

$$\therefore \quad PL : PK :: FA_1 : A_1X$$

$$:: FA : AX.$$

But by supposition $FP : PK :: FA : AX$,

therefore $FP = PL$, and the angle $LFP = FLP =$ the alternate angle LFX;

i.e. FL bisects the angle PFX;

similarly FE bisects the angle between FX and PF produced,

therefore the angle EFH is a right angle, since it is made up of the two angles EFX and HFX.

By the similar triangles PAN, AEX,

$$PN : AN :: EX : AX,$$

also $PN : A_1N :: HX : A_1X,$

$$\therefore \quad \overline{PN}|^2 : AN \cdot NA_1 :: EX \cdot HX : AX \cdot A_1X$$

$$:: FX^2 : AX \cdot A_1X,$$

since EFH is a right angle ;

i.e. PN^2 is to $AN \cdot NA_1$ in a constant ratio.

Hence taking PN coincident with BC, in which case

$$AN = NA_1 = AC,$$

$$\overline{BC}|^2 : \overline{AC}|^2 :: \overline{FX}|^2 : AX \cdot A_1X,$$

and $\therefore \quad PN^2 : AN \cdot NA_1 :: BC^2 : AC^2.$

This of course shews that the point P is the same whether deter-mined as the locus of a fixed point on a line of constant length sliding between two fixed rectangular axes or as the locus of a point which moves so that its distance from a fixed point (F) is in a constant ratio to its distance from a fixed line (MX), i.e. the two definitions of the ellipse already given are really identical. From the symmetry of the curve it is evident that F_1 is a second focus and M_1X_1 a second directrix.

Five geometrical conditions are generally necessary to determine an ellipse, and the ellipse shares with the hyperbola the property of satisfying five geometrical conditions. One or other of these curves can generally be drawn to pass through five given points or to touch five given straight lines, or to pass through two given points and touch three given lines, or to fulfil any five similar conditions. Which curve will satisfy the given conditions depends of course upon the relative positions of the given points and lines, and the necessary limitations will be noticed in discussing the separate problems. As in the case of the parabola the giving of certain points and lines is really equivalent in each case to the giving of two geometrical conditions; of these may be mentioned the centre, the foci, and the axes.

The eccentricity of the ellipse is (p. 57) the numerical value of the above fixed ratio; it is generally denoted by e and calling

$$CA = a$$

and

$$CB = b,$$

its value is

$$e = \frac{\sqrt{a^2 - b^2}}{a},$$

as is evident from the similar triangles FBM, FCB.

PROBLEM 60. (Fig. 55.) *To describe an ellipse having given axes AA_1, BB_1.*

First Method. Draw two lines perpendicular to each other intersecting in C. Set off CA, CA_1 each equal to $\frac{1}{2} AA_1$, and CB, CB_1 each equal to $\frac{1}{2} BB_1$. Take a smooth edged slip of paper and mark off on it $Pa = CA$ and $Pb = CB$ (a and b may be on the same or on opposite sides of P). Keep the point a on the minor axis and the point b on the major axis and (as already demonstrated) the point P will be on the curve. Any number of points may thus be determined. In the lower portion of the figure the

Fig.55.

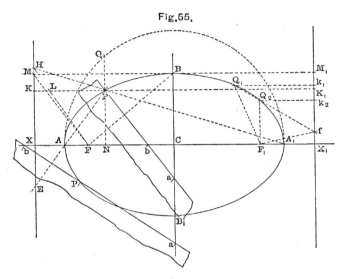

lengths CA, CB are shewn set off on opposite sides of P, and this arrangement is the better when the lengths AA_1, BB_1 are nearly equal, as in that case, when set off on the same side of P, the distance ab is too short to determine the direction of Pa with accuracy.

Second Method (f_3. 56). Arrange the axes as above, and on each as diameter describe a circle. Draw any number of radii as $C1$, $C2$, &c. From the extremities of the radii of the circle on the major axis draw lines parallel to the minor axis, and from the ends of the radii of the circle on the minor axis draw lines parallel to the major axis. The lines drawn from corresponding points (as $7P$, $7'P$) will intersect on the required ellipse, which can therefore be drawn through the points thus determined.

The proof is at once obvious by drawing through any point P on the curve a line parallel to the corresponding radius $C7$, cutting the axes in b and a. Then

$Ca\,P7$ is a parallelogram, and $\therefore Pa = C7 = CA$,

$Cb\,P7'$ is a parallelogram, and $\therefore Pb = C7' = CB$, so that the points found by this construction are identical with those found by the first.

Third Method (fig. 56). Determine the foci;—i.e. from the end of the minor axis (B_1) as centre describe an arc with radius $= CA$

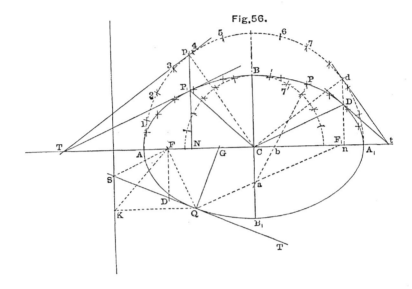

Fig. 56.

cutting AA_1 in F and F_1. Stick a pin firmly through the paper at each of the three points B_1, F, F_1, and tie a fine thread or piece of silk tightly round these pins, keeping it down in contact with the paper while doing so. Take out the pin at B_1 and keeping the string stretched with the point of a pencil, the curve may be drawn by moving the pencil round the circuit. This method is theoretically perfect, but it fails in practice to give a very exact result chiefly owing to the extensibility of the string and the impossibility of keeping it at a constant tension. It is difficult moreover to tie up the loop of the string to exactly the proper length and to keep the string continually in contact with the paper. Its use therefore cannot be recommended, but it illustrates a very important property of the ellipse, viz. *That the sum of the focal distances of any point on the ellipse is constant and equal to the major axis*, which may be proved thus :

In fig. 55, P is any point on the ellipse,

$$FP : PK :: FA : AX;$$

also

$$F_1P : PK_1 :: F_1A : AX_1,$$

$$\therefore FP + PF_1 : PK + PK_1 :: FA + F_1A : AX + AX_1$$

$$: XX_1 :: AA_1 : XX_1,$$

i.e.

$$FP + FP_1 = AA_1.$$

To draw the tangent at any point of the curve.

If Q_1 and Q_2 (fig. 55) be any two adjacent points of the curve, and the straight line drawn through them meets a directrix in f, draw Q_1k_1, Q_2k_2 perpendicular to the directrix and draw fF_2 to the corresponding focus.

Then

$$F_1Q_1 : F_1Q_2 :: Q_1k_1 : Q_2k_2$$

$$:: Q_1f : Q_2f,$$

therefore F_1f bisects the exterior angle between Q_1F_1 and Q_2F_1. (Euc. VI. Prop. A.)

Hence, exactly as in the case of the parabola (p. 59), when Q_2 moves up to and coincides with Q_1 so that the line through Q_1Q_2 becomes the tangent at Q_1 (Def. p. 30), the line F_1f becomes perpendicular to the line joining the focus to the point of contact of the tangent. *The tangent at any point Q_1 of an ellipse may therefore be drawn* by drawing a line from Q_1 to either focus, erecting a perpendicular to this line at the focus meeting the directrix, and drawing the tangent through this point and the proposed point of contact. It may also be drawn by using the known property *that the normal bisects the angle between the focal distances*, which may be proved thus. In fig. 56 Q is any point of the curve, F is a focus, and FS is perpendicular to QF meeting the corresponding directrix in S so that QS is the tangent at Q. Draw the normal QG perpendicular to QS meeting the major axis in G, and draw FD perpendicular to the major axis meeting QS in D, and QK perpendicular to the directrix. Join FK.

The angle QFG is the complement of QFD and is therefore equal to the angle SFD; the angle FQG is the complement of SQF and is therefore equal to the angle FSD, and therefore the triangle QFG is similar to the triangle SFD.

Hence $FG : FQ :: FD : FS$ ....(1).

But since SFQ, SKQ are right angles, a circle can be described round $FSKQ$, and therefore the angle FSQ = the angle FKQ.

Also the angle QFG = the angle FQK since GF is parallel to QK, therefore the angle $FQK = SFD$, therefore the triangle SFD is similar to the triangle KQF, and

$$\therefore FD : FS :: FQ : QK :: FA : AX,$$
$$\therefore FG : FQ :: FA : AX \qquad \text{from (1)};$$

similarly $\qquad\qquad F_1G : F_1Q :: FA : AX,$

and $\qquad\qquad \therefore FG : F_1G :: FQ : F_1Q,$

or the angle FQF_1 is bisected by the normal QG. (Euc. VI. 3.)

Hence SQT being the tangent the angle SQF is equal to the angle TQF_1 or *the tangent is equally inclined to the focal distances of the point of contact.* It follows that if F_1Q be produced to L *the tangent bisects the angle FQL.*

PROBLEM 61. *To describe approximately by means of circular arcs, an ellipse having given axes.*

First Method (fig. 57). CA, CB, CA_1, CB_1 are the semi-axes. Draw A_1M parallel to CB and BM parallel to CA meeting in M.

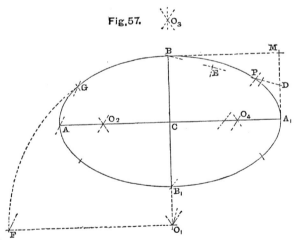

Fig. 57.

Bisect A_1M in D. Join BD and draw MB_1 cutting BD in P. P will be a point on the true ellipse with axes AA_1 and BB_1. Bisect

PB in *E*. Draw EO_1 perpendicular to *PB* meeting BB_1 in O_1, and with centre O_1 and radius to *B* or *P* draw the arc *PBF* meeting in *F* a line through O_1 parallel to AA_1. Draw *FA* and produce it to meet the arc in *G*. Draw GO_1 cutting AA_1 in O_2, and with centre O_2 and radius O_2G draw an arc which will be found to pass through *A*, since by the similar triangles GO_2A, GO_1F,

$$GO_2 : AO_2 :: GO_1 : FO_1,$$
$$\text{i.e. } O_2G = O_2A.$$

The two arcs *AG* and *GB* form one quadrant of the approximate ellipse and the remainder can of course be put in by symmetry, taking centres O_3 and O_4 in corresponding positions to those already obtained.

Second Method (fig. 58). Draw *AM*, *BM* parallel respectively to *BC*, *AC*, meeting in *M*. Draw MO_1 perpendicular to *AB*,

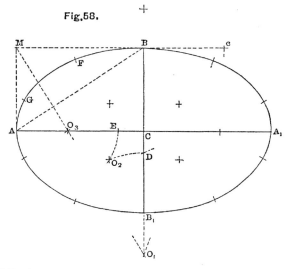

Fig.58.

cutting BB_1 in O_1 and AA_1 in O_3. Find a mean proportional (*BD*) between *CA* and *CB*. (This may conveniently be done by making *Bc* on *MB* produced equal to *BC*, and describing a semi-circle on *Mc* cutting *BC* in *D*.) Make *AE* equal to *BD*. With centres O_1, O_3 and radii O_1D, O_3E describe arcs intersecting in O_2. Then O_1, O_2, O_3 are points which can be used as centres for successive arcs of the required curve. The arc struck from O_1 will pass through B and extend of course to F on the line O_1O_2, that from O_2 will pass through F and extend to G on O_2O_3, and that from O_3 will start from G and pass through A. Thus each quadrant will consist of three arcs, and the centres for the other three quadrants can be taken by symmetry.

The arc struck with centre O_3 and radius O_3G will evidently pass through A, since $GO_2 = FO_2 = BD = AE$ and

$$GO_3 = GO_2 - O_2O_3 = GO_2 - O_3E = AE - O_3E = AO_3.$$

It will be shewn hereafter that the points O_1, O_3 are the *centres of curvature* at B and A respectively; the circular arcs struck with these centres through B and A coincide therefore more nearly with the true ellipse at those points than any others which can be drawn.

DEFINITION. Any line drawn through the centre of the ellipse and terminated both ways by the curve is called a diameter, and a semi-diameter CD parallel to the tangent at the extremity of a semi-diameter CP is said to be conjugate to CP. Every diameter is evidently bisected by the centre.

The following important properties of the ellipse should be carefully noticed.

PROP. 1. *Tangents drawn at the extremities of any chord subtend equal angles at the focus.*

Let PP_1 (fig. 59) be any chord of an ellipse, and let the tangents at P and P_1 meet in T. Let F be the focus, and from T draw TM, TM_1 perpendicular to FP, FP_1, and draw TN perpendicular to the directrix XS. Let the tangent at P_1 meet the directrix in S, then FS is perpendicular to FP_1 and therefore parallel to TM_1,

$$\therefore FM_1 : FP_1 :: ST : SP_1$$
$$:: TN : P_1K,$$

where P_1K is perpendicular to the directrix;

$$\therefore FM_1 : TN :: FP_1 : P_1K$$
$$:: FA : AX.$$

Similarly $FM : TN :: FA : AX,$

$$\therefore\ FM = FM_{1}.$$

Fig.59.

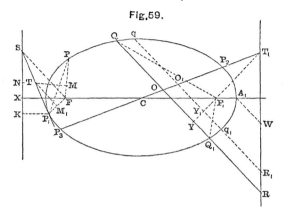

Hence in the right-angled triangles TFM, TFM_{1}, $FM = FM_{1}$ and TF is common, therefore the triangles are equal in all respects, i.e. the angle TFP equals the angle TFP_{1} and $TM = TM_{1}$.

Prop. 2. *A diameter bisects all chords parallel to the tangents at its extremities, i.e. all chords parallel to its conjugate.*

Let QQ_{1} (fig. 59) be any chord of an ellipse meeting the directrix in R and let O be the centre point of QQ_{1} and F_{1} the focus. Join $F_{1}Q$, $F_{1}Q_{1}$ and draw $F_{1}Y$ perpendicular to QQ_{1}, then

$$\overline{F_{1}Q}\,|^{2} - \overline{F_{1}Q_{1}}\,|^{2} = \overline{QY}\,|^{2} - \overline{Q_{1}Y}\,|^{2}$$
$$= (QY + Q_{1}Y)(QY - Q_{1}Y)$$
$$= 2QQ_{1}.OY\ \dots\dots\dots\dots\dots(1);$$

but since Q and Q_{1} are on the ellipse

$$F_{1}Q : F_{1}Q_{1} :: QR : Q_{1}R,$$

$$\therefore\ \frac{F_{1}Q^{2} - F_{1}Q_{1}^{2}}{\overline{F_{1}Q}\,|^{2}} = \frac{QR^{2} - Q_{1}R^{2}}{\overline{QR}\,|^{2}} = \frac{2OR.QQ_{1}}{QR^{2}}\ \dots\dots(2);$$

therefore from (1) and (2),

$$\frac{OY}{OR} = \overline{\frac{F_{1}Q}{QR}}\,\Big|^{2} = \overline{\frac{F_{1}A_{1}}{A_{1}W}}\,\Big|^{2},$$

where $A_{1}W$ is drawn through the vertex parallel to QR, meeting the directrix in W; i.e. $OY : OR$ in a constant ratio.

Take any second chord qq_1 parallel to QQ_1, meeting F_1Y in Y_1 and the directrix in R_1, let O_1 be its centre point, then since $\dfrac{OY}{OR} = \dfrac{O_1Y_1}{O_1R_1}$, it follows that the line OO_1 must pass through the point T_1 in which F_1Y meets the directrix and is therefore fixed for all chords parallel to QQ_1. This line T_1O will pass through the centre (i.e. will be a diameter), because the chord through the centre parallel to QQ_1 is bisected by the centre and also by T_1O. Let T_1O meet the ellipse in P_2 and suppose qq_1 to move parallel to itself till it approaches and ultimately passes through P_2. Since $O_1q = O_1q_1$ throughout the motion the points q, q_1 will evidently approach P_2 simultaneously, and in the limiting position qq_1 will be the tangent at P_2. It follows that if P_3 be the other extremity of the diameter through P_2, the tangent at P_3 is parallel to QQ_1, and therefore to the tangent at P_2.

COROLLARY. *The perpendicular on the tangent at any point from the focus meets the corresponding diameter in the directrix.*

PROP. 3. *If PCP_1 be a diameter and QVQ_1 a chord parallel to the tangent at P and meeting PP_1 in V, and if the tangent at Q meet PP_1 produced in T, then $CV \cdot CT = \overline{CP}|^2$* (fig. 60).

Let TQ meet the tangents at P and P_1 in R and r, and F being a focus draw RN perpendicular to the focal distance FP

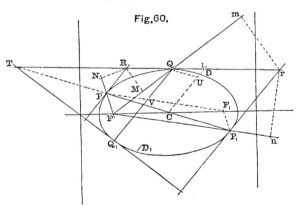

Fig. 60.

meeting FP in N, rn perperpendicular to FP_1 meeting it in n, and RM, rm perpendicular to the focal distance FQ.

Let F_1 be the other focus and join F_1P, F_1P_1.

Since $CF = CF_1$, $CP = CP_1$, and the angle FCP = the angle F_1CP_1, therefore the triangles FGP, F_1CP_1 are equal in all respects, and therefore the angle CPF = the angle CP_1F_1;

similarly CPF_1 = the angle CP_1F,

and therefore the whole angle FPF_1 = the whole angle F_1P_1F. But the tangents are equally inclined to the focal distances, and therefore also the angle FPR = the angle F_1P_1r,

$$\therefore \text{ the angle } FPR = \text{the angle } FP_1r,$$

i.e. the right-angled triangles RPN, rP_1n are similar, and therefore

$$RP \;:\; rP_1 \;::\; RN \;:\; rn.$$

But $RN = RM$ and $rn = rm$ (Prop. 1),

$$\therefore \; RP \;:\; rP_1 \;::\; RM \;:\; rm$$
$$:: \; RQ \;:\; rQ.$$

But $TR \;:\; Tr \;::\; RP \;:\; rP_1,$

$$\therefore \; TP \;:\; TP_1 \;::\; PV \;:\; P_1V,$$

or $CT - CP \;:\; CT + CP \;::\; CP - CV \;:\; CP + PV,$

$$\therefore \; CT \;:\; CP \;::\; CP \;:\; CV,$$
$$\therefore \; CT \cdot CV = CP^2.$$

Cor. 1.   Since CV and CP are the same for the point Q_1, the tangent at Q_1 passes through T or *the tangents at the extremities of any chord intersect on the diameter which bisects that chord.*

Cor. 2.   Since $TP_1 : TP :: P_1V : VP$, it follows that $TPVp$ is harmonically divided (p. 13).

The above proposition has been proved generally; it therefore holds when the diameter CP coincides with the major axis. Let P_1 be any point on an ellipse (fig. 56) and draw the ordinate P_1N perpendicular to CA, producing it to meet the auxiliary circle in p, and draw the tangent at P_1 meeting CA in T, then

$$CN \cdot CT = CA^2 = Cp^2,$$

and $\therefore \; CpT$ is a right angle,

and therefore pT is a tangent at p to the auxiliary circle: hence

Cor. 3. The tangents at the extremities of corresponding ordinates of the ellipse and auxiliary circle intersect on the major axis.

Draw CD (fig. 56) the diameter conjugate to CP_1, dDn the corresponding ordinate meeting the auxiliary circle in d, and the tangents at D and d meeting the major axis in t.

Then $\qquad P_1N : pN :: BC : AC :: Dn : dn,$

and $\qquad P_1N : NT :: Dn : Cn,$

since CD is parallel to P_2T,

$$\therefore\ pN : NT :: dn : Cn,$$

and therefore Cd is parallel to pT, i.e. pCd is a right angle, or

Cor. 4. Conjugate diameters in the ellipse project into diameters at right angles to each other in the auxiliary circle.

If the tangent at d meet the major axis in t, since dt is parallel to Cp, Dt (the tangent at D) will be parallel to CP_2, or,

Cor. 5. If CD be conjugate to CP_2, CP_2 is also conjugate to CD.

Since pCd is a right angle, the angle dCn is the complement of the angle pCN, and therefore equals the angle CpN, therefore the triangles CpN, dCn are equal in all respects, i.e. $Cn = pN$ and $dn = CN$,

$$CP_1{}^2 = P_1N^2 + CN^2 \text{ and } CD^2 = Cn^2 + Dn^2,$$
$$\therefore\ \overline{CP_1}|^2 + \overline{CD}|^2 = \overline{CN}|^2 + \overline{pN}|^2 + \overline{P_1N}|^2 + \overline{Dn}|^2$$
$$= \overline{CA}|^2 + \overline{P_1N}|^2 + Dn^2 \ldots\ldots\ldots\ldots(1).$$

But $\qquad P_1N : pN :: Dn : dn :: BC : AC,$

$$\therefore\ P_1N : Dn :: pN : dn,$$
$$\therefore\ P_1N^2 + Dn^2 : P_1N^2 :: pN^2 + dn^2 : pN^2,$$

and $\qquad pN^2 + dn^2 = AC^2;$

or $\qquad P_1N^2 + Dn^2 : \overline{AC}|^2 :: BC^2 : AC^2,$

$$\therefore\ \overline{P_1N}|^2 + Dn^2 = BC^2.$$

Therefore, from (1)

Cor. 6. $\overline{CP_1}|^2 + \overline{CD}|^2 = \overline{CA}|^2 + \overline{CB}|^2.$

PROP. 4.   If PCP_1, DCD_1 be conjugate diameters and QV be
rawn parallel to CD meeting the ellipse in Q and CP in V, then

$$QV^2 : PV . VP_1 :: CD^2 : CP^2.$$

[QV is called an ordinate of the diameter PCP_1.]

Let the tangent at Q (fig. 60) meet CP, CD in T and t, and
raw QU parallel to CT meeting CD in U.

Then $CV . CT = CP^2$ and $CU . Ct = CD^2$ (Prop. 3).

But $CU = QV$,

$$\therefore CD^2 : CP^2 :: QV . Ct : CV . CT$$

$$:: \overline{QV|}^2 : CV . VT.$$

ince $Ct : QV :: CT : VT$,

nd $CV . VT = CV . CT - CV^2$

$$= CP^2 - CV^2 = PV . VP_1,$$

$$\therefore QV^2 : PV . VP_1 :: CD^2 : CP^2.$$

PROBLEM 62.   *Given a pair of conjugate diameters to determine
he axes* (fig. 61).

$SD = CA , \ DZ = CB.$

$\text{Youv. Ann. } 1869 , \ 329.$

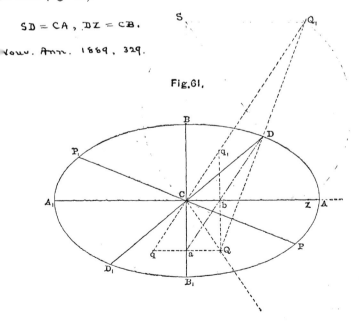

Fig. 61.

PCP_1, DCD_1 are the given conjugate diameters. Through D draw Q_1DQ perpendicular to CP. Make DQ and DQ_1 each equal to CP and draw the lines CQ, CQ_1. Then the major axis ACA_1 bisects the angle QCQ_1 and the minor axis (BCB_1) is of course a line through C perpendicular to ACA_1. The axes are therefore determined in direction. To determine them in magnitude:— On Q_1C on opposite sides of C make Cq and Cq_1 each equal to CQ, then Q_1q will be the length of the major axis AA_1 and Q_1q_1 will be the length of the minor BB_1. Bisect each of these lines and CA, CB will be given respectively.

Proof. Since $CQ = Cq$ and BC bisects the angle QCq, therefore a, the point in which Qq cuts BC, bisects Qq and therefore Da is parallel to Q_1q and $= \dfrac{Q_1q}{2} = CA$. Similarly b the point in which Qq_1 meets CA bisects Qq_1 and Db is parallel to Q_1q and $= \dfrac{Q_1q_1}{2} = CB$, and D, b, a are in the same straight line. Hence D is a point on the ellipse described with CA, CB as semi-axes. Also DQ is the normal at D, since Q is the instantaneous centre of rotation for the line ab moving along the axes. Therefore the tangent at D will be parallel to CP. Lastly, to shew that P will also be on the curve,

$$CQ^2 + CQ_1^{\,2} = 2CD^2 + 2DQ^2 \text{ (Euc. ii. 12 and 13)},$$
$$= 2\,(CD^2 + CP^2).$$

But $\qquad\qquad CQ_1 = AC + BC,$

and $\qquad\qquad CQ = AC - BC,$

$$\therefore\ CQ^2 + CQ_1^{\,2} = 2\,(AC^2 + BC^2),$$
$$\therefore\ CD^2 + CP^2 = AC^2 + BC^2,$$

a known property of conjugate diameters. (See Cor. 6, p. 109.)

PROBLEM 63. *To describe an ellipse having given conjugate diameters PCP_1, DCD_1.*

This might of course be done by the last problem: the curve may however be drawn independently, though none of the following constructions give any information as to the position of the axes, foci, or directrices.

First Method. By continuous motion (fig. 62). From C draw Ca perpendicular to CD and through P draw Pa parallel to CD meeting Ca in a.

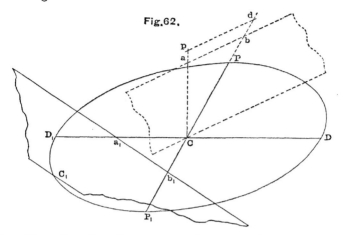

Fig.62.

On CP make $Cd = CD$ and on Ca make $Cp = CP$. Through a draw ab parallel to pd meeting CP in b. If a triangle equal and similar to the triangle abC be moved round so that the angle a is always on the diameter DCD_1 and the angle b on PCP_1, the angle C will be on the curve. The most convenient way of proceeding practically is to cut a strip of paper of breadth equal to the perpendicular distance between C and ab. The points a and b can then be marked off on one edge (as at $a_1 b_1$) and the point C on the other edge (as at C_1). The slip can easily be adjusted in any number of positions and the corresponding positions of C_1 marked. Any number of points on the curve may thus be determined*.

Second Method (fig. 63). Draw PM, $P_1 M_1$ parallel to CD and DMM_1 parallel to CP meeting PM in M and $P_1 M_1$ in M_1. Divide MD into any number of equal parts 1, 2, 3... and CD into the same number of equal parts. Then lines drawn from P to any of the points on MD intersect lines drawn from P_1 through the corresponding points on CD in points on the curve, and thus any number of points in the quadrant PD can be determined.

---

* I am indebted to Prof. Minchin for this construction.

Similarly if M_1D be divided into any number of equal parts $1', 2', 3'...$ and CD into the same number $1, 2, 3...$ lines drawn from P_1 to the points on M_1D intersect lines drawn from P to

Fig.63.

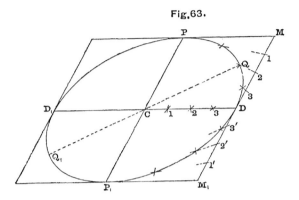

the corresponding points on CD in points on the required curve, and thus the quadrant DP_1 can be determined. When half the curve is drawn the remainder can be put in by symmetry, since every diameter is bisected by the centre; thus if QCQ_1 be drawn and CQ_1 be made equal to CQ, Q_1 will be a point on the curve and similarly for any other points on the semi-ellipse P, D_1, P_1.

Third Method (fig. 64). PCP_1, DCD_1 are the given conjugate diameters. Draw PM, P_1M_1 parallel to CD and MDM_1 parallel to CP meeting PM in M and P_1M_1 in M_1.

Draw the line PD and take on it any number of points $1, 2, 3...$

Draw the lines $1a, 2b, 3c...$ parallel to CD meeting DM in $a, b, c...$; and the lines $M_11, M_12, M_13...$ meeting MP in $a', b', c'...$. Then the lines $aa', bb', cc'...$ will be *tangents* to the curve, which must be drawn in to touch these lines, so giving the quadrant PD. A similar construction will give a second quadrant DP_1, and the remaining semi-ellipse can of course be put in similarly or by drawing any number of diameters.

Fourth Method (fig. 64). Draw PM_2, P_1M_3E parallel to CD_1 and $M_2D_1M_3$ parallel to PP_1 meeting PM_2 in M_2 and PM_3 in M_3. Make $M_3E = P_1M_3$ and divide PM_2 into any number of equal parts as at $1, 2, 3...$. Draw $E1, E2, E3...$ cutting D_1M_2 in f, g, h

E. 8

respectively. Then the lines joining corresponding points on PM_2 and M_2D_1, as $f3$, $g2$ and so on, will be tangents to the curve, which must therefore be drawn touching these lines.

Similarly for the remaining quadrants, or as before, when half the ellipse is obtained the other can be put in by symmetry.

To draw a tangent at any point of an ellipse having a given pair of conjugate diameters.

Let Q (fig. 64) be the point, PCP_1, DCD_1 the given conjugate diameters. Draw QN parallel to CP meeting CD_1 in N, so that

Fig. 64.

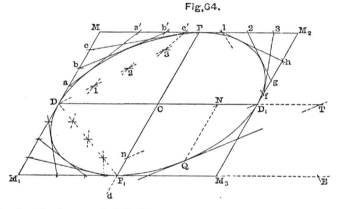

CN is the abscissa and QN the ordinate of Q referred to the given conjugate diameters as axes. Make Cn on CP_1 equal to CN and $Cd = CD_1$ and draw through d a line dT parallel to nD_1 cutting CD_1 in T. The line QT will be the tangent at Q, for by similar triangles

$$CT : Cd :: CD_1 : Cn,$$
i.e. $CT : CD_1 :: CD_1 : CN$ (Prop. 3, p. 107).

PROBLEM 64. *To describe an ellipse, one axis and a point* (P) *on the curve being given* (Fig. 55).

The axis is of course given in direction and magnitude, and this really involves the centre of the curve and the position of the other axis.

First, suppose the major axis AA_1 given. Bisect it in C and draw BCB_1 perpendicular to AA_1. From P with AC as radius mark the point a on BB_1 and draw Pa cutting AA_1 in b. Pb will be the length of the semi-minor axis, which can therefore be marked off from C to B and B_1.

Second, if the minor axis BB_1 is given. Bisect it in C, through C draw ACA_1 perpendicular to BB_1.   From P with radius BC mark off the point b on AA_1 and draw Pb, producing it to meet BB_1 in a.   Then Pa will be the length of the semi-major axis, which can be set off from C to A and A_1.

The construction is obvious from the original method of drawing the curve.

PROBLEM 65.   *To describe an ellipse, an axis ACA_1, and a tangent Tt being given* (Fig. 65).

T, t are the points in which the given tangent cuts the axes.

Draw the second axis BCB_1.

Take CN on CA, a third proportional to CT, CA (i.e. on CB make $Ca = CA$, draw An parallel to Ta, cutting CB in n, and

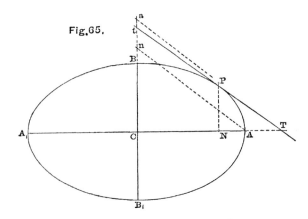

Fig.65.

make $CN = Cn$). Then N is the foot of the ordinate of the point of contact of the given tangent (Prop. 3, p. 107), and therefore by drawing NP perpendicular to CA meeting the tangent in P, a point on the curve is determined and the problem reduces to Problem 64.

PROBLEM 66. *To describe an ellipse, the directions of a pair of conjugate diameters CA, CB, a tangent PT and its point of contact P being given* (Fig. 65).

In the figure the given conjugate diameters are the axes, but the construction holds in any case.

Through P draw PN parallel to CB meeting CA in N. Take CA a mean proportional between CN and CT, which determines the length of the semi-diameter CA. Similarly determine the length CB.

PROBLEM 67. *To describe an ellipse, the centre (C), two points on the curve $(P$ and $Q)$, and the directions of a pair of conjugate diameters (CA, CB) being given. The lengths CA, CB are not given* (Fig. 66).

From P and Q draw PM, QN parallel to BC meeting CA in M and N. [In order that the problem may be possible, if PM is

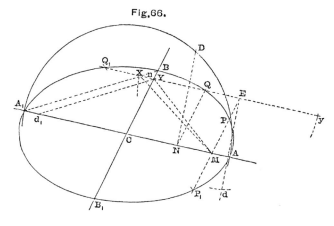

Fig.66.

less than QN, CM must be greater than CN.] Produce PM to E and P_1, making MP_1 equal to MP; P_1 will evidently be a point on the curve. Similarly, drawing $EQnQ_1$ parallel to CA meeting PM in E and CB in n, and making $nQ_1 = nQ$, Q_1 will be a point on the curve. Through M draw MX parallel to PQ and MY parallel to P_1Q_1 meeting EQ_1 in X and Y respectively. Find ND a mean proportional between EX and EY and set it up from N on a perpendicular to CA. [The mean proportional may conveniently be found by producing XE to y, making $Ey = EY$, and on Xy describing a semi-circle cutting Ed perpendicular from E to Xy in d. Ed is the required mean proportional.] Then a circle described with centre C and radius CD cutting CA in A and A_1 will determine A and A_1 the extremities of that diameter, and if Cd_1 be made $= ND$ on CA_1, and a parallel to d_1n be drawn through A_1 cutting CB in B, this will determine an extremity of the other. The curve can then be completed by preceding problems.

Proof. The construction depends on the known proposition that $EP . EP_1 : EQ . EQ_1 :: CB^2 : CA^2$; PP_1 and QQ_1 being any chords parallel to the conjugate diameters CB, CA and intersecting in E.   Admitting this, then by Prop. 4, p. 110,

$$QN^2 : AN . NA_1 :: EP . EP_1 : EQ . EQ_1.$$

By the construction
$$EX : EQ :: QN : EP,$$
and
$$EY : EQ_1 :: QN : EP_1,$$
$$\therefore \quad EX . EY : EQ . EQ_1 :: QN^2 : EP . EP_1;$$
but
$$EX . EY = ND^2 = AN . NA_1,$$
$$\therefore \quad AN . NA_1 : QN^2 :: EQ . EQ_1 : EP . EP_1,$$
which proves that AA_1 is the diameter parallel to EQQ_1.

Also by construction
$$CB : CA_1 :: QN : ND;$$
$$\therefore \quad CB^2 : CA_1^2 :: QN^2 : AN . NA_1,$$
or CB is the semi-diameter conjugate to CA_1.

That $EP . EP_1 : EQ . EQ_1 :: CB^2 : CA^2$ may be proved thus:—

Through E draw the diameter ERR_1 and draw the ordinate RU parallel to PP_1 or to CB, then by Prop. 4, p. 110,
$$CB^2 - RU^2 : CU^2 :: CB^2 : CA^2,$$
and
$$PM^2 : CA^2 - CM^2 :: CB^2 : CA^2;$$
$$\therefore \quad CB^2 - PM^2 : CM^2 :: CB^2 : CA^2,$$
so that
$$CB^2 - RU^2 : CU^2 :: CB^2 - PM^2 : CM^2;$$
but
$$RU^2 : CU^2 :: EM^2 : CM^2;$$
$$\therefore \quad CB^2 : CU^2 :: CB^2 - PM^2 + EM^2 : CM^2,$$
or $\quad CB^2 : CB^2 - PM^2 + EM^2 :: CU^2 : CM^2 :: CR^2 : CE^2;$

$$\therefore \quad CB^2 : EM^2 - PM^2 :: CR^2 : CE^2 - CR^2,$$

or $\quad CB^2 : EP . EP_1 :: CR^2 : ER . ER_1 .$

Similarly $\quad CA^2 : EQ . EQ_1 :: CR^2 : ER . ER_1 ,$

or $\quad EP . EP_1 : EQ . EQ_1 :: CB^2 : CA^2 .$

PROBLEM 68. *To describe an ellipse, the centre (C), direction of major axis CT, and two tangents (PT, Pt) being given* (Fig. 67).

Bisect the angle TPt between the given tangents by PR meeting CT in R, and draw PU perpendicular to PR meeting CT in U.

Fig. 67.

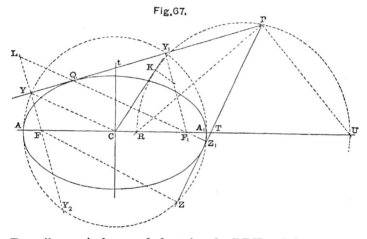

Describe a circle round the triangle RPU and draw a tangent from C to this circle meeting it in K. CK will be the distance of either focus from C, i.e. make $CF = CF_1 = CK$, and F and F_1 will be the foci of the required ellipse. From F draw FY perpendicular to Pt meeting it in Y, and make YL on FY produced $= YF$. Draw F_1L cutting Pt in Q, and Q will be the point of contact of Pt, i.e. Q will be a point on the ellipse, which can therefore be completed by preceding problems.

Proof. Since CK is a tangent to the circle RPU,

$$CK : CR :: CU : CK;$$

$$\therefore \quad CK + CR : CK - CR :: CU + CK : CU - CK,$$

or $\quad FR : RF_1 :: FU : F_1U,$

i.e. *FU is divided harmonically in* R *and* F_1 *or* $P\{FRF_1U\}$ *is* a harmonic pencil. But the angle RPU is a right angle, and therefore PF and PF_1 make equal angles with PR (p. 15). Therefore also the angle $FPQ =$ the angle F_1PT since PR bisects the angle QPT; or *the tangents from P make equal angles with the focal distances of P*: a known property of the ellipse.

F_1L is evidently the length of the major axis, for, by the construction $QL = FQ$, and therefore $F_1L = F_1Q + QF$, the sum of the focal distances (Prob. 60, p. 101).

It follows that Y is on the auxiliary circle, for $CF = CF_1$ and $FY = YL$; therefore CY is parallel to and equal to $\frac{1}{2}F_1L = CA$: and similarly if F_1Y_1, FZ and F_1Z_1 are perpendiculars from the foci on the tangents, Y_1, Z and Z_1 are all on the auxiliary circle. Produce YF to meet the auxiliary circle in Y_2, then FY_2 is equal to F_1Y_1, and therefore

$$FY \cdot F_1Y_1 = FY \cdot FY_2 = AF \cdot FA_1. \quad \text{(Euc. iii. 35.)}$$

Similarly $\qquad FZ \cdot F_1Z_1 = AF \cdot FA_1 = FY \cdot F_1Y_1,$

i.e. $\qquad\qquad FY : FZ :: F_1Z_1 : F_1Y_1;$

and since the angle YFZ is equal to the angle $Y_1F_1Z_1$, therefore the triangles YFZ, $Z_1F_1Y_1$ are similar (Euc. vi. 6), i.e. the angle

$$FZY = F_1Y_1Z_1.$$

Circles can be described about the figures

$$YFZP \text{ and } F_1Z_1PY_1,$$

and therefore the angle $FPY =$ the angle FZY,

,, ,, $F_1PZ_1 =$,, $F_1Y_1Z_1$; (Euc. iii. 21.)

therefore the angle $FPY =$ the angle F_1PZ_1, which proves the property above referred to.

PROBLEM 69. *To describe an ellipse, the centre C, the directions of a pair of conjugate diameters CT, Ct, a tangent Tt, and a point P being given* (Fig. 68).

[P must lie between the line Tt and a parallel corresponding line on the other side of C.]

Draw PCL meeting Tt in L, and make $CP_1 = CP$. P_1 is a point on the curve.

Take a mean proportional (Lm) between LP and LP_1 and

make *LM* on *LT* equal to *Lm*. On *Tt* describe a semicircle *Tqq₁t*; draw *Mn* perpendicular to *LM* and make *Mn* = *CP*. Draw *Ln* cutting the semicircle in *q* and *q₁*. From *q* draw *qQ*

Fig.68.

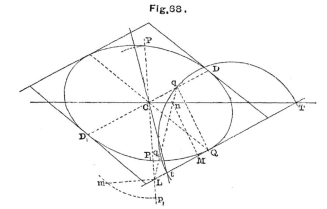

perpendicular to *LT* meeting it in *Q*; then *Q* will be the point of contact of *Tt*, and *Qq* will be the length of *CD* the semi-diameter conjugate to *CQ*; the curve can therefore be completed by Problems 62 or 63.

Since *Ln* cuts the semicircle in two points, there are two solutions.

Proof. The construction depends on the property of the ellipse proved in Problem 67, that the rectangles contained by the segments of intersecting chords are in the ratio of the squares of the parallel diameters; and on the further property that if the tangent at *Q* meet a pair of conjugate diameters in *T* and *t*, and *CD* be conjugate to *CQ*,

$$QT \cdot Qt = CD^2.$$

If *Q* be the point of contact of *Tt* it follows that

$$LP \cdot LP_1 : LQ^2 :: CP^2 : CD^2;$$

but $LP \cdot LP_1 = LM^2$ by construction,

$$\therefore LM : LQ :: CP : CD;$$

but by construction

$$LM : LQ :: Mn : Qq,$$

and *Mn* = *CP*, so that *Qq* = *CD*; also $Qq^2 = QT \cdot Qt$, since *Tqt* is a semicircle, therefore $CD^2 = QT \cdot Qt$ in the figure as drawn.

To prove that it does so in the ellipse, draw the ordinates QN, DK, parallel to Ct, and let the tangent at D meet CT in R, then by similar triangles,

$$QT \: : \: QN \: :: \: CD \: : \: DK,$$

and $$Qt \: : \: CN \: :: \: CD \: : \: CK;$$

$$\therefore \: QT . Qt \: : \: QN . CN \: :: \: CD^2 \: : \: DK . CK.$$

But $$CN . CT = CA^2 = CK . CR \text{ (Prop. 3, p. 107)},$$

$$\therefore \: CN \: : \: CK \: :: \: CR \: : \: CT$$

$$:: \: CD \: : \: QT$$

$$:: \: DK \: : \: QN;$$

$$\therefore \: CN . QN = CK . DK,$$

and $$\therefore \: QT . Qt = CD^2.$$

PROBLEM 70. *To describe an ellipse, the centre C, two tangents PT, QT, and a point on the curve (R) being given* (Fig. 69).

Fig. 69.

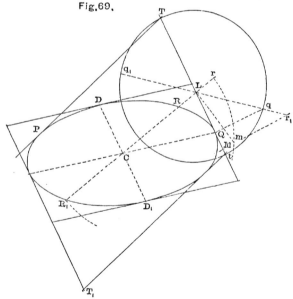

[It is of course possible to draw at once two more tangents by producing TC to T_1, making $CT_1 = CT$, and drawing through T_1 parallels to TP, TQ. The point R must lie within the quadrilateral thus formed. Let the parallel ($T_1 t$) to TP meet TQ in t.]

Draw RCR_1 and produce it to meet TQ in L; make $CR_1 = CR$. Take a mean proportional (Lm) between LR and LR_1 and make LM on $TQ = Lm$. Draw Mr_1 perpendicular to TQ and equal to CR, and join Lr_1, cutting the circle described on Tt as diameter in q and q_1; from q or q_1 drop a perpendicular (qQ) on Tt, and Q will be the point of contact of Tt. CD drawn parallel to Tt and equal to Qq will be the semi-diameter conjugate to CQ.

Proof. By construction,
$$LM^2 : LQ^2 :: Mr_1^2 : Qq^2,$$
$$\text{i. e. } LR.LR_1 : LQ^2 :: CR^2 : Qq^2;$$
therefore if Q is the point of contact of Tt, Qq must be the length of the semi-diameter parallel to Lt: and since
$$QT'.Qt = Qq^2 = CD^2,$$
Q is such point of contact. (See last problem.)

PROBLEM 71. *To describe an ellipse, the centre C and three tangents (SV, SW, VW) being given* (Fig. 70).

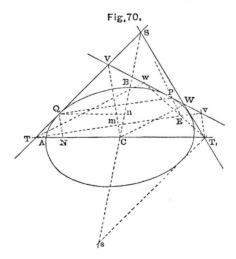

Fig.70.

Through C draw TCT_1 meeting SV in T and SW in T_1 so that TT_1 is bisected in C (Prob. 14, p. 19). CT will be conjugate to CS. Draw T_1v parallel to CV meeting VW in v, then Tv will be an ordinate of the diameter CV, for if it meets CV in m, $Tm = mv$, since $TC = CT_1$.

Similarly, if Tw be drawn parallel to CW meeting VW in w, T_1w will be an ordinate of the diameter CW.

Let Tv, T_1w intersect in E. Draw SE cutting VW in P, and P will be the point of contact of VW. Also PQ parallel to Tv meeting ST in Q will be the chord of contact of the pair of tangents VT, VW, i.e. P and Q are points on the curve; and the problem reduces to one of several previously given, or may be completed thus :—Draw QN parallel to CS meeting CT in N. QN is an ordinate of the diameter CT, and therefore CA the length of the semi-diameter is a mean proportional between CN and CT (Prop. 3, p. 107). Similarly if Qn be drawn parallel to CT meeting CS in n, CB must be taken a mean proportional between Cn and CS.

Proof. The only point in the construction requiring proof is that SE cuts VW in its point of contact.

Now the chords of contact PQ, PR, RQ of the given tangents are parallel respectively to TE, ET_1, T_1T, which is impossible unless EP passes through S the intersection of TQ and TR.

PROBLEM 72. *To describe an ellipse, the centre C, two points (A and B) of the curve and a tangent Tt being given* (Fig. 71).

Fig. 71.

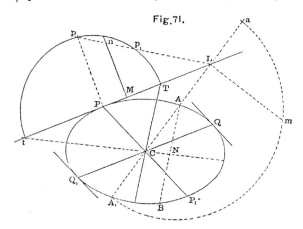

[A second tangent can at once be drawn parallel to Tt on the opposite side of C, and at the same distance from it; A and B must lie between these lines.]

Through C draw CT parallel to AB meeting the given tangent in T. Bisect AB in N and draw NCt meeting Tt in t. CT, Ct are a pair of conjugate diameters, and the problem reduces to Prob. 69. Draw the diameter ACA_1 meeting Tt in L. Take Lm a mean proportional between LA and LA_1. Make LM on Lt equal to Lm, draw Mn perpendicular to Lt and equal to CA and Ln cutting a circle on Tt as diameter in p and p_1. Perpendiculars from p and p_1 on Tt will determine two points, either of which can be taken as the point of contact of Tt, and the length pP will be the corresponding conjugate diameter CQ.

The construction is obvious from preceding problems.

PROBLEM 73.   *To describe an ellipse, the centre C and three points P, Q, R being given* (Fig. 72).

[Any one of the three points, as R, must lie *between* one pair of the parallel lines furnished by the remaining points and their corresponding points on the other side of the centre, and outside the other pair.]

Bisect PQ in p, QR in q, and RP in r, and draw Cp, Cq and Cr, producing each indefinitely. PR is a double ordinate of the

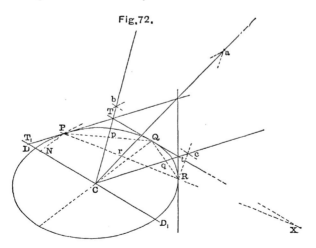

Fig. 72.

diameter Cr, and therefore the tangents at P and R will intersect on Cr produced; similarly the tangents at P and Q will intersect on Cp and those at Q and R on Cq. If therefore a triangle be drawn the sides of which pass through P, Q, R and the vertices of which lie on Cp, Cq, and Cr respectively, the sides of this triangle will be the tangents at P, Q and R. This can be done by Prob. 15, p. 20 :—Take *any point* a on Cr, draw Pa, Ra cutting Cp, Cq in b and c respectively ; join bc cutting PR in X, and draw XQ cutting Cb in T and Cc in t : PT, Tt, and Rt will be the tangents at P, Q, and R respectively, and the problem may be completed by preceding problems, or thus ; through C draw DCD_1 parallel to Tt so that CD is conjugate to CQ ; let TP meet CD in T'_1, draw PN parallel to CQ meeting CD in N. Take CD a mean proportional between CN and CT_1, and CD will be the extremity of the diameter CD (Prop. 3, p. 107).

The construction is obvious.

The given data are evidently equivalent to a diameter and two points of the curve.

PROBLEM 74. *To describe an ellipse, the foci F and F_1 and a point Q on the curve being given* (Fig. 56).

It has been shewn already that the foci lie on the major axis and that $FP + PF_1 =$ the major axis (p. 101).

Bisect FF_1 in C, and through C draw BCB_1 perpendicular to FF_1. On CF, CF_1 make $CA = CA_1 = \dfrac{FQ + QF_1}{2}$, and make $FB = FB_1 = CA$. AA_1, BB_1 will be the axes of the required ellipse.

PROBLEM 75. *To describe an ellipse, the foci F and F_1 and a tangent (PQ) to the curve being given* (Fig. 67).

[PQ must not lie between F and F_1.]

From F draw FY perpendicular to PQ and produce it to L making $YL = FY$. Draw F_1L cutting PQ in Q, which will be the point of contact of PQ and the problem reduces to the preceding.

The construction is obvious from Prob. 68.

PROBLEM 76.   *To describe an ellipse, a focus F, a tangent RT*
with its point of contact R, and a second point P on the curve
being given (Fig. 73).

From F draw FY perpendicular to RT meeting it in Y, and
produce FY to f making $Yf = YF$.

[F and P must lie on the same side of RT and the distance
of P from F must be less than its distance from a line drawn
through f perpendicular to fR. See Problem 106, Chap. v.]

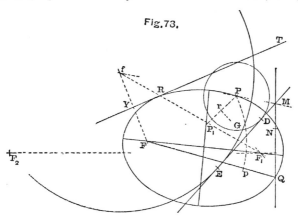

Fig. 73.

Draw fR, which will be a locus of the second focus. On fR
towards R make $fP_1 = FP$. Draw PP_1 and bisect it in r; through
r draw rF_1 perpendicular to PP_1 intersecting fR in F_1, which
will be the second focus. Hence both foci being known the problem may be completed by Probs. 74 or 75.

Proof.   That fR is a locus of the second focus has been
shewn in Prob. 68; that the second focus lies on rF_1 is evident
thus: it must be so situated that

$$FR + RF_1 = FP + PF_1 = fF_1 = fP_1 + P_1F_1.$$

But $FP = fP_1$, therefore PF_1 must be equal to P_1F_1, which
by construction it is; therefore F_1 is the second focus.

If fP_2 be made $= FP$ on Rf produced (i.e. on the side remote
from R), and a perpendicular to PP_2 be drawn through the centre
point of PP_2 meeting Rf in F_2, F and F_2 will be the foci of an
hyperbola fulfilling the given conditions.

PROBLEM 77. *To describe an ellipse, a focus F, a tangent RT', and two points P and Q of the curve being given* (Fig. 73).

[*F*, *P*, and *Q* must all lie on the same side of *RT*'.]

Let FQ be greater than FP, and on FQ make $Fp = FP$. With P as centre and radius $= pQ$ describe a circle DG, then evidently the second focus must be equidistant from this circle and from the point Q, since the sum of the focal distances is constant. From F draw FY perpendicular to the given tangent RT, produce it to f, make $Yf = YF$, and with f as centre and radius FQ describe a circle EG: the second focus will evidently be equidistant from this circle and from the point Q, for it has been shewn (Prob. 68) that the distance of f from the second focus is equal to the major axis, and therefore equal to the sum of the focal distances of any point on the curve.

The problem therefore is reduced to finding the centre of a circle to touch externally two given circles (DG, EG) and pass through a given point (Q), which is always possible since the circles must cut each other and Q lie outside both, i. e. the problem reduces to Prob. 32.

[Draw a common tangent EDM to the two circles meeting fP in M. Take MN on MQ such that

$$MN : MD :: ME : MQ,$$

and the second focus F_1 will lie on the line perpendicular to NQ and passing through the centre point of NQ.]

If the centre of the circle touching the above two circles *internally* be found (as F_2), F and F_2 will be the foci of an hyperbola which can be drawn through P and Q and touching RT'. (See Prob. 107.)

PROBLEM 78. *To describe an ellipse, a focus F, a point P on the curve, and two tangents TQ, TR being given* (Fig. 74).

[The points F and P must not lie on opposite sides of either tangent.]

From F draw FYf perpendicular to QT and FY_1f_1 perpendicular to RT', meeting them respectively in Y and Y_1. Make $Yf = YF$ and $Y_1f_1 = Y_1F$.

With centre P and radius PF describe the circle GH. Determine the centre (F_1) of a circle to touch this circle internally

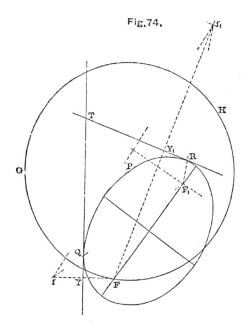

Fig. 74.

and to pass through f and f_1 (Problem 27): F_1 will be the second focus, and the axes can at once be determined by preceding problems.

Proof. It has been shewn (Prob. 68) that if F_1 is the second focus, $fF_1 = f_1F_1 =$ the major axis $= FP + PF_1$, which by construction it does.

Referring to Problem 27 it will be seen that if the line ff_1 cuts the circle GH and f and f_1 lie on opposite sides of it a second ellipse can be drawn with foci F and F_2. If this second solution is impossible, a circle can generally be drawn passing through f and f_1 and touching the circle GH externally. F and the centre of this circle will be the foci of an hyperbola fulfilling the conditions of the problem.

Hence either two ellipses or an ellipse and hyperbola can always be drawn to satisfy the given conditions.

PROBLEM 79. *To describe an ellipse, a focus F and three tangents TP, TQ and SR being given* (Fig. 74).

[The point F must lie within one of the three angles of the triangles (as PTQ), i.e. it must not lie within either of the angles (as PSY_1) where Y_1 is on RS produced.]

From F drop perpendiculars FYf, FY_1f_1, FY_2f_2 on the given tangents meeting them respectively in Y, Y_1, Y_2, and make $Yf = YF$, $Y_1f_1 = Y_1F$, $Y_2f_2 = Y_2F$; then f, f_1, f_2 must all be equidistant from the second focus (Prob. 68) and the problem therefore reduces to finding the centre (F_1) of a circle which will pass through three given points. (Prob. 20.) To do this it is not really necessary to bisect ff_1 and f_1f_2 because it will be found that the perpendiculars through their points of bisection will pass through the points S and K in which the given tangents intersect, so that it is only necessary to draw through S and K perpendiculars to ff_1 and f_1f_2, which will intersect in F_1 the second focus. The major axis is of course known since it is equal to F_1f.

PROBLEM 80. *To describe an ellipse, a focus F and three points P, Q, R on the curve being given* (Fig. 75).

[The point F must lie within one of the three angles PQR, QRP, RPQ, and if circles be described with two of the given

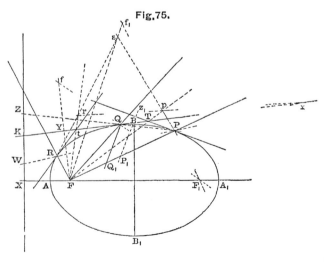
Fig.75.

points as centres passing through F and common tangents be drawn, the third point must be nearer to F than it is to the tangent more remote from F.]

First Method. It is a known proposition (Prop. 1, p. 105) that tangents drawn to an ellipse from any point subtend equal angles at the focus. The tangents at P and Q will therefore intersect on Fp the line bisecting the angle PFQ, those at R and Q will intersect on Fr the line bisecting the angle RFQ, and those at P and R will intersect on the line Fs bisecting the angle PFR. If therefore the three concurrent lines Fp, Fr, Fs be drawn and a triangle be constructed with its sides passing through P, Q and R and with its vertices on the corresponding lines respectively (Prob. 15), these sides will be tangents to the curve at those points.

On Fs take any point s. Draw Rs cutting Fr in r, and Ps cutting Fp in p. Let RP and rp meet in x, and draw xQ cutting Fp in T and Fr in t. PT, QT, Rt will be the tangents at P, Q, R respectively, and the second focus can then be easily determined and the problem completed by preceding problems.

Although there are generally six solutions to Prob. 15, one only is available here, since the sides through the points have to terminate on definite pairs of lines.

Second Method (same fig.).

Draw FP, FQ and FR and let FP be greater than FQ or FR.

Draw PQ and produce it to Z so that $PZ : QZ :: FP : FQ$,

      i.e. on FP make $FP_1 = PQ$ and $PQ_1 = FQ$.

Through P_1 draw P_1Z_1 parallel to QQ_1 meeting FQ in Z_1, and on PQ produced make $QZ = FZ_1$. Z will be a point on the directrix.

Similarly on PR produced take a point W such that

$$PW : RW :: FP : FR.$$

W will be a second point on the directrix, which is therefore determined.

From F draw a perpendicular FX to WZ meeting it in X, and on FX take points AA_1 such that $FA : AX :: FA_1 : A_1X :: FP$ is to the perpendicular distance of P from XZ. AA_1 will be the major axis.

The second focus and consequently the length of the major axis may perhaps be more easily determined thus. It is a known proposition (p. 102) that the tangent at any point, say Q, meets the directrix in a point K such that KFQ is a right angle. Therefore draw FK perpendicular to FQ meeting the directrix in K, and draw the tangent KQ. From F draw FYf perpendicular to KQ meeting it in Y, make $Yf = YF$, and draw fQ meeting XF in F_1, the second focus. fF_1 is of course the length of the major axis.

Proof. Since by construction

$$PF : PZ :: QF : QZ,$$

therefore evidently PF : dist. of P from $WZ :: QF$: dist. of Q from WZ, and since $\qquad PF : PW :: RF : RW,$

$\therefore PF$: dist. of P from $WZ :: RF$: dist. of R from WZ; therefore the distances of the given points from the focus are in a constant ratio to their distances from WZ, which is therefore the directrix.

If the lines PQ, PR are divided internally in the same ratio as above, two points are determined which being joined, either to each other or to the opposite points of the first pair, give three lines, either of which may be taken as the directrix of *an hyperbola* passing through the three given points and having F as focus. In each case one of the given points will lie on one branch of the curve and two on the other.

Thus generally four conics can be drawn fulfilling the given conditions, one of which is an ellipse.

PROBLEM 81. *To describe an ellipse, two tangents TQ, TR with their points of contact Q and R, and a point P on the curve being given* (Fig. 76).

[The point P must lie within the parabola which can be described touching TQ, TR at Q and R.]

This is of course a simple case of the more general problem to describe an ellipse to touch two given lines and to pass through three given points.

First Solution.   Let QP produced meet the tangent TR in S. From S draw a line passing through the intersection of PR and

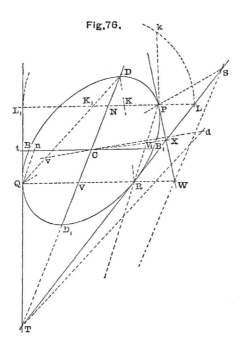

Fig.76.

the other tangent QT (Prob. 4) and meeting QR in W; then W will be a point on the tangent at P, which can therefore be drawn. Let it intersect TR in X.   Bisect QR in V and draw TVC, which will evidently be a diameter of the curve, i.e. is a locus of the centre.   Bisect PR in V_1 and draw XV_1C, which will similarly be a locus of the centre.   The centre is therefore at C, the intersection of TV and XV_1, and the centre being known the problem can be completed by Probs. 70, 71, &c.

Second Solution.   Bisect QR in V and through T draw TD_1VD, which will evidently be a diameter of the ellipse, i.e. will pass through the centre.   Through P draw $LPNL_1$ parallel to QR, meeting TR in L, TD in N and TQ in L_1.   Take Pk a mean proportional between PL and PL_1, and from L and L_1 towards N make $LK = L_1K_1 = Pk$; then RK or QK_1 will intersect TD in D,

the extremity of the diameter. On TD take a point C such that
$$TC : CD :: CD : CV,$$
i.e. $TC + CD : TC :: CV + CD : CD,$
or $TD : TC :: VD : CD.$

C will be the centre of the ellipse.

[The point C can easily be found by drawing any two parallels through T and D (as Td, Dv), making $Td = TD$ and $Dv = VD$, and joining dv cutting TD in C.]

The direction of the diameter CB conjugate to CD is known, since it is parallel to QR; its length can easily be determined by taking a mean proportional between Cn and Ct, where n is the foot of the ordinate from Q on CB and t the intersection of CB and of the tangent at Q.

Proof. Let DM be the tangent at D meeting TR in M, and let LP meet the curve again in p, so that $L_1P = Lp$.

Then $LP . Lp : LR^2$ is the ratio of the squares of the parallel diameters (p. 117); but $MD^2 : MR^2$ is the same ratio,
$$\therefore LP . Lp : LR^2 :: MD^2 : MR^2$$
$$:: LK^2 : LR^2 \text{ by similar triangles,}$$
$$\therefore LP . Lp = LK^2, \text{ which justifies the construction.}$$

PROBLEM 82. *To describe an ellipse, two tangents TP, TQ and three points A, B, C on the curve being given* (Fig. 77).

[The points ABC must not lie on opposite sides of either line.]

Draw the line AB cutting the given tangents in P and Q. Find X the centre, and E, E_1, the foci, of the involution A, B and P, Q (Prob. 13).

[In the figure, Pb on $TP = PB$, Aq_1 on a parallel to TP drawn through A is equal to AQ; then q_1b cuts AB in X, the required centre. XE is a mean proportional between XA and XB.]

E or E_1 will be a point on the chord of contact of the given tangents.

Similarly draw BC cutting the given tangents in p and q, and find X_1 the centre, and F, F_1 the foci of the involution B, C and p, q; then F or F_1 will be a second point on the chord of contact of the given tangents, the points of contact of which R, R_1 are therefore determined, and the problem reduces to the preceding*.   Since

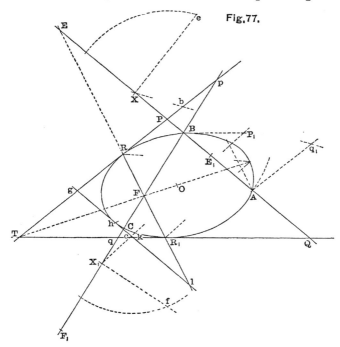

Fig. 77.

E and E_1 can be joined to either F or F_1 four chords of contact can in general be drawn, but one at least of the corresponding conics will be an hyperbola.

For proof that E and F are points on the chord of contact see Prop. 7, p. 143.

PROBLEM 83.   *To describe an ellipse, two points A, B on the curve, and three tangents PQ, QR, RP being given* (Fig. 78).

[A and B must not lie on opposite sides of either line.]

Draw a line through AB cutting the tangents through P in L and M and the remaining tangent in N.

Find X the centre, and D, D_1 the foci of the involution AB and LM (Prob. 13). D or D_1 will be a point on the chord of contact of the tangents PQ, PR.

* In the figure the point of bisection of RR_1 accidentally coincides with F.

[In the fig. *La* on $PR = LA$, *Bm* on a parallel to PR drawn through $B = BM$, and *ma* cuts AB in X, the required centre. XD is a mean proportional between XA and XB.]

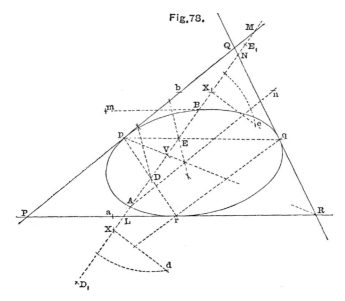

Fig.78.

Similarly find X_1 the centre, and E, E_1 the foci of the involution A, B and M, N (Prob. 13), and E or E_1 will be a point on the chord of contact of the tangents QP, QR.

[In the fig. *Mb* on $Qp = MB$, *An* on a parallel to QP through A is equal to AN, and *bn* cuts AB in X_1, the required centre. X_1E is a mean proportional between X_1M and X_1N.]

Find MV, the harmonic mean between ME and MD, M being the point on the given tangents which has appeared in each of the above involutions (Prob. 11); then RV will cut the opposite tangent PQ in its point of contact (p) with the curve, and therefore pEq will be the chord of contact of the tangents QP, QR and pDr that of PQ, PR. The problem therefore reduces to No. 81.

The construction depends on the property made use of in the last problem and proved in Prop. 7, p. 143, that the chord of contact of PQ, PR must pass through D or D_1, the foci of the involution AB and LM, and similarly that the chord of contact of QP and

QR must pass through E or E_1, the foci of the involution AB and MN.

Also if rq meets VR in u and the tangent PQ in T,
since $DVEM$ is harmonic (by construction) so also is $Truq$, and therefore uV is the polar of T and therefore determines p, the point of contact of PV (Prop. 5, p. 141).

Since either D or D_1 may be taken with E or E_1 there are in general four solutions.

PROBLEM 84. *To describe an ellipse to touch five given lines* AB, BC, CD, DE, EA.

[The lines must form a pentagon without a re-entering angle and the vertices are supposed to be lettered consecutively.]

Draw AC and BD intersecting in F. Then EF will intersect BC in P, the point of contact of BC. Similarly if BD and CE

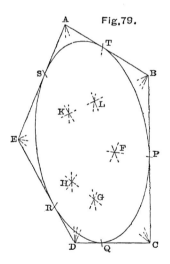

Fig.79.

intersect in G, AG will intersect CD in Q, the point of contact of CD; and continuing the construction R, T and V, the points of contact of DE, EA and AB may be determined.

The centre of the curve can easily be found and the curve completed by preceding problems.

The construction depends on Brianchon's well-known theorem:

"*The three opposite diagonals of every hexagon circumscribing a conic intersect in a point.*"

For if T be the point of contact of AB the pentagon may be considered as a hexagon AT, TB, BC, CD, DE, EA, and therefore AC, BE and DT must meet in a point L; and conversely if L is the point of intersection of AC and BE, DL must pass through T, the point of contact of AB, and similarly for the remaining sides.

PROBLEM 85.   *To describe an ellipse, four tangents AB, BC, CD, DA and a point E on the curve being given* (Fig. 80).

[The point E must lie within the quadrilateral $ABCD$, which must not be a parallelogram.]

Let BE, CE meet AD in B_1 and C_1 respectively.

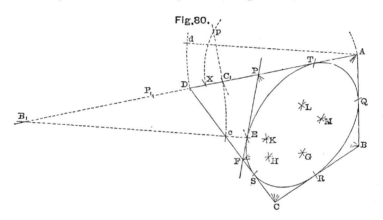

Fig.80.

Find X the centre, and P and P_1 the foci of the involution AC_1 and DB_1.   Prob. 13.

Then the tangent at E must pass through P or P_1 and the problem reduces to the preceding.

There are two solutions.

In the figure B_1c on $B_1B = B_1C_1$; Ad on a parallel to B_1B is equal to AD and cd intersects AB_1 in X, the required centre. XP is a mean proportional between XA and XC_1.

Also BP and AF intersect in L and CL will pass through T, the point of contact of AP.

PROBLEM 86. *To describe an ellipse to pass through five given points ABCDE* (Fig. 81).

[No point must lie inside the quadrilateral formed by the other four.]

Let *AB*, *DC* meet in *F* and *AC*, *BE* in *G*.

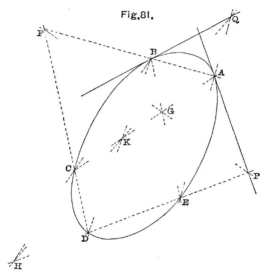

Fig. 81.

Draw *FG* meeting *DE* in *P*. *P* will be a point on the tangent at *A*.

Similarly if *BC* and *ED* meet in *H* and *AC*, *BD* in *K*, *HK* will meet *EA* in *Q*, a point on the tangent at *B*.

The problem can evidently be completed in various ways by preceding problems.

The construction depends on Pascal's well-known theorem : " *The three intersections of the opposite sides of any hexagon inscribed in a conic section are in one right line.*" For the tangent at *A* may be considered as meeting the curve in two consecutive points *A* and *a*, and therefore *P*, the intersection of *Aa* and *DE*, must lie on *FG*, the straight line through the intersections of *AB* and *DC* and of *BE* and *Ca*.

This line is known as the Pascal line.

There is only one solution.

PROBLEM 87. *To describe an ellipse, four points on the curve A, B, C, D and a tangent ad being given* (Fig. 82).

[All the points must lie on the same side of the tangent.]

Draw AB meeting ad in a, BC meeting ad in b, DC meeting it in c, and AD meeting it in d.

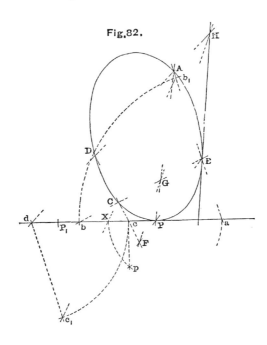

Fig.82.

Find X the centre, and P and P_1 the foci of the involution ac and bd.

P or P_1 will be the point of contact of the given tangent and the problem may be completed by several preceding ones.

In the fig. ab_1 on $aA = ab$; dc_1 on a parallel to $aA = dc$, and b_1c_1 intersects ad in X, the required centre. $XP = Xp$, a mean proportional between Xc and Xa.

If DC, BP meet in F, and BC, PA in G, then FG and DA will intersect in H, a point on the tangent at B.

There are of course two solutions, as either P or P_1 may be taken as the point of contact.

That P, the point of contact, is a focus of the involution is proved in Chapter 8.

POLE AND POLAR.

It has been shewn in the case of the circle (Cor. 3, p. 31) that the pairs of tangents drawn at the extremities of any chord through a fixed point intersect in a straight line.

This is also true in the case of any conic section, for let V (fig. 83) be any point in a conic and C the centre, and let CV

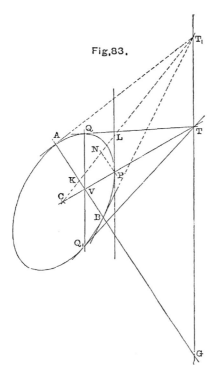

Fig. 83.

meet the curve in P. Take T in CV produced such that $CV : CP :: CP : CT$, and through V draw the chord QVQ_1 parallel to the tangent at P.

QQ_1 will be the chord of contact of the pair of tangents drawn from T to the conic, and will be bisected in V.

Through V draw any chord AVB and let the tangents at A and B intersect in T_1.

Join CT_1, and draw PN parallel to AB, meeting CT_1 in N. Then if CT_1 meet AB in K and the tangent at P in L,

$$CK \cdot CT_1 = CN \cdot CL. \quad \text{(Prop. 3, p. 107.)}$$

$$\therefore CT_1 : CL :: CN : CK$$
$$:: CP : CV$$
$$:: CT : CP;$$

hence TT_1 is parallel to PL, and therefore T_1, the intersection of the tangents at the extremities of *any* chord through V, lies on a fixed line.

DEF. As in the circle, the line TT_1 is called the *polar* of the point V with respect to the conic and the point V is called the *pole* of TT_1 with respect to the conic.

If the *pole* lies without the conic (as T), its *polar* is the line QQ_1 parallel to the tangent at the point (P) where CT meets the conic, and meeting CT in a point V such that

$$CV : CP :: CP : CT,$$

i. e. is the chord of contact of tangents from the pole.

If the conic be a parabola, since the centre may be considered as at an infinite distance, the line VT must be drawn parallel to the axis meeting the curve in P and PT be made equal to PV, the *polar* of V will then be parallel to the tangent at P and will pass through T.

If the pole be on the curve, the polar is the tangent at the point.

The directrix is the polar of the corresponding focus.

If a point (as T_1) lies on the polar of V, the polar of T_1 passes through V.

The following important harmonic properties should be noticed.

PROP. 5. A straight line drawn through any point is divided harmonically by the point, the curve, and the polar of the point.

a. Let the point be without the curve, as T (fig. 84), and let the line meet the curve in AB and the polar of T in C. Draw

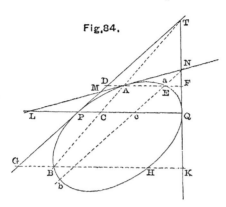

Fig.84.

the tangents TP, TQ meeting the curve in P, Q. C of course lies on the line PQ. Through A and B draw $DAEF$, $GBHK$ parallel to PQ meeting the tangents respectively in D, F and G, K and the curve in E and H.

Then the diameter through T bisects AE and PQ, and therefore also bisects DF;

hence $DA = EF$ and similarly $GB = KH$.

Also $\qquad\qquad GB : BK :: DA : AF$;

$\qquad \therefore GB . BK : \overline{GB}|^2 :: DA . AF : \overline{DA}|^2$,

$\qquad$ or $GB . GH : DA . DE :: \overline{GB}|^2 : DA^2$

$\qquad\qquad\qquad\qquad :: GT^2 : DT^2$;

but $\qquad GB . GH : DA . DE :: GP^2 : DP^2$ (p. 117);

$\qquad\qquad \therefore GP : PD :: GT : DT$,

and $\qquad\qquad \therefore TA : TB :: AC : CB$,

i.e. $TACB$ is divided harmonically.

β. Let the point be within the curve, as V (fig. 83), then drawing any chord $AVBG$ meeting in G the polar of V, the polar of G passes through V and therefore $AVBG$ is harmonically divided.

Prop. 6. If two tangents be drawn to a conic, any third tangent is harmonically divided by the two tangents, their chord of contact, and the point in which it touches the curve.

Let $LMAN$ (fig. 84) be the third tangent meeting PQ in L, and TP, TQ in M and N. Through N draw $Nacb$ parallel to TP meeting the curve in a, b and PQ in c.

Then
$$Na \cdot Nb : \overline{NQ}|^2 :: \overline{TP}|^2 : \overline{TQ}|^2 \text{ (p. 117)}$$
$$:: \overline{Nc}|^2 : \overline{NQ}|^2,$$
$$\therefore Na \cdot Nb = \overline{Nc}|^2;$$

but $\quad LN^2 : \overline{LM}|^2 :: \overline{Nc}|^2 : \overline{PM}|^2$ by similar triangles,

$$\therefore \overline{LN}|^2 : \overline{LM}|^2 :: Na \cdot Nb : \overline{PM}|^2$$
$$:: \overline{NA}|^2 : \overline{AM}|^2 \text{ (p. 117)},$$

i.e. $LMAN$ is divided harmonically.

Prop. 7. If a straight line meet two tangents to a conic in PQ and the curve in AB, the chord of contact of the tangents will pass through one of the foci of the involution P, Q and A, B (fig. 77).

Since X is the centre and E, E_1 the foci of the involution P, Q and A, B,
$$XP : XA :: XB : XQ;$$
$$\therefore XA - XP : XA :: XQ - XB : XQ,$$
$$\text{or } PA : XA :: BQ : XQ.$$

Similarly $\quad PB : XB :: AQ : XQ,$

$$\therefore PA \cdot PB : AQ \cdot BQ :: XA \cdot XB : \overline{XQ}|^2 :: \overline{XE}|^2 : \overline{XQ}|^2;$$

but (p. 18) $\quad EP : EQ :: PE_1 : E_1Q$, since EPE_1Q is harmonic;

$$\therefore EP : EP + PE_1 :: EQ : EQ + QE_1,$$
$$\text{or } EP : EQ :: 2XE : 2XQ;$$

$$\therefore PA \cdot PB : AQ \cdot BQ :: \overline{EP}|^2 : \overline{EQ}|^2 \dots\dots\dots\dots\dots\dots\dots(1).$$

Draw the tangent $ghkl$ parallel to PQ meeting TP, TQ in g and k, the chord of contact in l, and touching the curve in h; and if the chord of contact does not pass through E let it meet PQ in G.

$$PB \cdot PA : \overline{gh}|^2 :: \overline{PR}|^2 : \overline{Rg}|^2 \text{ (p. 117)}$$

$$:: \overline{PG}|^2 : \overline{lg}|^2 \text{ by similar triangles,}$$

and $\qquad QA \cdot QB : \overline{kh}|^2 :: \overline{QR_1}|^2 : \overline{kR_1}|^2$

$$:: \overline{QG}|^2 : \overline{lk}|^2 ;$$

but $lkhg$ is harmonic (Prop. 6),

and $\qquad\qquad \therefore \ \overline{lk}|^2 : \overline{lg}|^2 :: \overline{kh}|^2 : \overline{gh}|^2,$

$$\therefore \ PB \cdot PA : QA \cdot QB :: \overline{GP}|^2 : \overline{GQ}|^2 \dots\dots\dots\dots\dots (2);$$

but (1) and (2) cannot be simultaneously true unless the points E and G coincide.

PROP. 8.   If a quadrilateral be inscribed in a conic, its opposite sides and diagonals will intersect in three points such that each is the pole of the line joining the other two.

This follows at once from the harmonic properties of a complete quadrilateral, p. 16, combined with Prop. 5, p. 141. For since $ECfA$ (fig. 11) is harmonic it follows that f is a point on the polar of E with respect to any conic passing through A and C, and since EDf_1B is harmonic f_1 is a point on the polar of E with respect to any conic passing through BD.   Therefore ff_1, i.e. OF, is the polar of E with respect to a conic passing through $ABCD$.   Similarly OE is the polar of F.   Also since O is on the polar of E the polar of O must pass through E, and since it is also on the polar of F the polar of O must pass through F, i.e. EF is the polar of O.

The triangle EFG is of course *self-conjugate* with respect to any conic circumscribing the quadrilateral, Def. p. 32.

PROP. 9.   If a quadrilateral circumscribe a conic its three diagonals form a self-conjugate triangle (fig. 85a).

Let $ABCD$ be the quadrilateral and let AB and CD intersect in G, AC and BD in E, and AD and BC in F.   Let BD and AC meet FG in K and L respectively.   The triangle EKL is self-conjugate with respect to any conic inscribed in the quadrilateral $ABCD$.

Let the polar of F (i. e. the chord of contact PP_1) meet FG in R; then, since R is on the polar of F, it follows that F is on the polar of R.

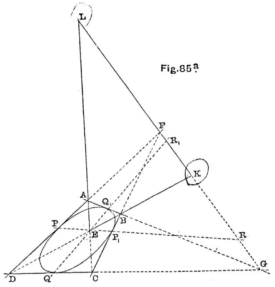

Fig.85ª

Now $F(AEBG)$ is a harmonic pencil (p. 16), and if PP_1 does not pass through E let FE meet PP_1 in T; then PTP_1R is a harmonic range; hence by (Prop. 5, p. 141) FE is the polar of R.

Similarly, if the other chord of contact QQ_1 meet FG in R_1, GE is the polar of R_1.

∴ E is the pole of RR_1, i.e. of LK.

Again, $DEBK$ is a harmonic range, and if QP meet AC in S and CK in V, $QSPV$ is harmonic, and therefore S is on the polar of V; but S is also on the polar of C, therefore CV or CK is the polar of S. Similarly, if P_1Q_1 meet AC in S_1, AK is the polar of S_1.

∴ K is the pole of LS_1, i.e. of EL;

∴ ELK is a self-conjugate triangle.

PROBLEM 88. *To determine the* centre of curvature *at any point P of a given ellipse* (see page 89), fig. 86.

CA, CB are the semi-axes, and F, F_1 the foci. Draw PG the normal at P meeting the major axis in G, and draw GK perpen-

E. 10

dicular to PG meeting PF or PF_1 the focal radii through P in K. KO perpendicular to PK will intersect PG in O, the required centre of curvature.

Fig. 86.

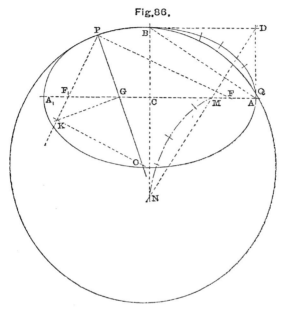

If AD, BD be drawn parallel to the axes and DN be drawn perpendicular to AB meeting the major axis in M and the minor in N, M and N will be the centres of curvature at A and B respectively. The evolute of the quadrant AB will therefore touch the axes at these points, and the evolute of the entire ellipse is made up of four curves similar to the chain dotted curve shewn in the figure between M and N.

As in the parabola, if the circle of curvature at P cuts the curve again in Q, PQ is inclined to the axes at the same angles as is the tangent at P.

The construction depends on the known value of the radius of curvature, $\dfrac{PG}{\cos^2 F_1 PG}$ (Salmon's *Conic Sections*, Chap. XIII.),

for
$$\cos F_1 PG = \frac{PK}{PO} = \frac{PG}{PK},$$
and therefore rad. of curvature $= PO$.

Examples on Chapter IV.

1. Describe an ellipse to touch a given straight line (QY) and pass through a given point (P); a focus F and the length $(2a)$ of the major axis being given.

[From F draw FY perpendicular to QY and produce it to T, making $YT = YF$. With T as centre and $2a$ as radius describe an arc, and with P as centre and $(2a - FP)$ as radius describe a second arc intersecting the former in F_1, which will be the second focus. There are two solutions.]

2. Describe an ellipse to touch two given straight lines; a focus and the length of the major axis being given (last question).

3. Describe an ellipse to touch two given lines OP, OQ at the points P and Q; one focus (F) being on the line PQ and the angle POQ less than a right angle.

[The second focus F_1 is the point of intersection of lines making with the given tangents angles equal to OPQ, OQP respectively, i. e. $OPF_1 = \pi - OPQ$ and $OQF_1 = \pi - OQP$. Bisect PQ in V; centre lies on OV. Draw F_1K parallel to PQ meeting OV in K. Bisect VK in C, which will be the centre of required elllipse.]

4. Given one focus F of an ellipse, the length $2b$ of the minor axis, and a point P on the curve; draw the locus of the centre.

[A parabola with the centre point of FP as focus, FP as axis and latus rectum $= 2\dfrac{b^2}{FP}$.]

5. Given one focus F of an ellipse, the length $2b$ of the minor axis and a tangent to the curve; shew that the locus of the second focus is a straight line parallel to the given tangent and at a distance from it $= \dfrac{b^2}{p}$, where p is the perpendicular from F on the given tangent.

6.   Any focal radius FP is drawn in an ellipse, and the point Q on the auxiliary circle corresponding to P is joined to the centre C.   Shew that the locus of the intersection of FP and CQ is an ellipse having F and C for foci.

7.   Given the base, and sum of sides of a triangle ; shew that the locus of centre of inscribed circle is an ellipse, having given base as major axis.

8. AB and BC are two equal rulers of length a, jointed at B. P is a point on BC distant b from B.   The end A of one ruler is fixed and the end C of the other moves along a right line AC through A.   Shew that the locus of P is an ellipse with semi-axes $a + b$ and $a - b$.

9.   An ellipse slides between two lines at right angles to each other ; shew that the locus of its centre is a circle of radius $\sqrt{a^2 + b^2}$, where a and b are the semi-axes of the ellipse.

10.   Draw an ellipse, and from any point P on it draw lines PD, PE equally inclined to the major axis and meeting the curve again in D and E ; draw PC perpendicular to the major axis meeting DE in C.   If the tangent at P meet DE in O, shew that the triangle POC is isosceles.

11.   Shew by construction that the normal PG at any point of an ellipse is an harmonic mean between the focal perpendiculars on the tangent at P.

12.   Given one focus F of an ellipse, the length $2b$ of the minor axis, and a point P on the curve ; draw the locus of the other focus.

[A parabola with focus P, axis FP and latus rectum $= 4\dfrac{b^2}{FP}.$]

13.   Shew that the locus of intersection of tangents at the ends of conjugate diameters of a given ellipse (semi-axes a and b) is an ellipse, the axes of which coincide in direction with the given ellipse, and the semi-lengths of which are $\sqrt{2}a$ and $\sqrt{2}b$.

14. AB is a line cutting in A and B a circle, centre C ; Q is a point on the perpendicular from C on AB on the same side of AB as C and outside the circle. Shew that the locus of the point P moving so that the tangent from P to the circle is in a constant ratio to the distance of P from AB (Q being a point on the locus) is an ellipse touching the circle at A and B.

15. Given any point P on an ellipse, inscribe in the ellipse a triangle PQR, the bisectors of the sides of which shall pass through the centre.

[Take p the point on the auxiliary circle corresponding to P. In the circle inscribe the equilateral triangle pqr ; the points corresponding to q and r will be the vertices of the required triangle.]

16. Given two tangents TP, TQ ; their points of contact P and Q and the radius of curvature (ρ) at one of them (P suppose) describe the ellipse.

[TC bisecting PQ is a locus of the centre. Draw the circle circumscribing the triangle TPQ and let d be its diameter. Draw a straight line through P such that p (the perpendicular distance of any point on it from PT) : q (the perpendicular distance of the same point from QP) :: $PT . d$: $QT . \rho$, i.e. determine the ratio $\dfrac{p}{q} = \dfrac{PT . d}{QT . \rho}$ (p. 10). This line is a second locus of the centre, which is therefore known.]

17. Draw an ellipse, a focus F, a tangent PT, its point of contact P and the radius of curvature (ρ) at P, being given.

[Reverse the construction of Prob. 88 to determine G, the foot of the normal at P, and consequently the direction of the major axis.]

18. If P is any point on an ellipse and the ordinate Pp perpendicular to the major axis meets the auxiliary circle in p, the angle between the major axis and the radius of the circle through p is called the eccentric angle of P.

Shew that if P be any point on an ellipse, the eccentric angle of which is α, three points A, B, and C on the curve, the eccentric angles of which are $-\dfrac{\alpha}{3}$, $-\dfrac{\alpha}{3} + 120^0$ and $-\dfrac{\alpha}{3} + 240^0$, are such that the circle of curvature at each passes through P; and verify that a circle can be described through A, B, C, and P, and that the bisectors of the sides of the triangle ABC pass through the centre of the ellipse.

19. Draw in a given ellipse a pair of conjugate diameters making a given angle with each other.

[On any diameter of the ellipse describe a segment of a circle containing the given angle (Prob. 30). If the points where the circle meets the ellipse be joined to the ends of the chosen diameters, the required conjugate diameters will be parallel to these chords. The least possible angle between conjugate diameters of a given ellipse is the angle between the diagonals of the rectangle formed by the axes.]

CHAPTER V.

THE HYPERBOLA.

As in the case of the ellipse, the definition of the curve given on page 56 does not immediately exhibit the property of the curve which furnishes the most convenient method of constructing it. It may also be defined as the locus of a point which moves in a plane, so that the difference of its distances from two fixed points in the plane is constant, and that the two definitions are really identical may be shewn thus:—

In fig. 87 let F be the focus and MX the directrix (Definitions, page 56).

Fig.87.

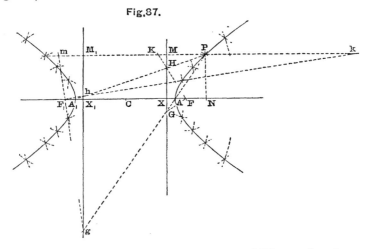

From F draw FXF_1 perpendicular to MX meeting it in X, and let A, A_1 be points on FX such that $\dfrac{FA}{AX} = \dfrac{FA_1}{A_1X} =$ the given

onstant ratio (greater than unity) for all points on the curve:
he points A and A_1 are called the vertices of the curve, and AA_1
he *transverse axis*, and if AA_1 be bisected in C, C is the *centre* of
he hyperbola.

To shew that the curve can be constructed from a second
ocus and directrix corresponding to the vertex A_1.

Let P be a point on the curve, i.e. let
$$FP : PM :: FA : AX,$$
where PM is the perpendicular from P on the directrix.

Draw AP, A_1P meeting the directrix in G and H, and let
FH meet PM in K.

Then
$$PK : FA_1 :: PH : A_1H$$
$$:: PM : A_1X,$$
or
$$PK : PM :: FA_1 : A_1X :: FA : AX;$$
$$\therefore PK = FP \text{ and the angle } PKF = \text{the angle } PFK$$
$$= \text{the angle } KFA_1.$$

Similarly FG bisects the angle between FA_1 and PF produced,
therefore the angle HFG is a right angle.

In AA_1 take a point X_1 such that $A_1X_1 = AX$, and through
X_1 draw a straight line perpendicular to AA_1, and in FA_1 produced take a point F_1 such that $A_1F_1 = AF$.

Let PA_1 and PA produced meet the perpendicular through
X_1 in h and g and join F_1g, F_1h,
then
$$gX_1 : GX :: AX_1 : AX$$
$$:: A_1X : A_1X_1$$
$$:: HX : hX_1,$$
$$\therefore gX_1 . hX_1 = GX . XH = FX^2 = F_1X_1^2;$$
$$\therefore gF_1h \text{ is a right angle.}$$

Let PK (parallel to axis) meet gX_1 in M_1, gF_1 in m, and F_1h
produced in k,
$$Pm : PM_1 :: F_1A : AX_1,$$
and
$$Pk : PM_1 :: F_1A_1 : A_1X_1,$$
$$\therefore Pm = Pk;$$

and mF_1k being a right angle,

$$F_1P = Pm = Pk,$$
$$\therefore F_1P : PM_1 :: F_1A_1 : A_1X_1,$$

and the curve can therefore be described by means of the focus F_1 and the directrix X_1M_1.

It follows that the curve is symmetrical with regard to the centre C, and that it lies wholly without the tangents at the vertices A and A_1, which are perpendicular to CA.

We have at any point P of the hyperbola,

$$FP : PM :: FA : AX,$$
$$F_1P : PM_1 :: F_1A_1 : A_1X_1$$
$$:: F_1A : AX_1;$$
$$\therefore F_1P - FP : PM_1 - PM :: F_1A - FA : AX_1 - AX;$$

but $\qquad PM_1 - PM = MM_1 = XX_1 = AX_1 - AX,$

$$\therefore F_1P - FP = F_1A - FA = AA_1,$$

i.e. the difference of the focal distances is constant and equal to the transverse axis.

PROBLEM 89. *To describe an hyperbola, the foci and a vertex, or the vertices and a focus, or the transverse and conjugate axes being given* (Fig. 88).

Bisect the distance between the given foci F, F_1 or the given vertices A, A_1 in C.

With centre F and any radius greater than FA describe arcs as at Q and q, and with centre F_1 and the same radius describe arcs as at Q_1 and q_1. On any convenient line on the paper mark off a length $aa_1 = AA_1$, and with centre a and radius FQ mark off a point on this line on the opposite side from a_1 as at Q'. Take off the distance $Q'a_1$ from this line with a pair of dividers or compasses, and with centres F_1 and F mark off points on the arcs already described about the opposite foci as centres. These points will of course be on the curve, since the difference of the focal distances of each is equal to AA_1, and the process may be repeated and as many points obtained as is necessary to define the curve and allow it to be sketched through the points with accuracy.

Though somewhat tedious, it is the only method for construct-ing the hyperbola which can be recommended.

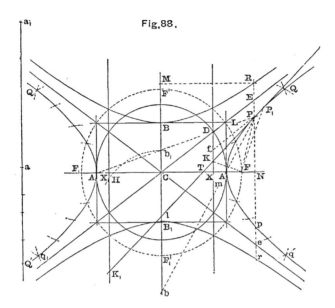

Fig.88.

Since the radii of the intersecting arcs may increase indefinitely, the curve evidently tends to infinity in both directions from C.

Through C draw BCB_1 perpendicular to AA_1, and let the circle described on FF_1 as diameter intersect the tangent at the vertex in L. Make $CB = CB_1 = AL$, then BB_1 is called the *con-jugate axis;* and if a second hyperbola be described with vertices at B and B_1 and with foci on BB_1 at F', F_1' the same distance from C as those of the original hyperbola, each curve is said to be conjugate to the other.

The eccentricity of the hyperbola (p. 57) is the numerical value of the ratio $\dfrac{FA}{AX}$. It is usually denoted by e, and its value in terms of the axes is $e = \dfrac{\sqrt{a^2 + b^2}}{a}$,

where $\qquad\qquad CA = a$ and $CB = b$.

For
$$\frac{FA}{AX} = \frac{FA_1}{A_1X} = \frac{CF}{CA} = \frac{CL}{CA} = \frac{\sqrt{a^2 + b^2}}{a}.$$

The diagonals of the rectangle formed by the tangents to the hyperbola and its conjugate at their vertices are called *asymptotes*. The axes therefore bisect the angles between the asymptotes.

In fig. 87 let PN drawn from any point P of the curve perpendicular to the transverse axis meet it in N, and, as before, let PA and PA_1 meet the directrix in G and H,

then
$$PN : AN :: GX : AX,$$

and
$$PN : A_1N :: HX : A_1X;$$

$$\therefore PN^2 : AN \cdot A_1N :: GX \cdot HX : AX \cdot A_1X$$
$$:: FX^2 : AX \cdot A_1X,$$

since GFH is a right angle,

i.e. $\dfrac{PN^2}{AN \cdot A_1N}$ is a constant ratio.

Since
$$FA : AX :: FA_1 : A_1X,$$

$$\therefore FA + FA_1 : FA :: AX + A_1X : AX,$$

or
$$CF : CA :: FA : AX \quad \dots\dots\dots\dots (1),$$

and
$$FA_1 - FA : FA :: A_1X - AX : AX,$$

or
$$CA : CX :: FA : AX \quad \dots\dots\dots\dots (2),$$

$$\therefore CF : CA :: CA : CX :: FA : AX \dots\dots\dots (3).$$

Also
$$CF : CX :: CF^2 : CF \cdot CX$$
$$:: CF^2 : CA^2 \quad \dots\dots\dots\dots\dots (4).$$

Let the directrix meet the asymptotes in D (fig. 88): then by the similar triangles CDX, CLA,

$$CL : CA :: CD : CX;$$

but $CL = CF$, therefore from (3) $CD = CA$, or the circle on AA_1 as diameter will cut the asymptote in a point on the directrix.

DEF. The circle on AA_1 as diameter is called the auxiliary circle.

Since $CD = CA$, $CF = CL$, and the angle DCF is common to the two triangles DCF and ACL,

$\therefore$ the angle $CDF =$ the angle $CAL =$ a right angle,

or the perpendicular from the focus on the asymptote is a tangent to the auxiliary circle at the point of intersection.

COROLLARY. $DX^2 = CX \cdot FX$.

Again, from (4),

$$CF^2 - CA^2 : CA^2 :: CF - CX : CX$$
$$:: FX^2 : CX(CF - CX);$$

but $CF \cdot CX = CA^2$ from (3), and $CA^2 - CX^2 = AX \cdot A_1X$.

Also $CF^2 - CA^2 = CB^2$,

$$\therefore CB^2 : CA^2 :: FX^2 : AX \cdot A_1X;$$

and comparing this with the constant ratio above given for

$\dfrac{PN^2}{AN \cdot NA_1}$, we have $PN^2 : AN \cdot NA_1 :: BC^2 : AC^2$, which may also be written

$$PN^2 : CN^2 - AC^2 :: BC^2 : AC^2 \ldots\ldots\ldots(5).$$

Let PN (fig. 88), where P is any point on the curve and PN the ordinate, meet the asymptotes in E, then

$$EN^2 : CN^2 :: BC^2 : AC^2, \text{ by similar triangles } \ldots\ldots(6),$$
$$\therefore EN^2 - PN^2 : AC^2 :: BC^2 : AC^2,$$

or $Ep \cdot EP = BC^2 = EP \cdot Pe,$

where p is the point in which PN meets the curve again, and e is the point in which it meets the other asymptote.

Let the ordinate through P meet the conjugate hyperbola in R (same fig.), and let RM be the ordinate of R perpendicular to BC, then of course

$$RM^2 : CM^2 - BC^2 :: AC^2 : BC^2,$$

or $CM^2 : BC^2 :: RM^2 + AC^2 : AC^2;$

but $CM = RN$ and $RM = CN$,

$$\therefore RN^2 : BC^2 :: CN^2 + AC^2 : AC^2 \ldots\ldots\ldots\ldots(7);$$

and combining (6) and (7), we get

$$RN^2 - EN^2 = BC^2 = RE \cdot Er = RE \cdot Re,$$

where r is the point on the other branch of the conjugate hyperbola corresponding to R, and e is the point in which Rr meets the other asymptote.

To draw a tangent and normal at any point of the curve (Fig. 88).

Let P_1 be a point on the curve adjacent to any point P, and let the chord PP_1 meet the directrices in K and K_1. Draw KF to the corresponding focus: then $FP : FP_1 :: PK : P_1K$, or PK bisects the exterior angle between PF and P_1F produced (Euc. VI. prop. A). Hence, exactly as in the case of the ellipse (p. 102), when P_1 moves up to and coincides with P, so that the chord PP_1 becomes the tangent at P, the line FK becomes perpendicular to the line FP drawn from the focus to the point of contact of the tangent. *The tangent at any point P of an hyperbola may therefore be drawn* by drawing a line from P to either focus, erecting a perpendicular to this line at the focus meeting the directrix, and drawing the tangent through this point and the proposed point of contact. It may also be drawn by making use of the known property that *it bisects the angle between the focal distances.* For in the two triangles PFK, PF_1K_1

$$FP : PK :: F_1P : PK_1,$$

and the angle $PFK =$ the angle PF_1K_1, each being a right angle,

$$\therefore \text{ the angle } FPK = F_1PK_1. \quad \text{(Euc. VI. 7.)}$$

Hence the normal bisects the exterior angle between the focal distances.

PROBLEM 90. *To describe an hyperbola, an asymptote CD, a focus F, and a point P being given* (Fig. 88).

From F draw FD perpendicular to CD, then D will be a point on the directrix as has been previously proved. Through P draw Pf parallel to CD and make $Pf = PF$, then f will be a second point in the directrix, which is therefore determined. Draw CF

perpendicular to Df meeting the given asymptote in C, which will evidently be the centre of the curve.   Make CA, CA_1 on CF each equal CD and AA_1 will be the transverse axis, and the curve is completely determined.

Since Pf can be measured on either side of P there are generally two solutions.

Proof. The only step in the construction which is not obvious is taking f as a point on the directrix.   It can easily be shewn to hold in the hyperbola, for draw Am parallel to the asymptote meeting the directrix in m, then in the hyperbola

$$FP \ : \ FA \ :: \ PM \ : \ AX$$
$$:: \ Pf \ : \ Am,$$

where PM is a perpendicular on the directrix.

But $$Am = DL = AF, \ \therefore \ FP = Pf;$$

and conversely, if Pf be made $= PF$, f will be a point on the directrix.

PROBLEM 91.   *To describe an hyperbola, an asymptote CT, a tangent Tt, and a focus F being given* (Fig. 89).

From F draw FD perpendicular to CT meeting it in D, and FY perpendicular to Tt meeting in Y.   Then D and Y are points on the auxiliary circle.   Bisect DY in K and draw KC perpendicular to DY meeting CD in C. C will be the centre of the curve, CF the direction of the transverse axis, and CD or CY its semi-length.

PROBLEM 92.   *To describe an hyperbola, an asymptote CD, a directrix DD_1 and a point P being given* (Fig. 89).

From D draw DF perpendicular to CD. DF will be a locus of the focus.   Through P draw Pf parallel to CD meeting DD_1 in f, and with centre P and radius Pf describe an arc cutting DF in F. F will be a focus, and FC drawn perpendicular to DD_1 will intersect CD in C, the centre of the curve; which is therefore completely determined.

[The problem is exactly the converse of Prob. 90.]

PROBLEM 93. *To describe an hyperbola, the asymptotes* CD, CD_1 *and a point P on the curve being given* (Fig. 89).

Bisect the angles between the asymptotes by the lines ACA_1, BCB_1; then ACA_1 in the angle in which P lies is the position of

Fig. 89.

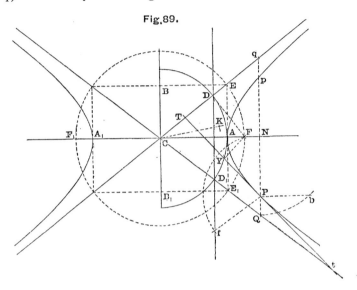

the transverse axis. Through P draw QPq perpendicular to AA_1 and meeting the asymptotes in Q and q. Take a mean proportional, as Pb, between PQ and Pq. Pb will be the length CB of the conjugate semi-axis.

Draw BE parallel to AA_1 meeting the asymptote in E; then BE is the length CA of the transverse semi-axis and $CE = CF$, the distance of either focus from C.

Proof. The only step in the construction requiring demonstration is that in the hyperbola $BC^2 = PQ \cdot Pq$.

Let N be the foot of the double ordinate Pp; by similar triangles CAE, CNQ.

$$QN^2 : AE^2 :: CN^2 : AC^2 \text{ and } AE = BC,$$
$$\therefore QN^2 - BC^2 : BC^2 :: CN^2 - AC^2 : AC^2;$$

but $CN^2 - AC^2 = AN.NA_1$ and (p. 156) $PN^2 : AN.NA_1 :: BC^2 : AC^2$,

$$\therefore QN^2 - BC^2 : BC^2 :: PN^2 : BC^2;$$

$$\therefore \ QN^2 - BC^2 = PN^2 \ \text{ or } \ QN^2 - PN^2 = BC^2,$$

i. e. $(QN + PN)(QN - PN) = BC^2 = PQ \cdot Pq,$

for by the symmetry of the curve $Nq = NQ$.

If qp be made equal to QP, p will evidently be a point on the curve.

PROBLEM 94.   *To describe an hyperbola, the asymptotes CT, Ct, and a tangent Tt to the curve being given* (Fig. 89).

Bisect Tt in P. P will be the point of contact of Tt, i. e. will be a point on the curve, and the problem therefore reduces to Problem 93.

The proof will be found on p. 163.

DEFINITION.   Any straight line drawn through the centre and terminated both ways either by the original curve or by the conjugate hyperbola is called *a diameter*, and by the symmetry of the curve every diameter is bisected by the centre.   A diameter CD parallel to the tangent at the extremity of a diameter CP is said to be *conjugate* to CP.

The following important properties of the hyperbola should be carefully noticed.

PROP. 1.   *If from any point Q in an asymptote $QPpq$ be drawn meeting the curve in P, p and the other asymptote in q, and if CD be the semi-diameter parallel to Qq,*

$$QP \cdot Pq = CD^2 \text{ and } QP = pq \ \text{(Fig. 90)}.$$

Through P and D draw RPr, DTt perpendicular to the transverse axis, and meeting the asymptotes in R, r and T, t; let Rr meet the axis in N.

Then $QP : RP :: CD : DT$ ⎫
and $Pq : Pr :: CD : Dt$ ⎬ by similar triangles,

$$\therefore \ QP \cdot Pq : RP \cdot Pr :: CD^2 : DT \cdot Dt.$$

But $RP \cdot Pr = BC^2 = DT \cdot Dt$ (p. 159),

$$\therefore \ QP \cdot Pq = CD^2.$$

Similarly $qp \cdot pQ = CD^2 = QP \cdot Pq$;

or, if V be the middle point of Qq,

$$QV^2 - PV^2 = QV^2 - pV^2.$$

Hence $PV = pV$, and therefore $PQ = pq$.

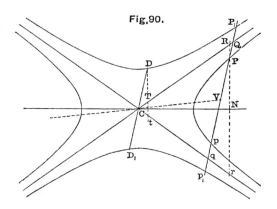

Fig.90.

COR. *If a straight line $PP_1 p_1 p$ meet the hyperbola in P, p, and the conjugate hyperbola in P_1, p_1, $PP_1 = pp_1$.*

For if the line meet the asymptote in Q, q,

$$QP_1 = p_1 q \text{ and } PQ = qp, \therefore PP_1 = pp_1.$$

PROP. 2. *A diameter bisects all chords parallel to the tangents at its extremities, i. e. all chords parallel to its conjugate.*

This can be proved exactly as in the analogous proposition for the ellipse.

Let QQ_1 (fig. 91) be any chord of an hyperbola meeting the directrix in R, and let O be the centre point of QQ_1 and F the focus.

Join FQ, FQ_1, and draw FY perpendicular to QQ_1.

Then
$$FQ^2 - FQ_1^2 = QY^2 - Q_1Y^2$$
$$= (QY + Q_1Y)(QY - Q_1Y)$$
$$= 2 \cdot QQ_1 \cdot OY \quad\ldots\ldots\ldots\ldots(1);$$

but since Q and Q_1 are on the hyperbola,

$$FQ : FQ_1 :: QR : Q_1R;$$

E.

11

therefore
$$\frac{FQ^2 - FQ_1^{\,2}}{FQ^2} = \frac{QR^2 - Q_1R^2}{QR^2} = \frac{2QQ_1 \cdot OR}{QR^2} \quad \ldots\ldots\ldots(2);$$

therefore, from (1) and (2),

$$\frac{OY}{OR} = \frac{FQ^2}{QR^2} = \frac{FA^2}{AW^2},$$

Fig. 91.

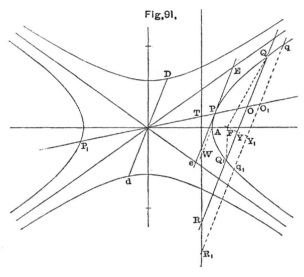

where AW is drawn through the vertex parallel to QR meeting the directrix in W.

I. e. $OY : OR$ in a constant ratio.

Take any second chord qq_1 parallel to QQ_1 meeting FY in Y_1 and the directrix in R_1. Let O_1 be its centre point; then, since $\dfrac{OY}{OR} = \dfrac{O_1Y_1}{O_1R_1}$, it follows that the line OO_1 must pass through the point T in which FY meets the directrix, and is therefore fixed for all chords parallel to QQ_1. This line will evidently pass through the centre (i.e. will be a diameter), for by the last proposition it bisects all chords of the conjugate hyperbola parallel to QQ_1, i.e. it bisects the diameter Dd, which is also bisected by C.

Let TO meet the hyperbola in P and suppose qq_1 to move parallel to itself till it approaches and ultimately coincides with P. Since $O_1q = O_1q_1$ throughout the motion, the points q, q_1 will evidently approach P simultaneously, and in the limiting position qq_1 will be the tangent at P. It follows that if P_1 be the other extremity of the diameter through P, the tangent at P_1 is parallel to QQ_1, and therefore to the tangent at P.

COROLLARY 1. The perpendicular on the tangent at any point from the focus meets the corresponding diameter in the directrix.

COR. 2. If the tangent at P meet the asymptotes in E and e, $PE = Pe$, for by the last proposition the intercept between q and one asymptote is always equal to the intercept between q_1 and the other asymptote, and when q and q_1 ultimately coincide with P these intercepts become PE and Pe respectively, i.e. the portion of any tangent between the asymptotes is bisected at the point of contact.

COR. 3. If PE be the tangent at P meeting the asymptote in E, $PE^2 = CD^2$, where CD is the semi-diameter conjugate to CP. For taking a parallel chord very near the tangent meeting the curve in p, p_1 and the asymptote in e, we have, by Prop. 1,

$$ep \cdot ep_1 = CD^2,$$

and therefore when p and p_1 coincide in P,

$$EP^2 = CD^2.$$

COR. 4. The asymptotes are the diagonals of the parallelogram formed by the tangents at the extremities of a pair of conjugate diameters. For E and e, which are on the asymptotes, are also angular points of such a parallelogram.

PROP. 3. *Tangents drawn at the extremities of any chord subtend equal angles at the focus.*

Let PQ (fig. 92) be any chord of an hyperbola and let the tangents at P and Q meet in R. Let F be the focus, and from R draw RN, RM perpendicular respectively to FP, FQ; draw RW perpendicular to the directrix and let the tangent at P meet the directrix in E.

Then EF is perpendicular to FP (p. 157), and therefore parallel to RN.

Therefore $FN : FP :: ER : EP$

$:: RW : PK,$

where PK is the perpendicular from P on the directrix.

Fig.92.

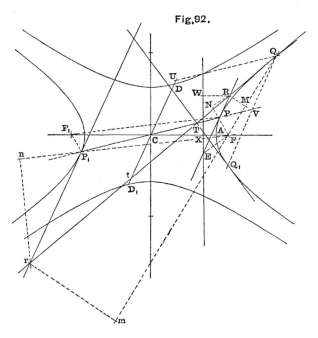

Therefore $FN : RW :: FP : PK$

$:: FA : AX.$

Similarly $FM : RW :: FA : AX;$

therefore $FN = FM.$

Hence in the right-angled triangles RFN, RFM, $FN = FM$, and FR is common.

Therefore the two triangles are equal in all respects, i.e. the angle RFP = the angle RFQ, and $RN = RM$.

PROP. 4.   *If PCP_1 be a diameter and QVQ_1 a chord parallel to the tangent at P and meeting PP_1 produced in V, and if the tangent at Q meet PP_1 in T, then $CV.CT = CP^2$ (Fig. 92).*

Let TQ meet the tangents at P and P_1 in R and r, and F being a focus draw RN perpendicular to the focal distance FP meeting it in N, rn perpendicular to FP_1 meeting it in n, and RM, rm perpendicular to the focal distance FQ. Let F_1 be the other focus, and join F_1P, F_1P_1.

Since $CF = CF_1$, $CP = CP_1$, and the angle $FCP =$ the angle F_1CP_1, therefore the triangles FCP, F_1CP_1 are equal in all respects; and therefore the angle $CPF =$ the angle CP_1F_1.

Similarly the angle $CPF_1 =$ the angle CP_1F.

Therefore the whole angle $FPF_1 =$ the whole angle F_1P_1F; but the tangents bisect the angles between the focal distances, therefore the angle $FPR =$ the angle FP_1r; i.e. the right-angled triangles RPN, rP_1n are similar, and therefore

$$RP : rP_1 :: RN : rn;$$

but $RN = RM$ and $rn = rm$ (Prop. 3), therefore

$$RP : rP_1 :: RM : rm$$
$$:: RQ : rQ.$$

But $\qquad TR : Tr :: RP : rP_1$
$$:: RQ : rQ;$$

therefore $\qquad TP : TP_1 :: PV : P_1V$

by similar triangles,

or $\qquad CP - CT : CT + CP :: CV - CP : CV + CP,$

i.e. $\qquad CT : CP :: CP : CV;$

therefore $\qquad CT . CV = CP^2.$

Cor. 1. Since CV and CP are the same for the point Q_1, the tangent at Q_1 passes through T, or the tangents at the extremities of any chord intersect on the diameter which bisects that chord.

Prop. 5. *If PCP_1, DCD_1 be conjugate diameters, and QV be drawn parallel to CD meeting the hyperbola in Q and CP in V, then*

$$QV^2 : PV . P_1V :: CD^2 : CP^2.$$

Let the tangent at Q (fig. 92) meet CP and CD in T and t respectively, and draw QU parallel to CP meeting CD in U.

Then $\quad CV . CT = CP^2$ and $CU . Ct = CD^2$ (Prop. 4);

but $\qquad CU = QV,$

therefore $\qquad CD^2 : CP^2 :: QV . Ct : CV . CT;$

but $\qquad Ct : QV :: CT : VT,$

$\therefore \quad CD^2 : CP^2 :: QV^2 : CV . VT,$

and $\quad CV \cdot VT = CV(CV - CT) = CV^2 - CP^2 = PV \cdot P_1V;$

therefore $\quad\quad QV^2 : PV \cdot P_1V :: CD^2 : CP^2.$

PROBLEM 95. *To describe an hyperbola, the transverse axis AA_1 and a point P on the curve being given* (Fig. 88).

Bisect AA_1 in C, which will of course be the centre of the curve. Draw the conjugate axis BCB_1. Let PA_1, PA cut BB_1 in b_1 and b respectively. Take a mean proportional CH between Cb and Cb_1, which will be the length (CB or CB_1) of the semi-conjugate axis. The foci can then be determined, since $CF = AB$.

Proof. Let PN be the ordinate at P.

Then $\quad\quad\quad PN : b_1C :: NA_1 : CA_1,$

and $\quad\quad\quad\; PN : bC :: NA\; : CA,$

or $\quad\quad\quad PN^2 : NA \cdot NA_1 :: bC \cdot b_1C : CA^2;$

therefore $\quad\quad bC \cdot b_1C = BC^2$ (p. 156).

PROBLEM 96. *To describe an hyperbola, the transverse axis ATA_1 and a tangent PT being given* (Fig. 88).

Bisect AA_1 in C, the centre of the curve. On CA towards CT take CN a third proportional to CT and CA. N will be the foot of the ordinate of the point of contact of the given tangent; i.e. if NP be drawn perpendicular to AA_1 meeting TP in P, P will be a point on the curve, and the problem therefore reduces to the preceding.

It may also be completed by Prob. 19, p. 23, determining two lines PF, PF_1 making equal angles with PT and meeting AA_1 in points equidistant from C; since it has been already shewn (p. 157) that the tangent bisects the angle between the focal distances.

The proof follows from Prop. 4, p. 164, which of course applies to the principal axes.

PROBLEM 97. *To describe an hyperbola, a pair of conjugate diameters being given* (Fig. 93).

PCP_1, DCD_1 are the given conjugate diameters.

First Method. Complete the parallelogram $QtqT$ formed by the tangents at their extremities; then the diagonals of this parallelo-

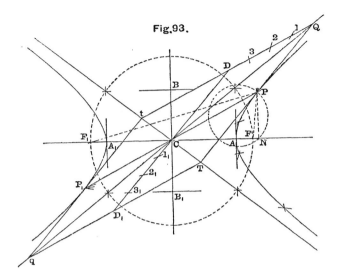

Fig. 93.

gram are the asymptotes (p. 163), and the axes therefore bisect the angles between them. Thus CA and CB are determined in direction.

From P draw two lines PF, PF_1 making equal angles with PT, the tangent at P, and meeting AA_1 in points F and F_1 equidistant from C (Prob. 19, p. 23). Then F and F_1 are the foci, and the vertices can be determined by dropping perpendiculars on AA_1 from the points in which the circle on FF_1 as diameter intersects the asymptotes.

The curve can therefore be drawn by the general method.

Second Method. Points on the curve can also be determined without finding the foci thus:

Complete the parallelogram $QtqT$ as before.

Divide QD into any number of equal parts as at 1, 2, 3. Divide CD_1 into the same number of equal parts as at 1_1, 2_1, 3_1; then $P1$ and $P_1 1_1$ will, when produced, intersect in a point on the curve, and similarly with the other corresponding points.

This method can also of course be applied to the principal axes; it cannot however be recommended, because a slight inaccuracy in the position of either line makes a considerable alteration in the position of the point on the curve, since in producing the lines the error is magnified, and the lines must often be produced to a considerable distance.

PROBLEM 98.   *To describe an hyperbola, the centre C, the directions of a pair of conjugate diameters CA, CB, and two points on the curve P and Q being given* (Fig. 94).

Draw PN, Qn parallel to CB meeting CA in N and n.   (Let PN be less than Qn; then CN must be less than Cn.)   Produce

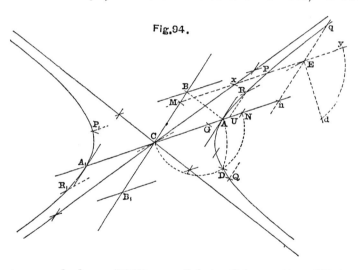

Fig. 94.

Qn to q and draw PMP_1 parallel to CA, meeting CB in M. Make $MP_1 = MP$ and $nq = nQ$.   Then P_1 and q are points on the curve.   Let PP_1 meet Qq in E.   Through n draw nx parallel to QP_1 meeting PP_1 in x,· and through n draw ny parallel to Pq meeting PP_1 in y.   Take Ed a mean proportional between Ex and Ey.   On CN describe a semi-circle CDN and make $ND = Ed$. CD will be the length CA of the diameter parallel to PP_1.   On CA make $CG = Ed$, and through A draw BA parallel to MG. CB will be the diameter conjugate to CA, and the problem reduces to the preceding.

Proof. The construction, as in the similar problem for the ellipse, depends on the property of the curve, that "the rectangles contained by the segments of any two chords which intersect each other are in the ratio of the squares on the parallel diameters,"

i.e. $EP \cdot EP_1 : EQ \cdot Eq :: CA^2 : CB^2$,

which may be thus proved :

Through E draw the diameter ERR_1, and draw the ordinate RU parallel to Qq or to CB; then, by Prop. 5, p. 165,

$$RU^2 : CU^2 - CA^2 :: CB^2 : CA^2,$$

$$\therefore CB^2 + RU^2 : CB^2 :: CU^2 : CA^2,$$

and

$$qn^2 : Cn^2 - CA^2 :: CB^2 : CA^2;$$

$$\therefore CB^2 + qn^2 : CB^2 :: Cn^2 : CA^2,$$

so that

$$CB^2 + RU^2 : CU^2 :: CB^2 + qn^2 : Cn^2.$$

But

$$RU^2 : CU^2 :: En^2 : Cn^2,$$

$$\therefore CB^2 : CU^2 :: CB^2 + qn^2 - En^2 : Cn^2,$$

or

$$CB^2 : CB^2 + qn^2 - En^2 :: CU^2 : Cn^2$$
$$:: CR^2 : CE^2;$$

$$\therefore CB^2 : qn^2 - En^2 :: CR^2 : CE^2 - CR^2,$$

or

$$CB^2 : EQ \cdot Eq :: CR^2 : ER \cdot ER_1.$$

Similarly

$$CA^2 : EP \cdot EP_1 :: CR^2 : ER \cdot ER_1,$$

$$\therefore EP \cdot EP_1 : EQ \cdot Eq :: CA^2 : CB^2.$$

But by construction $EQ : EP_1 :: En : Ex$,

and

$$Eq : EP :: En : Ey,$$

$$EQ \cdot Eq : EP \cdot EP_1 :: En^2 : Ex \cdot Ey;$$

but

$$Ex \cdot Ey = Ed^2 = ND^2 = CN^2 - CA^2 = AN \cdot NA_1,$$

$$\therefore En^2 \text{ or } PN^2 : AN \cdot NA_1 :: EQ \cdot Eq : EP \cdot EP_1,$$

which proves that AA_1 is the diameter conjugate to PN.

Also by construction

$$CB : CA :: CM : CG :: PN : ND,$$

$$\therefore CB^2 : CA^2 :: PN^2 : AN \cdot NA_1,$$

or CB is the semi-diameter conjugate to CA.

PROBLEM 99. *To describe an hyperbola, the centre C, the directions of a pair of conjugate diameters CT, Ct, a tangent Tt, and a point P on the curve being given* (Fig. 95).

[If a line be drawn parallel to Tt and at an equal distance from C, it will of course be a second tangent, and P must not

Fig. 95.

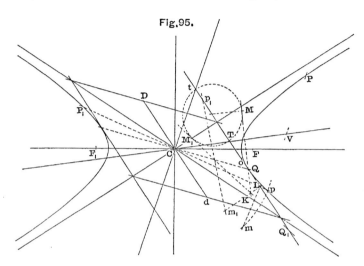

lie between these lines.] Draw PVp parallel to Ct cutting CT in V, and make $Vp = VP$. p will be a point of the curve. One of the two diameters CP or Cp (in the figure Cp) will always intersect Tt in a point (L) outside Tt; draw such diameter and on it make $CP_1 = Cp$. P_1 will be a point on the curve.

Take Lm a mean proportional between Lp and LP_1. On Tt as diameter describe a circle; through L draw LK perpendicular to Lt and on it take a point K such that $Cp : Lm :: \frac{1}{2}Tt : LK$, i.e. on LK make $Lm_1 = Lm$, and on Lt make $Lo = \frac{1}{2}Tt$ and $Lp_1 = Cp$. Through o draw oK parallel to m_1p_1, K will be the point required ; then tangents KQM, Q_1KM_1 from K to the circle on Tt will intersect Tt in points $(Q,$ and $Q_1)$ either of which may be taken for its point of contact with the curve. There are therefore two solutions.

Through C draw DCd parallel to Tt, make $CD = Cd = QM$, the tangent from Q to the circle. CQ and CD will be conjugate semi-diameters, and the problem reduces to Problem 97.

PROBLEM 100. *To describe an hyperbola, the centre C, two tangents PT, QT' and a point on the curve (R) being given* (Fig. 96).

Through C draw TCT_1 and make $CT_1 = CT$. Draw T_1t parallel to PT meeting QT in t, and draw T_1t_1 parallel to QT' meeting PT

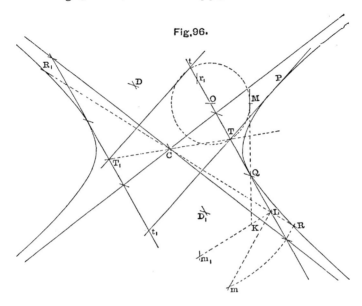

Fig.96.

in t_1. tT_1 and t_1T_1 will be tangents to the curve and TCT_1, tCt_1 will be the directions of a pair of conjugate diameters; and the problem therefore reduces to the preceding.

[The point R must lie outside the parallelogram TtT_1t_1 and within one of the exterior angles, such as PTQ.]

In the figure $RC = CR_1$ and RC meets Tt in L; Lm is a mean proportional between LR and LR_1; and $LK : Lm :: OT : CR$, where $OT = \frac{1}{2}Tt$, and LK is perpendicular to Tt. Then a tangent KM from K to the circle on Tt as diameter cuts Tt in its point of contact (Q) with the curve, and CD drawn through C parallel to QT' and equal to QM will be the semi-diameter conjugate to CQ.

There are two solutions, as two tangents can be drawn from K to the circle on Tt.

PROBLEM 101. *To describe an hyperbola, the centre C, two points (A and B) of the curve and a tangent Tt being given* (Fig. 97).

[A second tangent can at once be drawn parallel to Tt on the other side of C and at the same distance from it; the points A and B must not lie between these lines.] If the given points lie on opposite branches of the curve, as e.g. A and B_1, i.e. if they are on opposite sides of Tt, draw $B_1 C B$ and make $CB = CB_1$, then B will be on the same branch as A.

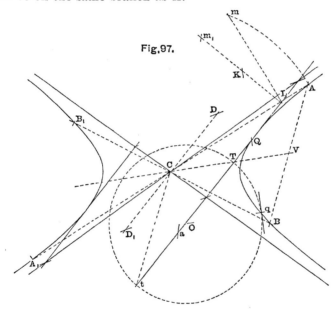

Fig. 97.

Draw AB and bisect it in V. Draw CV meeting the given tangent in T, and Ct parallel to AB meeting it in t. Then CT, Ct are the directions of a pair of conjugate diameters, and the problem reduces to Prob. 99.

In the figure $CA_1 = CA$ and ACA_1 meets Tt in L; Lm is a mean proportional between LA and LA_1; $LK : Lm :: OT : CA$, where LK is perpendicular to Tt and $OT = \frac{1}{2} Tt$.

Then a tangent (Kq) from K to the circle on Tt as diameter cuts Tt in Q, its point of contact with the curve. CD parallel to Tt and equal to Qq is the semi-diameter conjugate to CQ.

PROBLEM 102. *To describe an hyperbola, the centre C, and three tangents (SV, VW, WS) being given* (Fig. 98).

Through C draw TCT_1 meeting SV in T and SW in T_1, so that $TC = CT_1$ (Prob. 14, p. 19). *CT* will be conjugate to CS. Draw

Fig. 98.

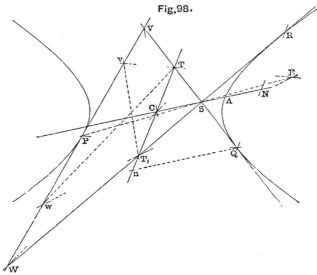

T_1v parallel to CV meeting VW in v, Tw parallel to CW meeting VW in w, and draw vT, wT_1 meeting in E. Then ES will cut VW in P, its point of contact with the curve. Also PQ parallel to vT will cut VS in Q, its point of contact, and QR parallel to CT or PR parallel to T_1w will cut WS in R, its point of contact. The problem can be completed by several of those previously given or thus;

Draw QN parallel to CT meeting CS in N. QN is an ordinate of the diameter CS, and therefore CA, the length of the semi-diameter, is a mean proportional between CS and CN (Prop. 4, p. 164). Similarly, if Qn be drawn parallel to CS meeting CT in n, CB must be taken as a mean proportional between Cn and CT.

PROBLEM 103. *To describe an hyperbola, the centre C and three points P, Q, R being given* (Fig. 99).

[Each of the points must lie either *between* both pairs of lines furnished by the remaining points and their corresponding points, or *outside* both these pairs of lines.]

Bisect PQ in p, QR in q, and RP in r, and draw Cp, Cq and Cr, producing each indefinitely. PQ is a double ordinate of the

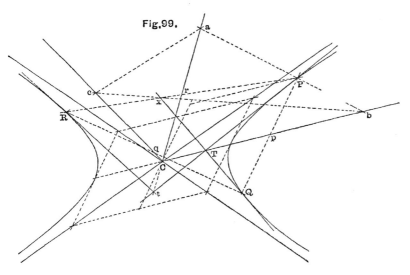

Fig.99.

diameter Cp, and therefore the tangents at P and Q will intersect on Cp; similarly the tangents at Q and R will intersect on Cq, and at R and P on Cr.   If therefore a triangle be drawn (Prob. 15, p. 20), the sides of which pass through P, Q and R, and the vertices of which lie on Cp, Cq and Cr respectively, the sides of this triangle will be the tangents at P, Q and R.   Take *any* point a on Cr; draw Pa, Ra cutting Cp, Cq in b and c respectively; join bc cutting PR in x, and draw xQ cutting Cb in T. QT, PT will be the tangents at Q and P respectively; and if PT meet Cr in t, Rt will be the tangent at R.   The problem may be completed by preceding problems.

PROBLEM 104.   *To describe an hyperbola, the foci F, F_1 and a point P on the curve being given* (Fig. 100).

It has been shewn already that the difference between the focal distances of any point on the curve is equal to the transverse axis (p. 153).

Let F_1P be greater than FP.   On PF_1 make $Pf = PF$.   Draw FF_1, bisect it in C and make $CA = CA_1 = \frac{1}{2}F_1f$. AA_1 will therefore be the vertices of the curve, and the problem reduces to Prob. 89.

Fig. 100.

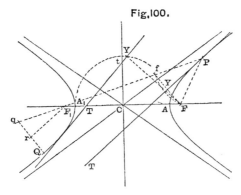

PROBLEM 105.   *To describe an hyperbola, the foci F, F₁ and a tangent Tt being given* (Fig. 100).

[The tangent must lie between F and F_1.]

Bisect FF_1 in C, the centre of the curve.   From F or F_1 drop a perpendicular (as FY) on the tangent.   On CF, CF_1 make $CA = CA_1 = CY$. A and A_1 will be the vertices of the curve, and the problem reduces to Prob. 89.

PROBLEM 106.   *To describe an hyperbola, a focus F, a tangent PT with its point of contact P, and a second point Q on the curve, being given* (Fig. 100).

If F and Q are on the same side of PT, the solution has already been given in the corresponding problem for the ellipse (Prob. 76). Hence the case of F and Q lying on opposite sides of PT need alone be considered here.

From F draw FY perpendicular to PT meeting it in Y, on FY produced make $Yf = YF$; then Pf will be a locus of the second focus.   From f on fP, on either side of f, make $fq = FQ$. Bisect Qq in r, and draw rF_1 perpendicular to Qq meeting Pf in F_1, which will be the second focus.   Hence, both foci being known, the problem may be completed by Probs. 104 or 105.

Since q may be taken on either side of f, there are in general two solutions.

Proof. That fP is a locus of the second focus has been shewn in p. 157 ; that the second focus is at the intersection of fP and rF_1 is evident thus :—it must be so situated that

$$F_1P \sim FP = FQ \sim F_1Q;$$

but $\qquad fQ = FQ$ and $F_1q = F_1Q,$

$$\therefore FQ \sim F_1Q = fq \sim F_1q = fF_1,$$

and $\qquad FP = fP, \therefore F_1P \sim FP = F_1P \sim fP = fF_1,$

i.e. F_1 is the second focus.

If F and Q are on opposite sides of PT, two hyperbolas can in general be drawn.

If F and Q are on the same side of PT, and the distance of Q from F is greater than its distance from the line drawn through f perpendicular to Pf, two hyperbolas can in general be drawn.

If F and Q are on the same side of PT, but the distance of Q from F is less than its distance from the above perpendicular, one hyperbola only can in general be drawn, but an ellipse can also be drawn.

If F and Q are on the same side of PT, and the distance of Q from F is equal to its distance from the above perpendicular, a parabola can be drawn fulfilling the required conditions, but no hyperbola or ellipse, since the second focus removes to an infinite distance.

PROBLEM 107.   *To describe an hyperbola, a focus F, a tangent RT and two points P and Q of the curve being given* (Fig. 101).

If F, P and Q are all on the same side of RT, the solution has already been given in Prob. 77, the corresponding problem for the ellipse.   Hence the cases of one or both of the points P, Q lying on the opposite side of RT to F need be considered.

Case 1.   Let F and P be on the same side of RT, and Q on the opposite side.   Produce PF to q, make $Fq = FQ$, and with centre P and radius Pq describe a circle qG.   From F draw FY perpendicular to RT, produce it to f, and make $Yf = YF$.   With centre f and radius FQ describe a circle GH, and find the centre (F_1) of a circle touching the circles qG and GH internally and passing through Q (Prob. 32). F_1 will be the second focus. The problem is always possible, since the circles must necessarily cut each other and the point Q be inside both.

Fig. 101.

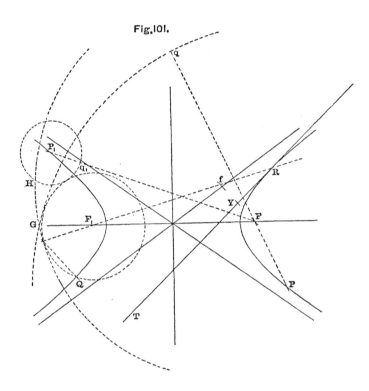

Proof. The second focus F_1 must be equidistant from Q and from the circle qG, since $F_1P - FP$ must be equal to $FQ - F_1Q$. But F_1P by construction $= Pq - F_1Q$ and $Pq = FP + Fq = FP + FQ$.

Also fF_1 must be equal to the transverse axis, p. 153, i.e. to $FQ - F_1Q$ or to $fG - F_1Q$, i.e. the second focus must be equidistant from the point Q and from the circle GH.

Case 2. Let P and Q be on the opposite side of RT to F, as P_1 and Q. Let FP_1 be greater than FQ. On FP_1 make $Fq_1 = FQ$, and with centre P_1 and radius P_1q_1 describe the circle q_1H. Determine the point f as in Case 1, and with centre f and radius FQ

E.   12

draw the circle GH. Determine F_1, the centre of a circle touching q_1H externally and GH internally. F_1 will be the second focus.

Proof. $FP_1 - F_1P_1 = Fq_1 + q_1P_1 - F_1P_1 = Fq_1 - (F_1P_1 - q_1P_1)$
$$= FQ - F_1Q$$
$$= fF_1, \text{ as in Case 1.}$$

PROBLEM 108.   *To describe an hyperbola, a focus F, a point P on the curve, and two tangents TQ, TR being given* (Fig. 102).

Fig.102.

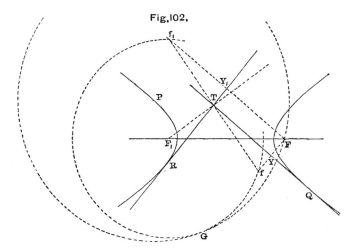

[F and P must be either both on the same side or both on opposite sides of each tangent.]

If F and P are on the same side of each tangent, the necessary condition for a possible solution has been explained in the corresponding problem for the ellipse, Prob. 78, p. 127, and the solution given. If they are on opposite sides, as in fig., draw FYf perpendicular to QT meeting it in Y, and FY_1f_1 perpendicular to RT meeting it in Y_1, and make $Yf = YF$ and $Y_1f_1 = Y_1F$.

With centre P and radius PF describe a circle FG, and find F_1 the centre of a circle to touch FG and to pass through f and f_1. Prob. 27. Since f and f_1 will necessarily lie within the circle FG, two solutions can generally be obtained.

Proof. If F_1 is the second focus, $fF_1 = f_1F_1$ the transverse axis $= FP - F_1P$, which by construction it does.

PROBLEM 109. *To describe an hyperbola, a focus F and three tangents PT, QT and RS being given* (Fig. 103).

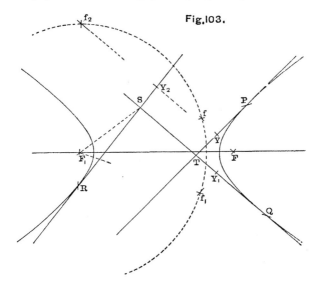

Fig.103.

[*F* must not lie within the triangle formed by the tangents.]

From F drop perpendiculars FYf, FY_1f_1, FY_2f_2 on the given tangents, meeting them respectively in Y, Y_1 and Y_2, and make $Yf = YF$, $Y_1f_1 = Y_1F$, and $Y_2f_2 = Y_2F$; then, as f, f_1 and f_2 must all be equidistant from the second focus (p. 153), and the problem therefore reduces to finding the centre (F_1) of a circle passing through three given points (Prob. 20), F_1 will be the second focus, and the transverse axis is of course known, since it is equal to $F_1'f$.

PROBLEM 110. *To describe an hyperbola, a focus F and three points P, Q, R on the curve being given* (Fig. 104).

[With two of the points as centres describe circles passing through F. The three given points cannot lie on the same branch of an hyperbola, unless

(1) F lies in one of the three angles PQR, QRP, and RPQ; and (2) the third point is more distant from F than it is from the common tangent to the above circles remote from F.

Whatever the relative position of the points and focus three hyperbolas can always be drawn.]

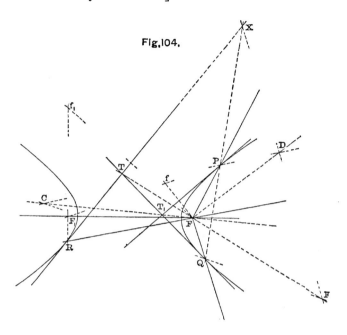

Fig.104.

The points being as in the figure, the above conditions for the points lying on the same branch are not complied with; an ellipse and three hyperbolas can be drawn by the first solution of the corresponding problem in the preceding Chapter, Problem 80.

The second solution there given can be adapted to the present case thus: Let P and Q lie on one branch of the required hyperbola and R on the other.

Bisect the angle PFQ by the line FC, bisect the angle between PF and RF *produced* by FD, and the angle between QF and RF *produced* by FE.

Determine the triangle whose sides pass through P terminating on FC and FD, through Q terminating on FE, FC, and through R terminating on FD and FE (Problem 15). The sides of this triangle will be tangents to the required curve at P, Q and R respectively.

To determine the triangle. Take any point C on FC, draw CP, CQ cutting CD, CE in D and E, and draw ED, QP intersecting in X. RX will be the tangent at R, and if it meets FE in T, QT will be the tangent at Q; similarly, if QT meets FC in T_1, PT_1 will be the tangent at P, passing also through the intersection of RT' and DF.

The construction depends on the well-known property of the hyperbola, that the angles subtended at the focus by a pair of tangents are equal or supplementary according as the tangents touch the same or opposite branches of the curve.

PROBLEM 111. *To describe an hyperbola, two tangents TQ, TR, with their points of contact Q and R, and a point P on the curve being given* (Fig. 105).

[The point P must lie outside the parabola which can be described touching TQ, TR at Q and R.]

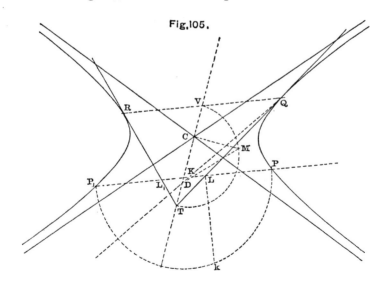

Fig.105.

The construction is exactly similar to the corresponding problem for the ellipse. Prob. 81.

Bisect QR in V and through T draw TDV. Through P draw PLL_1 parallel to QR meeting QT in L and RT in L_1.

Find a mean proportional (Lk) between PL and PL_1. (If P_1L_1 be made equal to PL, P_1 will be a point on the curve.) On PP_1 make $PK = Lk$, then QK will intersect TV in D, the extremity of the diameter TV.

On TV take a point C such that $TC : CD :: CD : CV$; and if, as in the figure, Q and R are on opposite branches of the hyperbola, C must be taken between T and V; i.e. on TV as diameter describe a semi-circle; draw DM making an angle of $45°$ with DV and meeting the semi-circle in M, and from M draw MC perpendicular to TV. Evidently MC is a mean proportional between CT and CV, and is equal to CD. C will be the centre of the hyperbola, and the asymptotes can easily be determined and the curve completed by preceding problems.

The proof is identical with that for the ellipse.

PROBLEM 112. *To describe an hyperbola, two points A and B on the curve and three tangents PQ, QR, RP being given* (Fig. 106).

[Either no one of the three tangents must pass between the

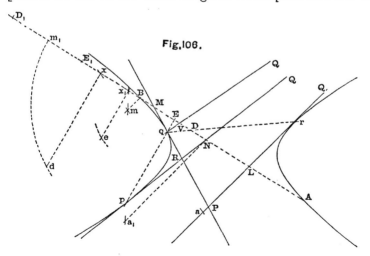

Fig.106.

points or all three must do so, and the points must not lie within the triangle formed by the tangents.]

Draw a line through AB cutting the tangents through P in L and M and the remaining tangent in N.

Find X the centre and D, D_1 the foci of the involution A, B and L, M (Prob. 13). D or D_1 will be a point on the chord of contact of the tangents PL, PM.

[In the figure La on $PQ = LA$, and Bm on a parallel to $PQ = BM$; am cuts AB in X, the required centre, and $XD = XD_1 = $ a mean proportional between XM and XL.]

Similarly, find X_1 the centre and E, E_1 the foci of the involution A, B and M, N (Prob. 13), and E or E_1 will be a point on the chord of contact of the tangents RM and RN.

Find MV the harmonic mean between ME and MD, M being the point of intersection of AB with the given tangents which has appeared in each of the above involutions, then QV (Q being the intersection of tangents through N and L) will meet the tangent through M in its point of contact (q) with the curve.

Therefore qDr will be the chord of contact of the tangents PQ, PR, and Eqp the chord of contact of the tangents RP, RQ.

The proof is identical with that for the ellipse, p. 135.

PROBLEM 113. *To describe an hyperbola, two tangents TP, TQ and three points A, B, C on the curve being given* (Fig. 107).

[The points A, B, C being taken together in pairs, each pair

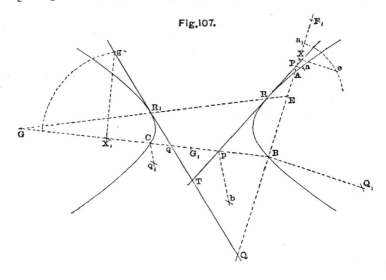

Fig.107.

of points must be either both on the same side or both on opposite sides of both tangents. In the figure A and B are both on the same side, and B and C on opposite sides of both TP and TQ, as also C and A.]

Draw the line AB cutting the given tangents in P and Q. Find X the centre and E, E_1 the foci of the involution A, B and P, Q (Problem 13).

[In the figure $Pa = PA$ and BQ_1 parallel to $Pa = BQ$. $Q_1 a$ cuts AB in X, the required centre. $XE = XE_1 =$ a mean proportional between XA and XB.]

E or E_1 will be a point on the chord of contact of the given tangents.

Again, draw BC cutting the given tangents in p and q, and find X_1 the centre and G, G_1 the foci of the involution B, C and p, q. G or G_1 will be a second point on the chord of contact of the given tangents, the points of contact of which R, R_1 are therefore determined, and the problem reduces to several preceding.

Since E and E_1 can be joined to either G or G_1 four chords of contact can in general be drawn, so that there are four solutions.

The construction depends on Prop. 7, p. 143.

PROBLEM 114. *To describe an hyperbola, five tangents AB, BC, CD, DE, EA being given* (Fig. 108).

[The pentagon formed by the given tangents must contain a re-entering angle.]

Draw AC, BD intersecting in F; and through the remaining angular point E of the pentagon draw EF meeting BC in P. P will be the point of contact of the given tangent BC. Similarly, if BD and CE intersect in G, AG will intersect DC in Q, the point of contact of the given tangent CD; and if CE and DA intersect in H, BH will intersect ED in R, its point of contact.

The problem therefore reduces to Problem 111, or the points of contact S and T of the remaining tangents can easily be determined.

The construction depends (as in the corresponding problem for the ellipse, p. 136) on Brianchon's theorem.

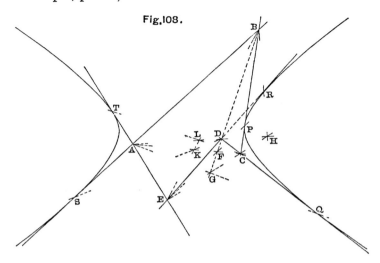

Fig. 108.

PROBLEM 115. *To describe an hyperbola, five points ABCDE being given* (Fig. 109).

Draw *AB*, *DE* intersecting in *F*, and *BC*, *EA* intersecting in *G*; then, if *FG* meet *CD* in *H*, *H* will be a point on the tangent at *A*, which can therefore be drawn.

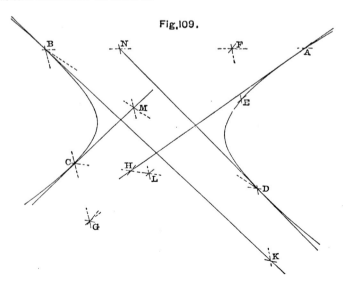

Fig. 109.

If a line be drawn through G and the intersection of AB and DC, meeting ED in K, K will be a point on the tangent at B. Hence two tangents with their points of contact being known and also (at least) one other point on the curve, the problem may be completed by Prob. 111, or the tangents at C, D and E may also be found by a similar construction to the above.

[If CD and EA intersect in L, and through L a line LM be drawn passing also through the intersection of BC and DE and meeting BD in M, M will be a point on the tangent at C; and if LM meet AB in N, N will be a point on the tangent at D.]

The construction of the tangent at E is left as an exercise for the student.

The construction (as in the corresponding problem for the ellipse, p. 138) is an adaptation of Pascal's theorem.

PROBLEM 116. *To describe an hyperbola, four tangents AB, BC, CD, DA and a point E on the curve being given* (Fig. 110).

Join EC and ED, cutting AB in c and D_1 respectively. Find X the centre and F and F_1 the foci of the involution A, c and B, D_1

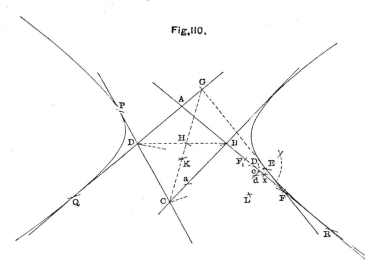

Fig. 110.

(Prob. 13); F or F_1 will be a point on the tangent at E, which can therefore be drawn and the problem completed by Prob. 114.

[In the figure Ba on $BC = BA$, and cd on a parallel to BC $= cD_1$; then ad meets AB in X, the required centre of the involution, and $XF = XF_1 = $ a mean proportional between XD_1 and XB.

If FE meets DA in G, the points of contact of the given tangents may be determined by drawing GC, DB intersecting in H, when FH will meet CD in P, the point of contact of CD; GC, DF intersecting in K, when BK will meet GD in Q, its point of contact; CF and GB intersecting in L, when DL will meet AB in R, its point of contact; the determination of the point of contact of CB is left as an exercise for the student.]

PROBLEM 117. *To describe an hyperbola, four points A, B, C, D of the curve and a tangent ad being given* (Fig. 111).

Let AB meet the given tangent in a, and BC, CD, DA meet it in b, c, and d respectively. Find X the centre and P, P_1 the

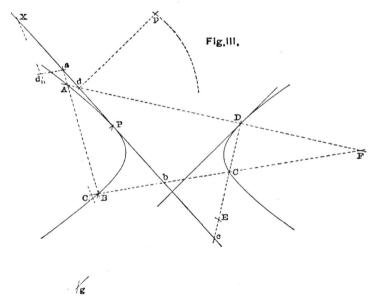

Fig. III.

foci of the involution a, c and b, d; P or P_1 will be the point of contact of the given tangent, so that five points being known the problem reduces to Prob. 115.

[In the figure bc_1 on $bB = bc$, and ad_1 on a parallel to $bB = ad$; then $c_1 d_1$ meets ad in X, the centre of the required involution, and XP is a mean proportional between Xd and Xb; P_1, the other focus, of course lies outside the limits of the figure.

If AP and DC meet in E, and AD, CB in F, EF will meet PB in g, a point on the tangent at D.]

PROBLEM 118.   *To find the centre and radius of curvature at any point P of a given hyperbola* (Fig. 112).

The construction is identical with that for the ellipse (Prob. 88).

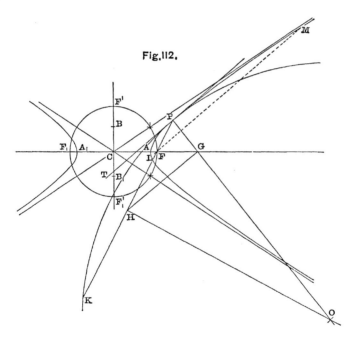

Fig. 112.

Draw PG the normal meeting the axis in G, GH perpendicular to PG meeting the focal chord PF in H, and HO perpendicular to PF meeting the normal in O, the required centre of curvature.

CHAPTER VI.

THE RECTANGULAR HYPERBOLA.

IF the axes of an hyperbola be equal, the angle between the asymptotes is a right angle, and the curve is called equilateral or rectangular.

If C is the centre, A a vertex, and F the corresponding focus, it follows that $CF^2 = 2AC^2$, for it has been shewn (p. 154) that $CF^2 = CA^2 + CB^2$, and in the rectangular hyperbola $CB = CA$.

Similarly $FA^2 = 2AX^2$, where X is the foot of the directrix, i.e. *the eccentricity* is always $\sqrt{2} : 1$.

Conjugate diameters are equal to one another and are equally inclined to either asymptote, for in any hyperbola

$$CP^2 - CD^2 = CA^2 - CB^2 \text{ and } \therefore CP = CD.$$

Also $CPLD$ (fig. 113) is a rhombus and therefore CL bisects the angle PCD.

Diameters at right angles to one another are equal, for if CE be perpendicular to CP the angle $BCE =$ the angle $PCA =$ the angle BCD, and therefore by symmetry $CE = CD$.

COROLLARY. The rectangles contained by the segments of chords which intersect at right angles are equal since they are in the ratio of the squares of the parallel diameters (p. 169).

Given three points on an equilateral hyperbola, a fourth is also given, for if the curve pass through the three points A, B, C it will also pass through the *orthocentre* of the triangle ABC, i.e.

through the intersection of the perpendiculars from A, B, C on the opposite sides.

This follows at once from the above corollary, for if ABC be a triangle, and O the orthocentre, and if CO meets ABC in D, the triangles DOA and DBC are similar, and

$$DO : DA :: DB : DC;$$
$$\therefore DO.DC = DA.DB,$$

so that O must be a point on the curve.

If P, Q, R are three points on the curve, the centre must lie on the circle passing through the middle points of the sides of the triangle PQR. For (fig. 113) let an asymptote meet the sides

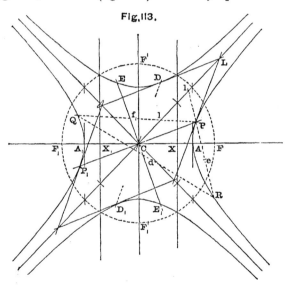

Fig. 113.

PQ, PR in l and l_1, and let d, e, f be the middle points of QR, RP and PQ respectively.   Let C be the centre of the hyperbola. Then Cf is conjugate to PQ and Ce to PR,

$$\therefore \text{ the angle } fCe = fCl + l_1Ce$$
$$= el_1C + Clf$$
$$= Pl_1l + Pll_1$$
$$= fPe$$
$$= fde,$$

since $fdeP$ is a parallelogram, i.e. the circle through fde passes also through C (Euclid III. 21).

Four points are therefore in general sufficient to determine a rectangular hyperbola, for the orthocentre of the triangle formed by any three is necessarily a fifth point on the curve, which can then be completed by the general method of Prob. 115, p. 185 ; or the centre can at once be determined as one of the points of intersection of the two circles which can be described through the centre points of the sides of the triangles formed by taking any three of the four given points in succession.

Similarly a rectangular hyperbola can generally be determined from four conditions, and the curve cannot in general be described to satisfy a greater number.

If QV be an ordinate of a diameter PCP_1, $QV^2 = PV \cdot VP_1$.

For in any hyperbola (Prop. 5, p. 165)
$$QV^2 : PV \cdot VP_1 :: CD^2 : CP^2;$$
but in the rectangular hyperbola $CD = CP$,
$$\therefore QV^2 = PV \cdot VP_1.$$

Hints for the solution of particular cases are given in the following examples, but as they are usually simple it has not been considered necessary to illustrate them by figures.

Given the following data, construct rectangular hyperbolas fulfilling them.

a. An asymptote and focus.

[A line through the focus making $45°$ with the asymptote meets it in the centre.]

b. An asymptote LC, a tangent PL and its point of contact P.

[Let the given tangent PL meet the asymptote in L; on it make $PL_1 = PL$, and draw L_1C perpendicular to the asymptote meeting it in C, the centre of the curve.]

c. The centre C, a tangent PT and its point of contact P.

[From C draw CY perpendicular to PT meeting it in Y.

The transverse axis bisects the angle PCY, and its semi-length CA is a mean proportional between CP and CY.]

d. The centre C and two points P, Q on the curve.

[Produce PC to p and make $Cp = CP$, so that Pp is a diameter. Describe a circle through the three points P, Q, p. The tangent to this circle at Q is parallel to the tangent to the curve at P, which is therefore known.]

e. The centre C, a tangent PT and a point Q of the curve.

[From Q drop a perpendicular QN on the given tangent, meeting it in N: bisect QN in n, and draw nt parallel to PT. A circle passing through C and N and touching nt will meet PT again in its point of contact.]

f. The centre C and two tangents PT, QT.

[Produce TC to T_1 and make $CT_1 = CT$; through T_1 draw T_1t parallel to QT and meeting PT in t. CT and Ct will be the directions of a pair of conjugate diameters, which determine the asymptotes.]

g. A focus F and two points P, Q.

[With centre P describe a circle, the radius of which

$$: FP :: 1 : \sqrt{2},$$

and with centre Q describe a circle, the radius of which

$$: FQ :: 1 : \sqrt{2}.$$

The directrix will be a common tangent to these two circles.]

h. A focus F, a tangent PT and its point of contact P.

[With centre P describe a circle, the radius of which

$$: FP :: 1 : \sqrt{2};$$

draw FT perpendicular to PT meeting it in T. A tangent from T to the circle will be the directrix.]

i. A focus F and two tangents PT, QT.

[From F draw GY perpendicular to PT meeting it in Y; produce FY to f, and make $Yf = YF$. Draw the circle which is the locus of the vertex of the triangle on base Ff, and with the sides terminating in F and f respectively in the ratio of $\sqrt{2}:1$, (Prob. 17, p. 21). This circle is a locus of the second focus. Similarly the tangent QT will furnish a second locus, so that the second focus must be at one of the points of intersection of the two circular loci.]

k.   A focus F, a tangent QT, and a point P.

[From F draw FY perpendicular to QT, produce it to f, and make $Yf = YF$; a circular locus of the second focus can be determined from Ff as in the last example. With P and f as foci and with distance between the vertices $= FP$, describe an hyperbola, which will be a second locus of the second focus, which is therefore at one of the intersections of the hyperbola and circle.]

l.   Two tangents PT, QT and their points of contact P and Q.

[Bisect PQ in V; then VT is a locus of the centre. On PQ describe a segment of a circle containing an angle equal to the supplement of the angle PTQ; the segment must be on the same side of PQ as T, and is then a second locus of the centre, which is therefore known.]

m.   Given three points and a tangent.

[From the three points a fourth can be determined (p. 189), and the curve can be drawn by the general method. Prob. 117, p. 187.]

n.   Given four tangents, AB, BC, CD, DA.

[Draw the circle to which the triangle formed by some three of the four tangents is self conjugate (Ex. 18, p. 55); it is a locus of the centre. A second locus is the straight line joining the points of bisection of the diagonals of the quadrilateral formed by the tangents. The centre is therefore known.]

o.   Given two points A, B and two tangents PT, QT. (Fig. 114.)

[Let AB meet PT in a and QT in b. Find X the centre, and O, O_1 the foci of the involution A, B and a, b. The chord of contact of PT and QT will pass through O or O_1, and if it passes through O, TO_1 will be the polar of O and conversely. Through

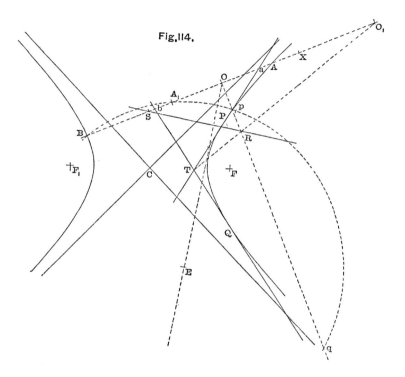

Fig. 114.

O draw Opq perpendicular to AB. On AB make $OA_1 = OA$, and find OS an harmonic mean between OA_1 and OB, let Oq and TO_1 meet in R and join SR. A circle described with its centre on OE perpendicular to SR and to pass through A_1 and B will cut Opq in points p, q of the required curve.]

p. Given three tangents AB, BC, CA and a point P. (Fig. 115.)

[The circle (centre S, radius SO) to which the given triangle ABC is self-conjugate (Ex. 18, p. 55) is one locus of the centre. Bisect AB, BC, CA in c, a, b respectively, and draw PA cutting bc in L, PB cutting ca in M, and PC cutting ab in N. The conic described to touch the sides of the triangle abc in the points LMN (Probs. 81 or 111) is a second locus of the centre. In the figure, the required conic is an ellipse and the circular locus cuts

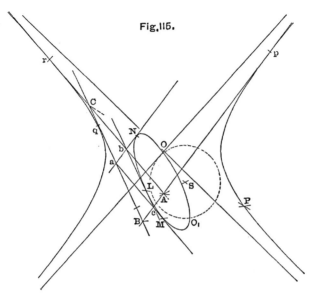

Fig. 115.

it in the points O and O_1, either of which may be taken as the centre. The points of contact of the given tangents are p, q, r.]

Examples on Chapters V. and VI.

1. Draw an hyperbola, the centre (C), one asymptote (CL) and a directrix LL_1 being given.

[Draw the axis CF perpendicular to LL_1, meeting it in X. The vertex A is at a distance CL from C.]

· 2. Draw an hyperbola, the asymptotes CL, CL_1 and the distance CF of a focus F being given.

3. Given the base AB of a triangle and point of contact, F, with base of the inscribed circle; shew that the locus of vertex of triangle is an hyperbola with foci A and B and vertex F.

4. Shew that the tangent at any point P of an hyperbola bisects any straight line perpendicular to the axis AA_1 and terminated by AP, A_1P.

5. Draw the locus of the foci of parabolas passing through two fixed points P and P_1 and having their axes parallel to a fixed line AB.

[The hyperbola described with P and P_1 as foci and with length of transverse axis $= PM$; the side parallel to AB of a right-angled triangle on PP_1 as hypotenuse.]

6. Given the centre C, vertex A, and a tangent PT meeting CA in T, describe the hyperbola.

[The foot N of the ordinate of the point of contact (P) may be determined from $CT : CA :: CA : CN$. P is then known. The asymptotes cut off equal distances on PT on each side of P and make equal angles with CA (Prob. 19).]

7. Given the centre C, the axis CT, a tangent PT and its point of contact P, draw the hyperbola. (See last example.)

8. Determine the locus of the intersection of the bisectors of the sides of the triangle formed by the asymptotes and any tangent to a hyperbola.

[A similar and similarly placed hyperbola with axes reduced in ratio 2 : 3.]

9. Given a focus F, tangent PT and point Q on an hyperbola, draw the locus of the second focus.

[From F draw FY perpendicular to PT meeting it in Y: produce FY to f and make $Yf = FY$. The required locus is the hyperbola with foci f and Q, and transverse axis $= FQ$.]

10. Given a line QT and two points P and F. From F draw a perpendicular FY to QT meeting it in Y, and produce FY to f, making $Yf = YF$. With P and f as foci and with PF as the distance between the vertices describe an hyperbola. With F and any point on this hyperbola as foci describe an ellipse to pass through P, and shew that it will touch QT:

i.e. Given a focus, tangent and point of a conic, the locus of the second focus is an hyperbola.

11. Given two tangents *PT*, *QT* to a rectangular hyperbola and their points of contact *P*, *Q*. Shew that if *QR* be drawn perpendicular to *PT*, and *PR* to *QP*, *R* will be a point on the curve.

12. In a given ellipse determine the pair of equal conjugate diameters.

[They coincide with asymptotes of hyperbola having the same axes.]

13. Draw the loci of the points of trisection of a series of circular arcs described on the straight line *AB*.

[Branches of two hyperbolas having their centres at the internal points of trisection of *AB* and asymptotes inclined 60° to axis.]

14. Given the asymptotes and a point on a directrix, draw the hyperbola.

15. From a given point *P* in an hyperbola draw a straight line, such that the segment intercepted between the other intersection with the hyperbola and a given asymptote shall be equal to a given line.

[With *P* as centre and the length of the given line as radius describe a circle cutting the other asymptote. Either point of intersection joined to *P* gives the line required.]

16. Given a focus *F*, and tangent *PY* to an hyperbola and the length 2*a* of the transverse axis, shew that the locus of the second focus is a circle.

[From *F* draw *FY* perpendicular to *PY* meeting it in *Y*; produce *FY* to *f* and make *Yf* = *FY*. *f* is the centre and 2*a* the radius of the required circle.]

17. Shew that any point on the circle through the middle points of the sides of a triangle *ABC* may be taken as the centre of an equilateral hyperbola passing through *A*, *B* and *C*.

18.   If four tangents to an equilateral hyperbola be given, shew that either of the *limiting points* (p. 46) of the system of circles described on the diagonals of the quadrilateral as diameters may be taken as the centre of the hyperbola.

19.   Given a focus F, a tangent PT, its point of contact P, and the eccentricity, draw the conic.

[From F draw FT perpendicular to FP and meeting PT in T which will be a point on the directrix. With P as centre and with radius r such that $\dfrac{FP}{r} =$ the given eccentricity, describe a circle. Tangents from T to this circle will be positions of the directrix. Two solutions are generally possible.]

20.   Draw normals to an ellipse, from a given point P.

[The normals pass through the intersections of the ellipse with the rectangular hyperbola passing through P and the centre of the ellipse, and having its asymptotes parallel to the major and minor axes at distances respectively

$$-\frac{b^2\beta}{a^2 - b^2}, \text{ and } \frac{a^2 a}{a^2 - b^2},$$

where a and b are the semi-axes and a, β the co-ordinates of P.]

21.   Draw normals to an ellipse from a point on the minor axis.

[They will pass through the intersections of the ellipse with the circle described through the foci and point.]

CHAPTER VII.

In page 31, it has been shewn how to find the pole of a given line and the polar of a given point with regard to a given circle, and the principal properties of poles and polars have been explained.

In pages 140 et seq. an extension has been made to the case of an ellipse, and the properties there noticed are applicable to all conic sections.

The pole of a line with regard to any conic being a point and the polar of a point a line, it follows that any system of points and lines can be transformed into a system of lines and points.

This process is called *reciprocation*, and it is clear that any theorem relating to the original system will have its analogue in the system formed by reciprocation.

Def. Being given a fixed conic section (Σ) and any curve (S), we can generate another curve (s) as follows; draw any tangent to S, and take its pole with regard to Σ; the locus of this pole will be a curve s, which is called the *reciprocal polar* of S with regard to Σ. The conic Σ with regard to which the pole is taken is called the *auxiliary conic*.

A point (of the reciprocal polar curve s) is said to *correspond* to a line (of the reciprocated figure S) when we mean that the point is the pole of the line with regard to the auxiliary conic Σ; and since it appears from the definition that every point of s is the pole with regard to Σ of some tangent to S, this is briefly expressed by saying that every point of s *corresponds* to some tangent of S.

THEOREM. *The point of intersection of two tangents to S will correspond to the line joining the corresponding points of s.*

This follows from the property of the conic Σ, that the point of intersection of any two lines is the pole of the line joining the poles of these two lines. (p. 141.)

Now if the two tangents to S be indefinitely near, then the two corresponding points of s will also be indefinitely near, and the line joining them will therefore be a tangent to s; and since any tangent to S intersects the consecutive tangent at its point of contact, the above theorem becomes: *If any tangent to S correspond to a point on s, the point of contact of that tangent to S will correspond to the tangent through the point on s.*

Hence we see that the relation between the curves is *reciprocal*, that is to say, that the curve S might be generated from s (through the auxiliary conic) in precisely the same manner that s was generated from S. Hence the name "reciprocal polars*."

Being given then any theorem *of position* concerning any curve S (i. e. one not involving the magnitudes of lines or angles), another can be deduced concerning the curve s. For example, if we know that a number of points connected with the figure S lie on a right line, we know also that the corresponding lines connected with the figure s meet in a point (the pole of the line with regard to Σ), and *vice versâ*.

From any one such theorem another can be derived by suitably interchanging the words "point" and "line," "inscribed" and "circumscribed," "locus" and "envelope," &c., understanding by the term envelope "the curve to which a series of lines drawn according to any given rule are tangents."

The *evolute* of a curve, e.g. is the *envelope* of normals to the curve.

* Salmon's *Conic Sections*, chap. xv.

Although the auxiliary conic Σ has hitherto been spoken of as any conic whatever, it is most common to make this conic a circle, considerable simplification being thereby introduced, and generally unless the contrary is specially mentioned, reciprocal polars may be understood to be polars *with regard to a circle.* It has been shewn, p. 31, that the polar of any point with regard to a circle is a line perpendicular to the line joining the point to the centre, and conversely that the pole of any given line with regard to a circle is on the line through the centre perpendicular to the given line; in either case the product of the distances of the pole and polar from the centre being equal to the square of the radius, so that the polar of a given point or the pole of a given line with regard to a given circle may always be found by merely drawing tangents to that circle. The centre of the auxiliary circle is frequently called the *origin.*

The advantage of using a circle for the auxiliary conic chiefly arises from the two following theorems, which enable us to transform by this method, not only theorems of position, but also theorems involving the magnitude of lines and angles.

THEOREM. *The distance of any point P from the origin O is the reciprocal of the distance Ot from the origin of the corresponding line pt;*

$$\text{i. e. } OP . Ot = r^2,$$

where Ot is perpendicular to pt and r is the radius of the auxiliary circle.

THEOREM: *The angle TQT_1 between any two lines TQ, T_1Q is equal to the angle subtended at the origin by the corresponding points p, p_1; for Op is perpendicular to TQ and Op_1 to T_1Q.*

PROBLEM 119. To find the polar reciprocal of one circle, centre C, radius CA, with regard to another, centre O, radius OM, i. e. to find the locus of the pole p with regard to the circle (O) of any tangent PT to the circle C. (Fig. 116.)

Find MM_1 the polar with respect to the auxiliary circle (centre O) of C, the centre of the circle to be reciprocated; i. e. if

C is, as in the figure, outside the auxiliary circle, draw CM a tangent to that circle and draw MM_1 perpendicular to OC, meet-

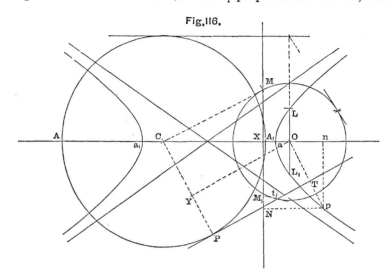

Fig, 116.

ing it in X. Draw any tangent PT to (C); draw OT perpendicular to PT, and find the pole p with respect to the auxiliary circle of PT. Then by definition, $OC \cdot OX = r^2 = Op \cdot OT$, where r is the radius of the auxiliary circle,

i.e. $Op : OC :: OX : OT$.

From p draw pN perpendicular to MM_1 meeting it in N, and pn perpendicular to OC meeting it in n. Also draw OY perpendicular to CP meeting it in Y, so that $OT = PY$. Then by similar triangles Opn, OCY,

$$Op : OC :: On : CY,$$
$$\therefore\ Op : OC :: OX + On : PY + CY$$
$$:: nX : CP.$$

But $$nX = pN,$$
$$\therefore\ Op : pN :: OC : CP;$$

but the ratio $\dfrac{OC}{CP}$ is constant, since both OC and CP are fixed distances.

Therefore the point p moves so that its distance (Op) from a fixed point O is in a constant ratio to its distance (pN) from a fixed right line MM_1; i.e. the locus of p is a conic section of which O is a focus, MM_1 the corresponding directrix, and the eccentricity of which is $\dfrac{OC}{CP}$. The eccentricity is evidently greater, less than, or equal to unity according as O is outside, inside, or on the circumference of the reciprocated circle.

Hence, *the polar reciprocal of a circle is a conic section, of which the origin is the focus, the line corresponding to the centre is the directrix, and which is an hyperbola, an ellipse, or a parabola, according as the origin is outside, inside, or on the circle.*

The tangents at A and A_1, the extremities of the diameter through O, *correspond* to the vertices at a and a_1 of the reciprocal polar. [In the figure At touches the auxiliary circle and at is perpendicular to OC].

The extremities of the latus rectum LL_1 *correspond* to the tangents parallel to OC. Therefore $OL . CP = r^2$, where r is the radius of the auxiliary circle.

The centre of the reciprocal conic is the pole with respect to (O) of the polar of O with respect to (C), i.e. if O is outside (C) it is the pole of the chord of contact of tangents from O to the circle (C), and in that case the asymptotes are perpendicular to these tangents. Of course if O is inside (C) real tangents from it to (C) cannot be drawn, and consequently the ellipse has no real asymptotes.

Conversely of course the reciprocal of a conic section with regard to a circle which has one of the foci for its centre is a circle, with its centre at the pole of the corresponding directrix and of radius (R) such that the ratio, $R :$ distance between its centre and the focus, is the eccentricity of the conic.

The above important property enables us to deduce from any property of a circle, a corresponding property of a conic; and since the proof of the existence of the relation in the circle will usually be much simpler than a direct proof of the corresponding relation in the conic, the method is frequently of great value. It will soon be found that the operation of forming the reciprocal theorem will reduce itself to a mere mechanical process of interchanging the words "point" and "line," "inscribed" and "circumscribed," "locus" and "envelope," &c., as has been already noticed; but the method also furnishes admirable examples and tests of draughtsmanship, and the actual construction of reciprocal figures should I think be much more largely practised than it is.

Of course a little care is required in taking the original circles so that the resulting conic may be of convenient proportions, but a very little practice will enable this to be done and there is no real difficulty in the construction itself.

A convenient ratio for the eccentricity of an ellipse is one not very different from 3 : 4, which may therefore be taken as a guide for the ratio of the radius of the circle to be reciprocated to the distance of the origin from its centre; and the auxiliary circle should then be taken of such radius as to bring the length between the poles of the tangents at the extremities of the diameter through the origin, i.e. the length of the major axis, a convenient one. The approximate position of these poles relatively to any assumed radius is easily seen. The *size* of the reciprocal conic depends entirely on the radius of the auxiliary circle.

As an example, fig. 117 gives the figure illustrating the following reciprocal theorems:

THEOREM.	RECIPROCAL.
If a chord of a circle subtend a constant angle at a fixed point on the curve, the chord always touches a circle.	If two tangents to a conic move so that the intercepted portion of a fixed tangent subtends a constant angle at the focus, the locus of the intersection of the moving tangents is a conic having the same focus and directrix.

C is the centre of the circle, M the fixed point on it, and PP_1 the chord which moves so that the angle PMP_1 is constant, and which therefore always touches a circle described with centre C.

F is the centre of the auxiliary circle, and since it is taken inside the circle (C) the reciprocal polar of this circle will be an ellipse.

Find K the point corresponding to the line MP, i.e. the pole

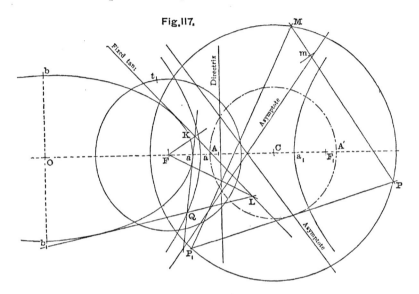

Fig. 117.

of MP with respect to the auxiliary circle, (in other words draw Fm perpendicular to MP meeting it in m, draw mt a tangent to the auxiliary circle touching it in t and draw tK perpendicular to Fm meeting it in K); find L the point corresponding to MP_1, i.e. the pole of MP_1 with respect to the auxiliary circle, (in other words, since MP_1 cuts the auxiliary circle, draw a tangent at one of the points of intersection meeting FL drawn perpendicular to MP_1 in L); then the line KL *corresponds* to the point M, and will therefore be a fixed tangent to the reciprocal conic.

Find Q the point corresponding to the line PP_1, then the line KQ corresponds to the moving point P, and the line LQ to the moving point P_1, and these lines are therefore moving tangents to the reciprocal conic, intercepting on the fixed tangent a length KL which subtends a constant angle at F, for since FK is perpendicular to MP and FL to MP_1, the angle KFL is equal to the angle PMP_1 which by supposition is constant.

Lastly, since Q corresponds to PP_1 which is a tangent to a circle centre C, the locus of Q must be the polar reciprocal of this circle, and is therefore a conic with focus F and the polar of C for directrix, i.e. a conic with the same focus and directrix as the polar reciprocal of the circle MPP_1.

As in the figure F lies outside the circle to which PP_1 is a tangent, the locus of Q is a hyperbola, the vertices of which are the poles of the tangents at A and A_1, the ends of the diameter through the origin F.

Examples on Chapter VII.

Below are given in parallel columns some examples of reciprocal theorems :

1. The angles in the same segment of a circle are equal.

If a moveable tangent of a conic meet two fixed tangents, the intercepted portion subtends a constant angle at the focus.

2. Two of the common tangents of two equal circles are parallel.

If two conics have the same focus, and equal latera recta, the straight line joining two of their common points passes through the focus.

3. If a circle be inscribed in a triangle, the lines joining the vertices with the points of contact meet in a point.

If a triangle be inscribed in a conic, the tangents at the vertices meet the opposite sides in three points lying in a straight line.

4. If two chords be drawn from a fixed point on a circle at right angles to each other, the line joining their ends passes through the centre.

If two tangents of a conic move so that the intercepted portion of a fixed tangent subtends a right angle at the focus, the two moveable tangents meet in the directrix.

5. Any two tangents to a circle make equal angles with their chord of contact.

The line drawn from the focus to the intersection of two tangents bisects the angle subtended at the focus by their chord of contact.

6. If two chords at right angles to each other be drawn through a fixed point on a circle, the line joining their extremities passes through the centre.

The locus of the intersection of tangents to a parabola which cut at right angles is the directrix.

[Take the fixed point on the circle as the centre of the auxiliary circle, and the circle reciprocates into a parabola.]

7. The envelope of a chord of a circle which subtends a given angle at a given point on the circle is a concentric circle.	The locus of the intersection of tangents to a parabola, which cut at a given angle, is a conic having the same focus and the same directrix.
8. The rectangle under the segments of any chord of a circle through a fixed point is constant.	The rectangle under the perpendiculars let fall from the focus on two parallel tangents is constant.

[Take the fixed point as centre of auxiliary circle.]

9. If lines be drawn from the end of a diameter of a circle making equal angles with a fixed straight line in the plane of the circle, the chords subtended by these lines are parallel.	The points of intersection of tangents to a parabola, which are equally inclined to a given straight line, lie on a fixed straight line passing through the focus.
10. The portion of any tangent to a circle intercepted between two parallel tangents subtends a right angle at the centre.	The portion of the directrix intercepted between chords drawn from the ends of any focal chord of a conic to any point of the curve subtends a right angle at the focus.

11. Shew that the polar reciprocal of a parabola with respect to a circle having any point (S) of the directrix as centre is an equilateral hyperbola.

[Draw the tangents to the parabola from the point S, which will be at right angles to each other since S is on the directrix. The reciprocals of their points of contact will be asymptotes to the reciprocal curve, because their points of contact (the poles of the tangents) are at an infinite distance. The tangents at the vertices can easily be drawn, since they are the polars of the points in which a line through S parallel to the bisector of the angle between the asymptotes meets the parabola.]

12. Given three points A, B and C, on a parabola, and a point L on the directrix, draw the curve.

[If the three points are reciprocated with respect to a circle described with centre L, and a rectangular hyperbola described passing through L and having the polars of A, B and C for tangents (Ex. p, p. 194), any point on the hyperbola when reciprocated with respect to the same circle becomes a tangent to the parabola.]

13.   If a conic be inscribed in a quadrilateral, shew that the angles subtended at a focus by the pairs of opposite sides are together equal to two right angles.

[Reciprocate the well-known theorem : The opposite angles of any quadrilateral inscribed in a circle are equal to two right angles.]

14.   With the centre of perpendiculars of a triangle as focus are described two conics, one touching the sides and the other passing through the feet of the perpendiculars; prove that these conics will touch each other, and that their point of contact will lie on the conic which touches the sides of the triangle at the feet of the perpendiculars.

15.   An hyperbola is its own reciprocal with respect to either circle which touches both branches of the hyperbola and intercepts on the transverse axis a length equal to the conjugate axis.

CHAPTER VIII.

ANHARMONIC RATIO AND ANHARMONIC PROPERTIES
OF CONICS.

Application of the signs + and − to determine the direction of segments of a right line.

If A, B are two points in a straight line and it is necessary to discriminate whether the length AB is to be measured from A to B or from B to A, it may be done by calling the one direction positive and the other negative, the starting point in each case being called the origin.

Regard being paid to this convention we may evidently say

$$AB = -BA \text{ or } AB + BA = 0,$$

and an obvious interpretation of this equation is that if we go from A to B and back again from B to A we are finally at zero distance from the starting point.

The same thing is evidently true of any number of segments; for if we take three points A, B, C *in any order* in a straight line and travel from A to B, then from B to C, and finally from C to A, we arrive at the point we started from, and really perform the operation expressed by the equation

$$AB + BC + CA = 0.$$

Since $-CA = AC$, this may also be written

$$AB + BC = AC.$$

When the position of a point A is determined by its distance from an origin O, if we wish to refer it to another origin O_1 anywhere on the line through O and A, we can always take

$$OA = O_1A - O_1O,$$

E.

for this is identical with the equation

$$OA - O_1A + O_1O = 0,$$

and, since $-O_1A = AO_1$, with

$$OA + AO_1 + O_1O = 0.$$

The difference of two segments OA, OB of a straight line with a common origin O is always equal to BA, whatever may be the magnitudes and directions of the segments.

For the equation $OA - OB = BA$

is identical with $OA + AB + BO = 0.$

If a is the middle point of a segment Aa and M any point on the line through Aa,

$$Ma = \frac{MA + Ma}{2} \text{ and } MA \cdot Ma = \overline{Ma}|^2 - \overline{aa}|^2,$$

for between the three points M, a, A the relation holds

$$Ma + aA + AM = 0,$$

$$Ma + aA = MA.$$

Similarly $Ma + aa = Ma$;

therefore, adding these equations and remembering that $aA = -aa$, since a is midway between A and a,

$$Ma = \frac{MA + Ma}{2};$$

also, multiplying together the right and left-hand members, we get

$$MA \cdot Ma = \overline{Ma}|^2 + Ma(aA + aa) + aA \cdot aa$$

$$= \overline{Ma}|^2 - \overline{aa}|^2,$$

since $aA = -aa$.

Let A, B, C, D be four points in a straight line, then the ratio of the distances of one point A from two others B and D, divided by the ratio of the distances of the remaining point C from the same two (B and D), is called the Anharmonic Ratio of the range A, B, C, D; i.e. the anharmonic ratio of the range $ABCD$ is the numerical value of the expression $\frac{AB}{AD} \div \frac{CB}{CD}$, which may also be written $\dfrac{AB}{AD} \cdot \dfrac{CD}{CB}$ or $AB.CD : CB.AD$. The sign of the ratio will depend on the signs of the segments of which it is composed, those which are measured in one direction being considered positive and those measured in the opposite direction negative.

Thus, if the four points are in the order from left to right $ABCD$, the three terms AB, CD and AD in the above ratio are positive and the term CB is negative; and the ratio itself is negative.

Since four points in a straight line taken in pairs give six segments, there are really six anharmonic ratios corresponding to any range, three of which however are merely the inverse values of the remaining three. Thus instead of taking the ratio of the distances of A from B and D and dividing by the ratio of the distances of C from B and D, we might take the ratio of the distances of A from C and D and divide by the ratio of the distances of B from C and D, giving the expression

$$\frac{AC}{AD} \div \frac{BC}{BD}, \text{ or } \frac{AC}{AD} \cdot \frac{BD}{BC},$$

and in this case if the points are in the order $ABCD$ all the segments are of the same sign and the ratio is positive.

Again, we might take the ratio of the distances of A from B and C and divide by the ratio of the distances of D from B and C, giving the expression

$$\frac{AB}{AC} \div \frac{DB}{DC}, \text{ or } \frac{AB}{AC} \cdot \frac{DC}{DB},$$

where two of the segments are of the same sign and two of opposite sign, so that the ratio is again positive.

In the above ratios the same point A has been associated successively with the three remaining C, B, D. In the first A and C may be said to be conjugate points, in the second A and B, and in the third A and D.

Of the three fundamental ratios formed as above, two are always positive and one negative, whatever the order of the points.

Besides these there are the three inverse ratios

$$\frac{AD}{AB} \div \frac{CD}{CB}, \quad \frac{AD}{AC} \div \frac{BD}{BC}, \quad \frac{AC}{AB} \div \frac{DC}{DB}.$$

It is of course necessary to retain throughout any investigation the particular order adopted at its commencement.

The anharmonic ratio of the range A, B, C, D is denoted by $\{ABCD\}$.

If the anharmonic ratio of a range $= -1$, the segments are in harmonic progression; for if the points occur in the order $ACBD$ and $\frac{AC}{AD} \div \frac{BC}{BD} = -1$, we have

$$\frac{AC}{AD} = -\frac{BC}{BD} = \frac{CB}{BD},$$

since BC and CB are measured in opposite directions, and therefore of course the three segments AC, AB, AD are such that the first : the third :: difference between first and second : difference between second and third. If one of the points (D suppose) is at an infinite distance, the anharmonic ratio $\frac{AC}{AD} \div \frac{BC}{BD}$ reduces to the simple ratio $\frac{AC}{BC}$, for it may be written $\frac{AC}{BC} \div \frac{AD}{BD}$, and AD is ultimately equal to BD.

PROP. 1. *If four fixed straight lines which meet in O be cut by any transversal in the points A, B, C, D* (fig. 118), *then will* $\{ABCD\}$ *be constant.*

Draw the straight line aBc parallel to OD, and meeting OA, OC in a and c.

Then $AB : AD :: aB : OD$ by similar triangles.

Similarly, $CD : CB :: OD : cB$,,   ,,

therefore $AB.CD : AD.CB :: aB : cB,$

or $\dfrac{AB}{AD} \div \dfrac{CB}{CD} = \dfrac{aB}{cB};$

but $\dfrac{aB}{cB}$ is a constant ratio for all positions of ac parallel to OD, therefore $\dfrac{AB}{AD} \div \dfrac{CB}{CD}$, which is the anharmonic ratio of the four points A, B, C, D, is also constant.

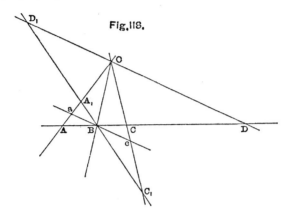

Fig. 118.

DEF. A bundle of lines drawn through one point is called a *pencil of rays*, or shortly *a pencil*.

The *anharmonic ratio of a pencil* of four rays is the anharmonic ratio of the range in which its rays are intersected by any transversal.

Pencils and ranges are said to be *equal* when their anharmonic ratios are equal, corresponding lines and points being taken for the comparison.

Equiangular pencils are evidently equal.

The anharmonic ratio of a pencil is denoted by $O\{ABCD\}$; O being the vertex and OA, OB, OC, OD the rays of the pencil.

PROP. 2. *The transversal may cut the rays of the pencil on either side of the vertex.*

For if, in the preceding article a transversal is drawn through B, cutting OA in A_1, OC in C_1, and OD in D_1, where D_1 lies in DO produced, then, exactly as before,

$$A_1B : A_1D_1 :: aB : OD_1,$$

and
$$C_1D_1 : C_1B :: OD_1 : cB;$$

therefore
$$\dfrac{A_1B}{A_1D_1} \div \dfrac{C_1B}{C_1D_1} = \dfrac{aB}{cB} = \dfrac{AB}{AD} \div \dfrac{CB}{CD}.$$

If a transversal meet AO produced in a, BO produced in β, CO produced in γ, and DO in δ,

$$\{ABCD\} = \{a\beta\gamma\delta\}.$$

If a transversal be drawn parallel to one of the rays of the pencil (OC) suppose, meeting the other rays in a, b, d, we have as before for the anharmonic ratio of the range $abcd$, where c is at an infinite distance, $\dfrac{ab}{ad}$, which is therefore $= \dfrac{AB}{AD} \div \dfrac{CB}{CD}$.

If the pencil is harmonic $\dfrac{ab}{ad} = -1$; therefore $ab = -ad$, or a is the centre point of bd.

PROBLEM 120. *Given the anharmonic ratio λ of four points, three of which are given in position, to determine the fourth* (Fig. 119).

Suppose that the three points A, C, and D of the anharmonic ratio $\dfrac{AC}{AD} \div \dfrac{BC}{BD} = \lambda$ are given and the point B required. Through A draw any line and on it set off from A segments Aa, Aa' which

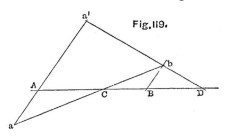

Fig.119.

are to each other in the ratio λ: the segments must be taken on the same side of A if λ is positive, and on opposite sides (as in figure) if it is negative. Draw aC and $a'D$ meeting in b, and draw bB parallel to Aa meeting the line ACD in B, which will be the required fourth point of the range; for by similar triangles we have

$$\frac{AC}{BC} = \frac{Aa}{Bb}, \quad \text{and} \quad \frac{AD}{BD} = \frac{Aa'}{Bb};$$

$$\therefore \frac{AC}{AD} \div \frac{BC}{BD} = \frac{Aa}{Aa'} = \lambda,$$

the ratio being negative, since AC, AD and BD are measured in one direction and BC in the opposite.

The same construction determines the points C or D if the points A, B, D or A, B, C and the ratio $\dfrac{AC}{AD} \div \dfrac{BC}{BD} = \lambda$ are given. To determine C, e.g. draw Bb parallel to Aa meeting $a'D$ in b, and draw ab to meet AB in C.

If the points B, C, D are given, the given anharmonic ratio may be written $\dfrac{BD}{BC} \div \dfrac{AD}{AC} = \lambda$, and the construction may be made by substituting the point B for the point A; by drawing, i.e. through the point B any line and setting off on it from B segments Bb', Bb in the ratio λ, and joining b' to D and b to C.

If λ, instead of being a number positive or negative, is the ratio of two lines of given length, these lengths may themselves be set off from A to a and a', on the same or on opposite sides of A according as the ratio is positive or negative.

PROP. 3. *If A, B, C, D are four points in a straight line, then $AB \cdot CD + AC \cdot DB + AD \cdot BC = 0$, the general rule of signs being observed* (Fig. 120).

Divide by $AB \cdot CD$, and the equation becomes

$$\frac{AC}{AB} \div \frac{DC}{DB} + \frac{AD}{AB} \div \frac{CD}{CB} = 1.$$

Fig. 120.

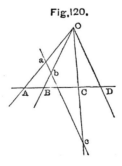

Draw the lines OA, OB, OC, OD, O being any point, and draw a transversal parallel to OD meeting OA, OB, OC in a, b, c;

then
$$\frac{AC}{AB} \div \frac{DC}{DB} = \frac{ac}{ab},$$

and
$$\frac{BC}{BA} \div \frac{DC}{DA} = \frac{bc}{ba} = \frac{AD}{AB} \div \frac{CD}{CB},$$

so that the above equation may be written

$$\frac{ac}{ab} + \frac{cb}{ab} = 1,$$

or
$$ac + cb + ba = 0,$$

which is always true.

The above equation is formed by multiplying each term of the identity $BC + CD + DB = 0$ by the distance of A from the remaining point, the first term BC by AD, the second CD by AB, and the third DB by AC.

PROP. 4. *If the anharmonic ratios of two systems of four points A, B, C, D and a, b, c, d taken on two straight lines and corresponding each to each are equal, and the lines are so placed that two homologous points A and a coincide, the three straight lines joining the remaining pairs of homologous points will meet in a point* (Fig. 121).

For if not, let Bb and Cc meet in O, and let OD meet the line ac in d_1 : the pencil O, $ABCD$ is met by two transversals AD

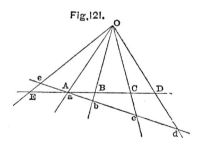

Fig. 121.

and ad_1, and therefore the anharmonic ratio

$$\frac{AB}{AC} \div \frac{DB}{DC} = \frac{ab}{ac} \div \frac{d_1 b}{d_1 c};$$

but by hypothesis

$$\frac{AB}{AC} \div \frac{DB}{DC} = \frac{ab}{ac} \div \frac{db}{dc},$$

therefore $\dfrac{db}{dc} = \dfrac{d_1 b}{d_1 c}$, which is impossible unless d and d_1 coincide.

Two lines divided so that the anharmonic ratio of any four points on the one is equal to the anharmonic ratio of the four corresponding points on the other are said to be divided *homographically*.

PROP. 5. *If the anharmonic ratios of two pencils of four rays, corresponding each to each, are equal, and the pencils are so placed that two corresponding lines coincide in direction, the three points of intersection of the remaining homologous rays lie on a straight line* (Fig. 122).

Let O and O_1 be the vertices of the pencils, the ray OA of the one coinciding in direction with the ray Oa of the other, and let the

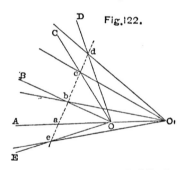

Fig. 122.

homologous rays OB, $O_1 b$ meet in b, and OC, $O_1 c$ in c; the straight line bc will pass through the point d where OD intersects $O_1 d$, for if not, let it meet OD in D and $O_1 d$ in d_1; then, since the anharmonic ratios of the two pencils are equal, we have

$$\frac{ab}{ac} \div \frac{Db}{Dc} = \frac{ab}{ac} \div \frac{d_1 b}{d_1 c},$$

which is impossible unless d_1 and D coincide.

Two pencils such that the anharmonic ratio of any four rays of the one is equal to the anharmonic ratio of the corresponding four rays of the other are said to be *homographic*.

PROBLEM 121. *Given any number of points A, B, C, D, E...*
on a straight line, and any three corresponding points (as a, b, c)
on a second line, to complete the homographic division of the second
line (Fig. 121).

Place the lines at any angle with each other and with two
corresponding points (as A and a) coinciding. Let the lines
joining the remaining pairs of corresponding points (*Bb* and *Cc*)
meet in O, then the lines OD, OE...&c. will meet the second
line in d, e, &c., the required points of homographic division.

The construction is obvious from the known property of the
transversals of a pencil of rays.

It follows conversely that if a pencil of rays intersect any two
lines in points B, b ; C, c...... the lines are divided homographically,
and that the point A in which the two lines intersect is its own
homologue in both divisions.

PROBLEM 122. *Given a pencil of rays O . ABCDE... and*
any three corresponding rays O_1 . abc of a second pencil, to com-
plete the second pencil so that the two shall be homographic
(Fig. 122).

Place the pencils so that two corresponding rays (OA, O_1a suppose) shall be coincident in direction, let the homologous rays intersect in b and c ; the straight line bc will intersect the remaining
rays of the given pencil in points on the required completing rays
of the second. The construction is obvious from the known property of a transversal.

Conversely, when the corresponding rays of two pencils intersect in points on a straight line, the pencils are homographic, and
the line OO_1 joining the centres is common to both pencils and is
coincident with its own homologue.

PROP. 6. *If A, B, C, D are four points on the circumference of*
a circle, and from any point O on the circumference the pencil
O . ABCD is drawn, the anharmonic ratio of this pencil is constant.

For if O_1 is any other point on the circumference the pencil
O_1 . *ABCD* is equiangular with the pencil O . *ABCD*.

PROP. 7. *If four fixed tangents to a circle are met by any variable tangent in A, B, C, D, the anharmonic ratio of this range is constant.*

For the angles which the four points subtend at the centre are constant, and therefore the ranges are transversals of equiangular pencils.

If we reciprocate these theorems (Prob. 119), the four fixed points in the first correspond to four fixed tangents to a conic, the variable point O corresponds to a variable tangent, the *lines* OA, OB, &c. correspond to the *points* a, b, c, d in which the variable tangent cuts the fixed tangents; and since points corresponding to lines lie on lines through the centre of the auxiliary circle perpendicular to the lines to which they correspond, the pencil formed by joining a, b, c, d to the centre of the auxiliary circle is equiangular with the pencil $O . ABCD$, i.e. the anharmonic ratio of the range $abcd$ is constant.

PROP. 8. *The reciprocal theorem to Prop. 6 therefore is "The anharmonic ratio of the points in which four fixed tangents to a conic cut any variable tangent is constant."*

PROP. 9. *By exactly similar reasoning the reciprocal theorem to Prop. 7 is "The anharmonic ratio of the pencil formed by joining any four fixed points on a conic to a variable fifth is constant."*

If the reciprocal figures be drawn, by observing the angles which correspond to the constant angles in the circle, it will be seen that the angles which the four points of the variable tangent in the first theorem subtend at either focus are constant ; and that the angles are constant which are subtended at the focus by the four points in which the inscribed pencil meets the directrix in the second theorem.

HOMOGRAPHIC RANGES IN THE SAME STRAIGHT LINE.   DOUBLE POINTS.

When two lines divided homographically are superposed, there exist, in general, two points, each of which considered as belonging to the first division coincides with its homologue in the

second division. They may be called *double points*, since each
represents two coincident homologous points. The double points
may become imaginary.

Let *A*, *B*, *C*, *D*... (fig. 123) be any points on a straight line, *S*
any point, and *AJ* a line through *A* making any angle with
AD, and meeting *SB*, *SC*, &c. in *β*, *γ*... respectively.

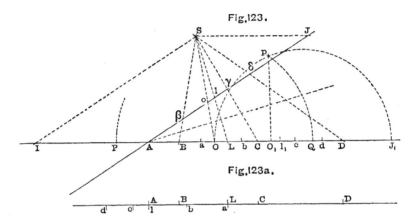

Fig,123.

Fig,123a.

The ranges *ABCD*... and *Aβγδ*... are of course homographic,
and if the second range be rotated round *A* till it coincides in
direction with *AD*, the point *A*, considered as belonging to the
first division, will evidently coincide with its own homologue in
the second division, as will also the point *L* determined by drawing
SL perpendicular to the line bisecting the angle *DAJ*.

Two homographic ranges in the same straight line formed as
above possess therefore two double points.

Instead however of the two ranges being formed merely by
the rotation of the second about *A*, the second may in addition
be moved along *AD* into any position to the right or left,
bringing (as in the figure) the point corresponding to *A* to *a*,
β to *b*, *γ* to *c*.... In this case also two double points in general
exist, which may be thus found :—

PROBLEM 123. *Given two homographic ranges ABCD...*, *abcd...*
in the same straight line, to determine the double points (Fig. 124).

Draw any circle whatever, and from any point *M* on it draw

MA, MB, MC cutting the circumference in A_1, B_1, C_1, and draw Ma, Mb, Mc cutting the circumference in a_1, b_1, c_1.

Fig. 124.

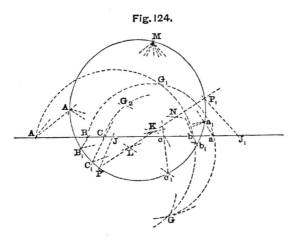

Draw A_1b_1, B_1a_1 intersecting in K, and A_1c_1, C_1a_1 intersecting in L, and draw KL cutting the circumference in P and P_1. The lines MP, MP_1 will cut Aa in the required double points J and J_1.

For $\{ABCJ\}$

$$= M\{A_1B_1C_1P\} = a_1\{A_1B_1C_1P\} \qquad \text{(Prop. 6.)}$$
$$= \{NKLP\},$$

where N is the point of intersection of KL and A_1a_1

and $\qquad \{abcJ\} = M\{a_1b_1c_1P\} = A_1\{a_1b_1c_1P\}$
$$= \{NKLP\},$$

i.e. the point J, considered as belonging to the first range, coincides with its own homologue in the second and is therefore a double point. Similarly for the point J_1.

It will be seen that the line PP_1 is a Pascal line (Prob. 86) in the circle, for C_1b_1 and B_1c_1 intersect on it.

The double points may also be determined thus:—On Ab, Ba as chords describe two circles passing also through any arbitrary point G and intersecting again in G_1, on Ac, Ca as chords describe circles passing through G and intersecting again in G_2. The circle through G, G_1, G_2 passes also through the required double points of the ranges.

A third construction for the double points is shewn in fig. 123. Through A, any point of the first range, draw AJ, a line making any angle with the given line. On it make $A\beta = ab$, $A\gamma = ac$, where a, b, c are the points of the second range corresponding to the points A, B, C of the first. Draw $B\beta$, $C\gamma$ intersecting in S. Through S draw SJ parallel to AC meeting AJ in J, so that J is the point on the range $A\beta\gamma$ ... corresponding to an infinitely distant point on the range ABC... ; and draw SI parallel to AJ, so that I is the point on the range ABC... corresponding to an infinitely distant point on the range $A\beta\gamma$.... Make aJ_1 on the superposed ranges $= AJ$, so that the range $A\beta\gamma$... J is identical with the range abc ... J_1. Bisect IJ_1 in O, which will be equidistant from the required double points. Find the point O_1 on the range abc... corresponding to the point O considered as belonging to the range ABC... [i.e. join SO cutting AJ in o, and make $aO_1 = Ao$]. Then the mean proportional between OO_1 and OJ_1 will be the distance from O of the required double points P and Q.

On page 17 a system of pairs of points on a straight line such that $XA . Xa = XB . Xb = XC . Xc = ... = XP^2 = XQ^2$ was defined as a system in Involution, any two corresponding points such as A, a being called conjugate points, the point X the centre, and the points P and Q the foci of the involution.

PROP. 10. *When three pairs of conjugate points are in involution, the anharmonic ratio of any four of the points is equal to the anharmonic ratio of their four conjugates, i.e. taking any four A, B, C, a and their four conjugates a, b, c, A,*

$$\frac{AB}{AC} \div \frac{aB}{aC} = \frac{ab}{ac} \div \frac{Ab}{Ac} ;$$

for if O is the centre of the involution

$$OA : OB :: Ob : Oa,$$
$$\therefore OA - OB : OB :: Ob - Oa : Oa,$$
or
$$AB : ab :: OB : Oa,$$

and
$$OA + Ob : Ob :: OB + Oa : Oa\;;$$
$$\therefore\; Ab : aB :: Ob : Oa,$$
$$\therefore\; \frac{AB \cdot Ab}{ab \cdot aB} = \frac{OB \cdot Ob}{Oa^2} = \frac{OA}{Oa}.$$

Similarly of course
$$\frac{AC \cdot Ac}{ac \cdot aC} = \frac{OA}{Oa} = \frac{AB \cdot Ab}{ab \cdot aB},$$
$$\therefore\; \frac{AB \cdot Ab}{AC \cdot Ac} = \frac{ab \cdot aB}{ab \cdot aC},$$

which may be written
$$\frac{AB}{AC} \div \frac{aB}{aC} = \frac{ab}{ac} \div \frac{Ab}{Ac},$$

which proves the proposition.

A series of points in involution consists of two homographic ranges, the directions of which coincide, and in which to any point whatever M of the line the same point m corresponds, whether M be considered as belonging to the first or second system.

For consider M as belonging to the range $ABC...$,

and $\quad\quad\quad m \quad\quad\quad ,, \quad\quad\quad ,, \quad\quad\quad abc...;$

then, since the ranges are homographic,
$$\frac{MA}{MB} \div \frac{CA}{CB} = \frac{ma}{mb} \cdot \frac{ca}{cb}.$$

If they are also in involution we must be able to interchange m and M, i.e. considering M as belonging to the range $abc...$ and m as belonging to the range $ABC...$, we must have
$$\frac{Ma}{Mb} \div \frac{ca}{cb} = \frac{mA}{mB} \div \frac{CA}{CB}.$$

Dividing each term of the first equation by the opposing term of the second,
$$\frac{MA}{MB} \div \frac{mA}{mB} = \frac{ma}{mb} \div \frac{Ma}{Mb},$$

i.e. the anharmonic ratio of the four points M, A, B, m is equal to the anharmonic ratio of their four conjugates m, a, b, M, or the points are in involution.

PROP. 11. *It is always possible to superimpose two homographic ranges, so that the two divisions shall be in involution.*

For it has been shewn (p. 220) that two pairs of corresponding points can be found equidistant from each other, by drawing viz. through S (fig. 123) a line Ll perpendicular to the line bisecting the angle between the ranges when the second is placed at any angle with the first and with two corresponding points A, a at the intersection: the pairs of points A, L and a, l are then equidistant. If now the two ranges are superimposed with the point a coinciding with the point L, and the point l coinciding with the point A (fig. 123a), the two ranges will be in involution.

The foci (p. 17) are points at which pairs of conjugate points coincide, and their existence is only possible when the points of any conjugate pair in the involution are both on the same side of the centre.

Thus if the points are in the order $ABab$, the centre X must fall between B and a in order that the products $XA \cdot Xa$ and $XB \cdot Xb$ may have the same sign, and that sign will be negative since the segments in each of the products are measured in opposite directions; but a square number is always positive, and therefore no foci exist.

If three segments Aa, Bb, Cc are in involution and one overlaps (as above) another, i.e. if the points are in the order $ABab$, it will also overlap the third. This is evident if we consider that if C lies to the left of X, and XC is greater than XA, c must be on the opposite side of X, and Xc must be less than Xa and vice versâ, and similarly with regard to Bb.

Conversely, if the segment Aa does not overlap Bb, it cannot overlap Cc, nor can Bb and Cc overlap.

The centre X forms with any two pairs of points A, a and B, b an involution in which the conjugate to the centre is at an infinite distance, for if x is conjugate to X, the anharmonic ratio of the four points $XABx =$ the anharmonic ratio of the four conjugate points $xabX$,

$$\text{i.e.} \quad \frac{XA}{XB} \div \frac{xA}{xB} = \frac{xa}{xb} \div \frac{Xa}{Xb};$$

but $\dfrac{XA}{XB} = \dfrac{Xb}{Xa}$, and therefore $\dfrac{xB}{xA} = \dfrac{xa}{xb}$,

or $\qquad\qquad xA \cdot xa = xB \cdot xb \dots\dots\dots\dots\dots\dots\dots (a).$

Now x cannot lie between b and A because the segment Xx must overlap both Aa and Bb, i.e. x must lie either to the right of b or to the left of A; if it lies to the right of b the segment xa is greater than the segment xb and the segment xA is greater than the segment xB, and therefore the equation (a) cannot hold unless x is at an infinite distance, in which case the segments xA, xa, xB, xb are ultimately equal.

Similarly x cannot lie to the left of A except at an infinite distance, and similar reasoning applies to points in the position shewn in figs. 12 and 13.

PROP. 12. *If on two segments Aa, Bb of a right line as chords, any two arcs of circles are described, their common chord passes through the centre X of the involution A, a and B, b (Fig. 125).*

For $\qquad XA \cdot Xa = XG \cdot Xg = XB \cdot Xb.$

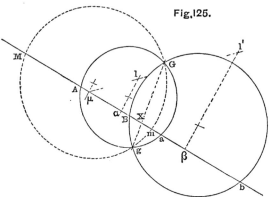

Fig. 125.

If the segments overlap as in the above figure, they may be taken as diameters of the intersecting circles, and the chord Gg will be perpendicular to the line $AaBb$. If the points are situated as in figs. 12 and 13, circles described on Aa and Bb as diameters will not intersect in real points, but the centre X will lie on the *radical axis* of the two circles.

E. 15

If a third circle be described passing through the points Gg and cutting Ab in the points M, m (fig. 125) it follows, since

$$XM . Xm = XG . Xg = XA . Xa = XB . Xb,$$

that M and m are another pair of conjugate points in the involution.

The same is evidently true of *any* line cutting the circumferences of all three circles, and we have the important proposition :—

If three circles pass through two given points, any straight line meeting the circles does so in a series of points in involution, the two points on the same circle being conjugate.

When the three circles described on three segments in involution as diameters intersect, straight lines drawn from either of the points of intersection to the ends of each segment are perpendicular to each other; it follows, that *when three segments of a straight line are in involution, two points (real or imaginary) exist, at each of which each segment subtends a right angle; and conversely, that if a right-angled triangle turns round that angular point as centre, the segments which it intercepts on a fixed right line in any three of its positions have their extremities in involution.*

PROBLEM 124. *Given A, a and B, b, two pairs of conjugate points, and C a fifth point of the involution, to determine c the point conjugate to C.*

Through any arbitrary point G describe segments of circles having Aa, Bb as chords; they will intersect in a second point g, and a circle described through the three points G, g and C will intersect AC in c, the required conjugate point.

Or thus :—Take any arbitrary point G and draw GA, GB, GC; draw any triangle with its vertices on these lines and two of its sides passing through a, b. The remaining side will pass through c.

If the point C be at infinity, the same method will give us the centre of the system.

The construction for this case is, " Through A, B draw any pair of parallels Ah, Bk, and through a, b a different pair of parallels ah, bk; then hk will pass through the centre of the system."

PROP. 13. *If Aa, Bb, Cc are any three fixed segments of a straight line, and a, β, γ their centre points, and if m is any point on the line, the function $mA \cdot ma \cdot \beta\gamma + mB \cdot mb \cdot \gamma a + mC \cdot mc \cdot a\beta$ is of constant value whatever the position of m, the general rule of signs being observed.*

Take M any other point on the line, then (p. 209)

$$mA = MA - Mm, \quad ma = Ma - Mm;$$

$$\therefore \quad mA \cdot ma = MA \cdot Ma - (MA + Ma) Mm + Mm^2$$

$$= MA \cdot Ma - 2Ma \cdot Mm + Mm^2,$$

and $\quad mB \cdot mb = MB \cdot Mb - 2M\beta \cdot Mm + Mm^2,$

and $\quad mC \cdot mc = MC \cdot Mc - 2M\gamma \cdot Mm + Mm^2.$

Multiply these equations by $\beta\gamma$, γa and $a\beta$ respectively, then since (p. 209) $\quad \beta\gamma + \gamma a + a\beta = 0,$

and (prop. 3) $\quad Ma \cdot \beta\gamma + M\beta \cdot \gamma a + M\gamma \cdot a\beta = 0,$

we get $\quad mA \cdot ma \cdot \beta\gamma + mB \cdot mb \cdot \gamma a + mC \cdot mc \cdot a\beta$

$$= MA \cdot Ma \cdot \beta\gamma + MB \cdot Mb \cdot \gamma a + MC \cdot Mc \cdot a\beta,$$

which proves the proposition.

PROP. 14. *If three conjugate pairs of points A, a; B, b; C, c are in involution, and a, β, γ the centre points of the segments Aa, Bb, Cc; if any point m be taken on the same straight line,*

$$mA \cdot ma \cdot \beta\gamma + mB \cdot mb \cdot \gamma a + mC \cdot mc \cdot a\beta = 0,$$

the general rule of signs being observed.

By the last proposition the value of the expression is constant whether the points are in involution or no. When they are in involution the value is zero when m coincides with the centre of the involution, since then

$$mA \cdot ma = mB \cdot mb = mC \cdot mc,$$

so that the equation may then be written

$$mA \cdot ma \, (\beta\gamma + \gamma a + a\beta) = 0,$$

which is evidently true since (p. 209)

$$\beta\gamma + \gamma a + a\beta$$

is always zero; and this proves the proposition.

PROP. 15.   *If A, a; B, b; C, c are three pairs of conjugate points in involution, and a, β, γ the centre points of the segments Aa, Bb, Cc,*

$$\frac{AB \cdot Ab}{AC \cdot Ac} = \frac{a\beta}{a\gamma} = \frac{aB \cdot ab}{aC \cdot ac},$$

with similarly formed equations for the remaining points.

In the equation proved in the last proposition, suppose that the point m coincides with the point A. The first term then becomes zero, since mA is zero, and the equation is

$$AB \cdot Ab \cdot \gamma a + AC \cdot Ac \cdot a\beta = 0;$$

or, since $\gamma a = -a\gamma$,

$$\frac{AB \cdot Ab}{AC \cdot Ac} = \frac{a\beta}{a\gamma} = \frac{aB \cdot ab}{aC \cdot ac},$$

if we make m coincide with a.

PROBLEM 125.   *Given two pairs of points A, a and B, b in a straight line, to find on the same line a fifth point such that the product of its distances from one pair shall be to the product of its distances from the other in a given ratio λ, i.e. given A, a and B, b, to determine a point M such that* $\dfrac{MA \cdot Ma}{MB \cdot Mb} = \lambda$ (Fig. 125).

Take any arbitrary point G and describe circles passing through A, a, G and B, b, G and intersecting again in g. Their centres will of course lie on lines perpendicular to Aa, Bb bisecting these segments; let a and β be the points of bisection. Divide $a\beta$ in the point μ, so that $\dfrac{a\mu}{\beta\mu} = \lambda$, i.e. on any parallel lines through a and β make $al =$ the numerator, and $\beta l' =$ the denominator of the given ratio, the lengths al, $\beta l'$ being set off on the same side of $a\beta$ if λ is positive, and on opposite sides if it is negative.

Describe a third circle to pass through G and g, and with its centre on a line through μ perpendicular to Ab. This circle will cut Ab in two points M and m, either of which fulfils the required conditions of the problem.

Proof. The points Mm as found are evidently in involution with the points Aa and Bb (p. 226).

$$\therefore \frac{MA \cdot Ma}{MB \cdot Mb} = \frac{\mu a}{\mu \beta} = \frac{mA \cdot ma}{mB \cdot mb} \quad \text{(prop. 15)};$$

but $\qquad \frac{\mu a}{\mu \beta} = \lambda$ by construction,

which proves the construction.

If the segments Aa, Bb overlap the problem is always possible, but otherwise cases of impossibility may arise owing to the position of the point μ. The problem becomes impossible if μ falls between P and Q, the foci of the involution A, a and B, b.

1. If one of the segments falls entirely within the other (as in fig. 12) their centre points a and β lie outside the segment PQ and both on the same side of it. If μ falls within the segment PQ the ratio $\frac{\mu a}{\mu \beta} = \lambda$ is positive, and its value lies between $\frac{Pa}{P\beta}$ $\frac{Qa}{Q\beta}$. In order that the problem may be possible in this case λ must be negative or must not be between these limits.

2. If the segments are entirely outside each other (as in fig. 13) their centre points lie outside the segment PQ, but on opposite sides of it. If μ falls on PQ the ratio $\frac{\mu a}{\mu \beta}$ is negative, and its absolute value is between $\frac{Pa}{P\beta}$ and $\frac{Qa}{Q\beta}$. In order that the problem may be possible in this case λ must be positive or must not be between these limits.

PROBLEM 126. *Given two straight lines AL, BL_1, and a fixed point on each A and B. Through a given point R to draw a straight line meeting AL in a and BL_1 in b, so that the segments Aa and Bb shall be to each other in a given ratio λ (Fig. 126).*

Imagine two variable points a_1, b_1 to move along Aa and Bb respectively, so that in corresponding positions $\frac{Aa_1}{Bb_1} = \lambda$. The points in corresponding different positions would form homographic ranges on the two lines, for if a_1, a_2, a_3; b_1, b_2, b_3 are corresponding positions of the moving points,

$$\frac{Aa_1}{Bb_1} = \frac{Aa_2}{Bb_2} = \frac{Aa_3}{Bb_3} = \frac{Aa_1 - Aa_3}{Bb_1 - Bb_3} = \frac{a_3a_1}{b_3b_1} = \frac{Aa_2 - Aa_3}{Bb_2 - Bb_3} = \frac{a_3a_2}{b_3b_2},$$

Fig. 126.

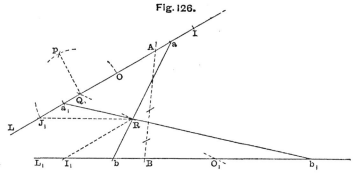

and therefore the anharmonic ratio

$$\frac{Aa_1}{Aa_2} \div \frac{a_3a_1}{a_3a_2} = \frac{Bb_1}{Bb_2} \div \frac{b_3b_1}{b_3b_2};$$

and the question therefore is to draw through R a line which will meet the two ranges in homologous points. If the points $b_1b_2b_3\ldots$ are joined to R, and the joining lines cut AL in $a_1a_2a_3\ldots$, the ranges $a_1a_2a_3\ldots$ and $a_1a_2a_3\ldots$ are also homographic, since $a_1a_2a_3\ldots$ is a transversal of the pencil $R \cdot b_1b_2b_3\ldots$ and the double points of the ranges $a_1a_2a_3\ldots$ and $a_1a_2a_3\ldots$ are extremities of lines fulfilling the conditions of the problem.

Determine the positions of I and J_1, the points which correspond to infinity. [Through R draw RI_1 parallel to AL meeting BL_1 in I_1, and make $AI : BI_1 = \lambda$; through R draw RJ_1 parallel to BL_1 meeting AL in J_1.]

Bisect IJ_1 in O, and on BL_1 take a point O_1 such that $AO : BO_1 = \lambda$. Draw RO_1 meeting AL in Q. Take a mean proportional (Op) between OJ_1 and OQ, and on AL make $Oa = -Oa_1 = Op$.

Either of the lines aR, a_1R fulfils the required conditions.

In making use of the ratio $\dfrac{Aa_1}{Bb_1} = \lambda$, signs must be given to the segments, measured from the two fixed points A and B; as otherwise to a point a_1 we might have corresponding points b_1 on either side of the origin B; so that if the directions in which the segments are measured is not prescribed, the problem admits of four solutions instead of two.

PROBLEM 127. *Given two straight lines AL, BL_1 and a fixed point A, B on each, to draw through a given point R a line meeting AL in a and BL_1 in b, so that the rectangle $Aa \cdot Bb$ shall have a given value v* (Fig. 127).

Exactly as in the last problem, if points $a_1 a_2 a_3 \ldots$ are taken on AD, and points $b_1 b_2 b_3 \ldots$ on BL_1, connected by the relation

$$Aa_1 \cdot Bb_1 = Aa_2 \cdot Bb_2 = Aa_3 \cdot Bb_3 \ldots = v,$$

Fig. 127.

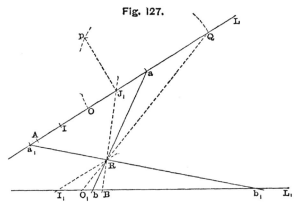

these points will form homographic ranges; and if the pencil $R \cdot b_1 b_2 b_3 \ldots$ be drawn meeting AL in $a_1 a_2 a_3 \ldots$ respectively, the double points of the homographic ranges $a_1 a_2 a_3 \ldots$, $a_1 a_2 a_3 \ldots$ will be points on the lines required.

Corresponding to the point at infinity on the range $a_1 a_2 a_3 \ldots$ we must evidently have the point B on the range $b_1 b_2 b_3 \ldots$, and therefore the line BR meets AL in the required point J_1. Corresponding to the point at infinity on the range $a_1 a_2 a_3 \ldots$ we have the point I_1 on BL_1 found by drawing RI_1 parallel to AL, and then I is determined by making $AI \cdot BI_1 = v$. Bisect IJ_1 in O and determine O_1 on BL_1, so that $AO \cdot BO_1 = v$. Draw RO_1 meeting AL in Q, and take a mean proportional (Op) between OJ_1 and OQ. Make $Oa = -Oa_1 = Op$, and Ra, Ra_1 will be lines fulfilling the conditions of the problem.

PROBLEM 128.   *To draw a triangle having its vertices on three
given lines and its sides passing through three given points* (Fig.
128).

Let JJ_1, KK_1, LL_1 be the given lines, and A, B, C the given
points.   Through one of the points, as A, draw any three lines

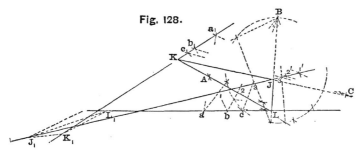

Fig. 128.

meeting two of the lines, as LL_1, KK_1, in a, b, c, $a_1b_1c_1$ respectively.
Draw the pencils B. abc, C . $a_1b_1c_1$ cutting the third line JJ_1 in
1, 2, 3, 1′, 2′, 3′ respectively, which will evidently be homographic
ranges.   Find the double points JJ_1 of the ranges (p. 221) and each
will be the vertex of a triangle fulfilling the required condition, for

$$\{123J\} = \{abcL\} = \{1′2′3′J\} = \{a_1b_1c_1K\},$$

and since the rays aa_1, bb_1, cc_1 pass through A so also must the
ray KL.

In the figure JKL, $J_1K_1L_1$ are the two triangles.

PROP. 16.   *If a quadrilateral $ABCD$ be inscribed in a conic,
and any transversal be drawn meeting the four sides in a, b, c, d
and the conic in e and g, then the three pairs of points ac, bd, eg
are in involution* (Fig. 85.)

Let $ABCD$ be the angles of the quadrilateral, AB, DC meeting
in E, and BC, DA in F.

Let a transversal cut AB in a, BC in b, CD in c, DA in d,
and the curve in e and g.

The rectangles de . dg, dA . dD are in the ratio of the squares
on parallel diameters, as also are the rectangles be . bg and bB . bC;
but the squares on the diameters parallel to AD and BC are in
the ratio

$$FA \; . \; FD : FC \; . \; FB \, ;$$

$$\therefore \frac{de.dg}{be.bg} = \frac{dA.dD}{bB.bC} \cdot \frac{FB.FC}{FA.FD}.$$

Fig. 85.

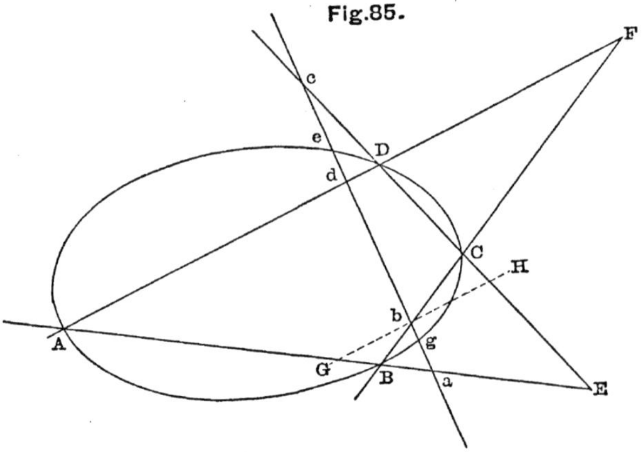

But
$$\frac{dA}{da} = \frac{\sin a}{\sin A}, \quad \frac{dD}{dc} = \frac{\sin c}{\sin D},$$

$$\frac{bB}{ba} = \frac{\sin a}{\sin B}, \quad \frac{bC}{bc} = \frac{\sin c}{\sin C};$$

$$\therefore \frac{dA.dD}{bB.bC} = \frac{da.dc}{ba.bc} \cdot \frac{\sin B \sin C}{\sin A \sin D}$$

$$= \frac{da.dc}{ba.bc} \cdot \frac{FA}{FB} \cdot \frac{FD}{FC},$$

i.e.
$$\frac{de.dg}{be.bg} = \frac{da.dc}{ba.bc},$$

or
$$\frac{de}{da} \div \frac{be}{ba} = \frac{bg}{bc} \div \frac{dg}{dc},$$

i.e. the anharmonic ratio of the four points d, e, a, b is equal to that of their four conjugates

$$b, \quad g, \quad c, \quad d,$$

or the three pairs of points are in involution.

Since the diagonals of the quadrilateral form a particular case of a conic passing through the four points, it follows that the points in which the transversal cuts the diagonals are another pair in involution with ac, bd, &c.

Cor. If the transversal be a tangent to the curve (meets it, that is, in two coincident points), it follows that the point of contact is a focus of the involution formed by the three pairs of points in which the tangent cuts the opposite sides and diagonals.

MacLaurin's method of generating conic sections :—

Triangles are described, whose sides pass through three fixed points A, B, C, and whose base angles move on two fixed lines Oa, Ob: the vertices will lie on a conic section (fig. 129).

Fig. 129.

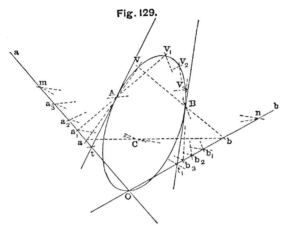

Suppose four such triangles drawn, then since the pencils through A and B are both homographic with the system through C, they are homographic with each other; therefore A, B, V, V_1, V_2, V_3, lie on the same conic section (Prop. 9). Now if the first three triangles be fixed, it is evident that the locus of V_3 is the conic section passing through

$$A, B, O, V_1, V_2.$$

It follows of course that the locus of the intersection of homologous rays in two homographic pencils is a conic section.

Newton's method of generating conic sections :—

Two angles of constant magnitude move about fixed points P, Q; the intersection of two of their sides traverses the right line AA_1; then the locus of V, the intersection of their other two sides, will be a conic passing through P, Q (fig. 130).

Take four positions of the angles, then

$$P \cdot \{AA_1A_2A_3\} = Q \cdot \{AA_1A_2A_3\};$$

but $$P.\{AA_1A_2A_3\}=P.\{VV_1V_2V_3\}$$
and $$Q.\{AA_1A_2A_3\}=Q.\{VV_1V_2V_3\},$$
since the angles of the pencils are the same;
$$\therefore\ P.\{VV_1V_2V_3\}=Q.\{VV_1V_2V_3\},$$
and therefore, as before, the locus of V_3 is a conic through P, Q, V, V_1, V_2.

Fig. 130.

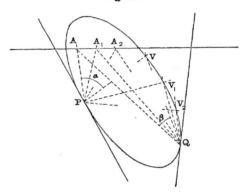

M. Chasles' extension of Newton's method.

If the point A instead of moving on a right line moves on any conic passing through the points P, Q, the locus of V is still a conic section, since
$$P.\{AA_1A_2A_3\}=Q.\{AA_1A_2A_3\}.$$

PROP. 17. *If there be any number of points a, b, c, d, &c. on a right line, and a homographic system a_1, b_1, c_1, d_1, &c. on another line, the lines joining corresponding points will envelope a conic.*

For if we construct the conic touched by the two given lines and by three lines aa_1, bb_1, cc_1, then, by the anharmonic property of the tangents of a conic (Prop. 8), any other of the lines dd_1 must touch the same conic.

PROBLEM 129. *Given two points A and B and a line L; given also two lines Sa, Sb, and a point O; to find on L a point, Q, such that if Om, On be drawn parallel respectively to AQ and BQ, meeting Sa in m and Sb in n, the line mn shall*

(α) *be parallel to a given direction R,*

(β) *pass through a given point P (Fig. 131).*

If two homographic pencils be drawn having O as common vertex, the envelope of the lines formed by joining the points in which the rays of the one meet Sa to the points in which the corresponding rays of the other meet Sb, is a conic section (Prop. 17).

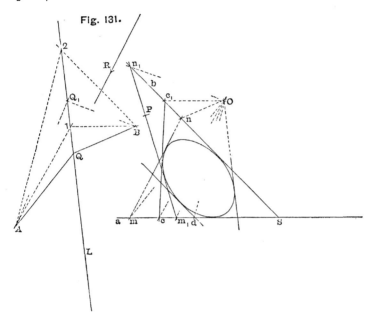

Fig. 131.

Draw therefore any lines $A1$, $A2$, $A3$, &c., meeting L in 1, 2, 3,... and through O draw parallels meeting Sa in c, d, e,... and parallels to $B1$, $B2$, $B3$,... meeting Sb in c_1 d_1 e_1.... The pencils $O(cde...)$, $O(c_1 d_1 e_1...)$ are homographic because the pencils $A(1, 2, 3...)$ and $B(1, 2, 3...)$ are so, and therefore cc_1, dd_1, ee_1 are tangents to a conic touching Sa and Sb, and which can therefore be constructed (Probs. 84 and 114).

In the figure the point d_1 is at an infinite distance (i.e. the tangent dd_1 is parallel to Sb) because the line $B2$ is drawn parallel to Sb.

A line through O parallel to the given line L is evidently a tangent to the conic to be constructed, so that it is only necessary to draw two pairs of lines $A1$, $B1$, $A2$, $B2$, since five tangents to the required conic are then known.

For the solution of the first part (a) draw mn, a tangent to this conic, parallel to the given direction R, and meeting Sa in m and Sn in n.

Then AQ drawn parallel to Om and BQ parallel to On will necessarily meet on the line L and determine the required point Q.

For the solution of the second part (β) it is evidently only necessary to draw a tangent from P to the conic cutting Sa in m_1 and Sb in n_1, and to draw through A and B parallels to Om_1 and On_1, which will meet in Q_1 on the given line L.

This problem is sometimes of importance in questions of Graphic Statics.

If A and B are on opposite sides of the line L, the conic is an hyperbola if O is situated in the acute angle formed by the lines Sa and Sb; and conversely if A and B are on the same side of L.

The conic will be a parabola when parallels to Sa, Sb, through A and B, meet in the same point on L.

EXAMPLES ON CHAPTER VIII.

1. Given on a conic three points A, B, C and three other points a, b, c, determine on the conic a point P such that $\{ABCP\}=\{abcP\}$.

[Either of the points in which the Pascal line (Prob. 85) meets the conic may be taken as the point P, i.e. draw Ac, Ca intersecting in K, Bc, Cb intersecting in L, and KL will cut the curve in the required point. For if cC meets KL in M, the anharmonic ratio of $ABCP$ is that of the pencil $c(ABCP)$, i.e. of the range $KLMP$, and the anharmonic ratio of $abcP$ is that of the pencil $C(abcP)$, i.e. again of the range $KLMP$.]

2. Inscribe in a given conic a triangle with its sides passing through three given points ABC.

[Draw any line through A meeting the conic in a and b, draw bB meeting the curve in c, and draw Cc, which will not in general pass through a but will meet the curve in d. Repeat this twice, giving a range aa_1a_2 and a second aa_1a_2. Find a point P such that $\{aa_1a_2P\} = \{aa_1a_2P\}$. P will be a vertex of one such triangle.]

3.　Given two straight lines AL, BL, draw a transversal meeting them in F and f, so that Ff shall subtend given angles a and β at two given points P and p.

[From the point A draw AP, Ap and construct the angles $APa = a$ and $Apb = \beta$, the points a and b being on BL. Imagine A to slide along AL and a and b will form two homographic divisions, and each of the double points gives a solution.]

4.　Given two straight lines AL, BL, draw a transversal meeting them in F and f passing through a given point P, and such that Ff subtends a given angle β at a second given point p.

[Last example, the angle a being zero.]

5.　Determine on a given straight line a segment which shall subtend given angles at two given points.

[The two lines of Ex. 3 coincide in direction.]

6.　Determine on a given straight line a segment of given length which shall subtend a given angle at a given point.

7.　Given two straight lines AL, BL and a point P, draw through P transversals cutting AL in F, G and BL in f, g, so that FG, fg are given lengths.

[Draw AP meeting BL in a. On AL make $AA_1 = FG$, and on BL make $aa_1 = fg$; draw Pa_1 cutting AL in a; A_1 and a will form homographic ranges, the double points of which give solutions.]

8.　Given on two straight lines AL, BL, two homographic ranges; draw through two given points P and p, lines Pa, pa_1 passing through homologous points a, a_1 of the ranges and containing between them a given angle θ.

[Take any point A on the first line and its homologous point B on the second. Draw pB and Pa meeting AL in a and making an angle θ with pB. Imagine A to slide along AL to A_1 and A_2, giving corresponding positions a_1, a_2, of a.

The range aa_1a_2 is homographic with AA_1A_2 because the pencils $p\,(BB_1B_2)$ and $P\,(aa_1a_2)$ are equiangular.

The double points of these ranges give two solutions.]

9. Given two lines Aa, Ab intersecting in A, the point a being fixed; given also a point S on the opposite side of Ab from a. Draw a line through S meeting Ab in P and Aa in p, and so that $AP = ap$.

[Problem 126, the fixed points being A and a, and the ratio one of equality.]

10. Two lines OAB, Oab meet in O; A, B, a and b are fixed points on the lines. If OAB remains fixed and Oab turns round O, shew that the locus of the intersection (S) of Aa and Bb is a circle having its centre (C) on AB, determined by drawing through any one position of S a parallel SC to the corresponding position of Oab.

[The anharmonic ratio of A, B, O, C is equal to the anharmonic ratio of abO and an infinitely distant point, so that C is fixed.]

11. Given two homographic ranges $ABC...$ $abc...$ on two lines, determine two homologous segments KL, kl which shall subtend given angles $KPL = a$, $kpl = \beta$ at two given points P, p.

[Take any point, as A, on the first range and construct the angle $APF = a$, and let a and f be the homologous points on the second range to A and F on the first. Construct the angle $apf_1 = \beta$, where f_1 is on the second range. Suppose the point A to slide along the first range and the points f and f_1 will form on the second range two homographic divisions, the double points of which will evidently determine two solutions of the question. Three angles, such as APF, have to be drawn to furnish three pairs of points on the second range.]

12. Given two homographic ranges $ABC...$ $abc...$ on two lines, determine two homologous segments KL and kl of given lengths.

[The principle of the solution of the last example is evidently applicable.]

CHAPTER IX.

PLANE SECTIONS OF THE CONE AND CYLINDER.

DEF. If any fixed point V be taken on a straight line passing through the centre O of a circle perpendicular to the plane of the circle, and a straight line move so as always to pass through the circumference of the circle and through the point V, the surface generated by the moving line is called a *Right Circular Cone*, and the line OV the axis of the cone. If any solid be conceived as divided into any two parts by any plane passing through the solid, the resulting plane surfaces of the solid in contact with the cutting plane are termed *sections* of the solid.

The most convenient way of treating any question on the sections of any solid figure, is by obtaining the projections of the solid on two planes at right angles to each other, the projection of a figure on any plane being, as already explained, the area traced out on the plane by perpendiculars drawn from all points of the figure to the plane.

The projection of any figure on a horizontal plane is called *its plan*, and on a vertical plane an *elevation* of the figure. In any given position therefore a solid can have but one plan but it may have any number of elevations, so that it is always possible to take the vertical plane on which an elevation is projected perpendicular to any plane of section of the solid.

For simplicity, the circular base of the cone will be supposed to be horizontal, and the vertical plane of projection perpendicular to the plane cutting the cone.

In figure 132 (p. 242) let o be the centre, and aob a diameter of a circle representing the base of a right circular cone resting on the plane of the paper; draw any line xy parallel to aob, and imagine the part of the paper above xy to be turned up along xy so as to stand perpendicularly to the part in front of that line; draw aa', $oo'v'$, and bb' all perpendicular to xy and meeting it in a', o and b' respectively; a' and b' will be respectively the elevations of a and b the extremities of the circular base, o' will be the elevation of the centre, and $o'v'$ will be the elevation of the axis of the cone. The plan of the axis is obviously the point o. Let the vertex of the cone be at the height $o'v'$ above the circular base ab, then v' will be the elevation of the vertex; and if the lines $a'v'$, $b'v'$ be drawn and produced indefinitely the triangle $a'v'b'$ will be the elevation of the portion of the cone between the vertex and the horizontal plane of projection. The angle $a'v'b'$ is called the vertical angle of the cone, and since the line $v'o'$ evidently bisects this angle either of the angles $a'v'o'$, $b'v'o'$ will be the semi-vertical angle.

It is evident that any section by a plane perpendicular to the axis, or parallel to the base of the cone, is a circle, the circle becoming infinitely small (i.e. the section being a point) when such plane passes through the vertex; and that the section by any plane through the vertex which cuts the cone in any other point (i.e. which lies within the vertical angle of the cone) will be two straight lines, the angle between which is greatest when the plane passes through the axis, in which case the angle is equal to the vertical angle, and the section is called a Principal Section.

PROBLEM 130. *To determine the section of a cone by a plane which does not contain the axis, and does not pass through the vertex.*

Case I. Suppose the angle which the plane makes with the horizontal plane to be equal to the angle $v'a'o'$, the base angle of the cone, fig. 132. Let the plane intersect the base of the cone in the line lm perpendicular to xy, the points l and m being on the base of the cone, i.e. on the circle ab, and let the line lm

E. 16

meet *xy* in *l'* ; draw *l'n'* parallel to *a'v'* meeting *b'v'* in *n'*.   The
line *lm* is the *horizontal trace,* and *l'n'* the *vertical trace* of the

Fig. 132.

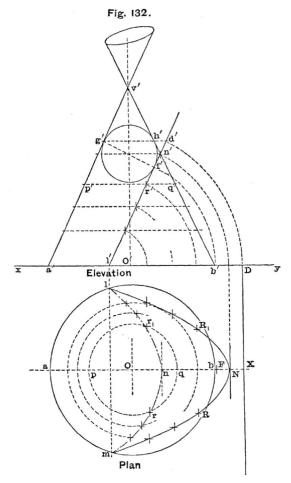

Elevation

Plan

section plane, those being the lines in which it cuts the planes of
projection respectively.   The *plan* of the point *n'* will evidently
be on the line *ob* vertically below *n'*, i.e. if *n'n* be drawn perpendicular to *xy* meeting *ob* in *n*, *n* will be the plan of *n'*.

Imagine a horizontal plane to cut the solid at any height
between the base and the point *n*, as at *p'q'* ; it will evidently
cut the cone in a circle of diameter *p'q'*, and which would in

plan have o for its centre, and it will cut the section plane in a horizontal line the elevation of which is the point r', and the plan of which is the line rr_1r' perpendicular to xy. The points of intersection of the circle and line will evidently be points on the desired curve of intersection, and therefore if r, r_1 are the points in which the plan of the line cuts the circle pq described with centre o and radius equal to $\frac{1}{2}p'q'$, these will be points on the projected curve of intersection. Similarly any number of additional points can be found by taking a series of planes parallel to $p'q'$. The curve lr_1nrm will be of course the plan of the required curve.

Now imagine the plane of section to be rotated round its horizontal trace lm until it coincides with the horizontal plane of projection, carrying with it the various points of intersection as found. In elevation they would of course travel over circular arcs described with l' as centre and with radii equal to the distances between l' and their respective elevations, while on plan they would travel along lines through their respective plans perpendicular to lm.

The point n would therefore reach N, the points r and r_1 would reach R and R_1 and so on, and the curve lR_1NRm would be the *true form* of the section made by the given plane.

Inscribe in the cone a sphere which will also touch the given plane of section. The *elevation* of such sphere will be the circle touching $v'a'$, $v'b'$ and $n'l'$; let it do so in the points g', h' and f', and let the line $g'h'$ meet $l'n'$ in d'.

d' will be the elevation of the line of intersection of the given section plane and of the plane through the circle of contact of the cone and the inscribed sphere. On being turned down along with the plane of section this line would therefore come into the position DX, while the point f' would come to F.

The required curve of intersection is a parabola having F for focus and DX for directrix.

Proof. The line whose elevation is $f'r'$, is a tangent to the inscribed sphere, since it lies in a tangent plane to that sphere (the given section plane) and passes through the point of contact

16—2

of that plane. It is therefore equal in length to any other tangent to the sphere drawn from the point whose elevation is r', and since r' is really on the surface of the cone, the length of the tangents drawn from it to the sphere must be equal to the line $h'q'$, which is evidently equal to $d'r'$, i.e. $FR = r'd' =$ the perpendicular distance of R from DX; therefore R is a point on the parabola described with focus F and directrix DX, and the same of course holds for any other point of the curve.

Case II. Let the angle which the plane of section makes with the horizontal plane be less than the angle $v'a'o'$, the base angle of the cone (fig. 133).

Proceeding exactly as before, let the plane intersect the plane of the base of the cone in the line lm perpendicular to xy, and draw $ln'n''$ making any angle less than the base angle of the cone with xy and meeting $v'a'$, $v'b'$ in n' and n''.

Take any horizontal plane (as $p'q'$) at any height between n' and n'', meeting $v'a'$ in p', $v'b'$ in q', and ln'' in r', and draw the plan of the circle in which this plane cuts the cone (the circle described with centre o and radius op, or $oq = \frac{1}{2}p'q'$) and of the line in which it cuts the section plane (through r' perpendicular to xy). The points of intersection r and r_1 of this circle and line will be the *plans* of two points on the required curve of section. Turning the plane round its horizontal trace until it coincides with the horizontal plane the point n' reaches N, the point n'' reaches N_1, and r and r_1 come to R and R_1 respectively. Similarly any number of points can be found, and it will be found that they lie on a closed curve.

Inscribe in the given cone spheres to touch also the given plane of section (two such can be drawn, one above and the other below the plane); let them touch the plane in f' and f'', and $v'a'$, $v'b'$ in g', g'', and h', h'' respectively: let $g'h'$ meet ln' in d', and $g''h''$ meet it in d''.

d' and d'' will be the elevations of the lines of intersection of the given plane of section with the planes of contact of the cone and its inscribed spheres.

Suppose f' and f'' and the lines through d' and d'' to be turned down along with the plane of section so that f' comes to F, f'' to F_1, and the lines to DX and D_1X_1 respectively, and the curve of section will be an ellipse with foci F and F_1 with directrices DX and D_1X_1.

Fig. 133.

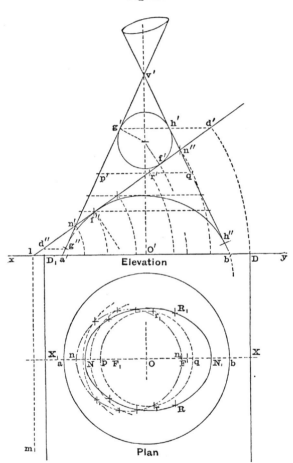

Elevation

Plan

Proof. The line whose elevation is $f'r'$ is a tangent to the inscribed sphere, since it lies in a tangent plane to that sphere (the given section plane) and passes through the point of contact of that plane. It is therefore equal in length to any other tangent to the sphere drawn from the point whose elevation is r'; and since r' is really on the surface of the cone, the length of the tangents drawn from it to the sphere must be equal to the line $h'q'$, which is always in a constant ratio to but is less than $d'r'$, since the angle $d'r'q'$ is less than $h'q'r'$, i.e. FR is always in a constant ratio, smaller than unity, to the perpendicular distance of R from DX.

Therefore R is a point on the ellipse described with focus F and directrix DX, and the same of course holds for any other point on the curve.

Case III. Let the angle which the plane of section makes with the horizontal plane be greater than the angle $v'a'o'$, the base angle of the cone (fig. 134).

The description of the last case applies exactly to the present, and the figure is lettered to correspond. The plane will necessarily cut both sheets of the cone, and the curve will consist of two infinite branches.

It will be found to be an hyperbola with foci F and F_1 and with directrices DX and DX_1.

Proof. In this case the line $h'q'$ is always in a constant ratio to but is greater than the line $d'r'$. Hence the distance of any point on the curve from the focus F is always in a constant ratio, greater than unity, to its distance from the directrix DX.

The two straight lines in which a cone is intersected by a plane through the vertex parallel to an hyperbolic section are parallel to the asymptotes of the hyperbola.

The asymptotes may be thus found. They of course pass through the point C midway between X and X_1. Draw the generators of the cone parallel to the given section plane, i.e. draw $v'w'$ parallel to $l'n'$, which will be the elevation of such generators, and project w' to w and w_1 on the base of the cone. The tangent planes to the cone along the generators whose plans are ow, ow_1 and whose elevations are $v'w'$ will intersect the given plane of section in the required asymptotes. If therefore a tangent at w to the circular base of the cone meet lm (the horizontal trace of the given section plane) in W, W will be a point on one asymptote, which will therefore be the line CW. Similarly the second asymptote can be obtained from the point w_1.

Fig. 134.

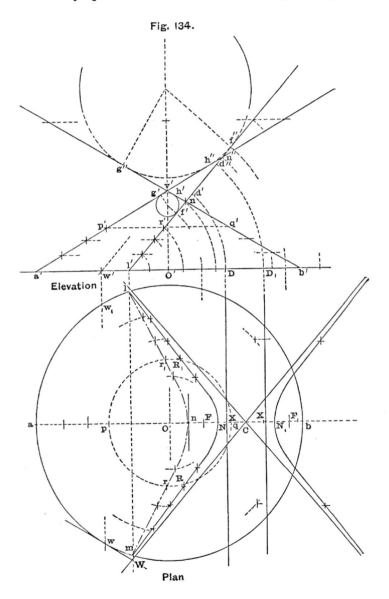

Elevation

Plan

PROBLEM 131. *To cut a conic of given eccentricity from a given cone* (Fig. 135).

Let $v'a'b'$ be the elevation of the given cone, and let the eccentricity be $\dfrac{m}{n}$ given by two lines m and n. From o', the foot of the axis of the cone, set off along the axis a length $o'd = n$ and

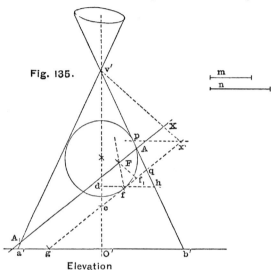

Fig. 135.

Elevation

$o'e = m$; through d draw dh parallel to the base of the cone meeting the slant side in h; from e with radius hb' (the distance between h and the foot of the slant side) describe an arc cutting $a'b'$ in g; the required section plane must be inclined to the horizontal plane at the angle ego', and all sections made by planes inclined at this angle will have the same eccentricity.

Proof. Produce ge to meet the slant side of the cone in q, and in the cone inscribe a sphere touching the plane of section geq in the point f and the slant side $v'b'$ in p: through p draw px parallel to the base of the cone meeting geq in x.

In the triangle pqx,
$$pq : qx :: \sin pxq : \sin qpx\,;$$
but $pq = fq$, the angle $pxq =$ the angle ego', and the angle $qpx =$ the angle $hb'g$.

$$\therefore \ \frac{fq}{qx} = \frac{\sin ego'}{\sin hb'g} = \frac{eo'}{eg} \div \frac{do'}{hb'} = \frac{m}{n}, \text{ since } eg = hb'\,;$$

but f is the focus, q the vertex, and x the trace of the directrix of the section made by the plane geq.

If the conic is to be an hyperbola, i.e. if $m > n$, there is a limit to the vertical angle of the cone in order that the problem may be possible.   It will be observed that the length eg is $\dfrac{n}{\cos a}$, where a is the semi-vertical angle of the cone, and eg must evidently be greater than eo' or m.

Therefore $\dfrac{n}{m}$ must be greater than $\cos a$ or $a > \cos^{-1} \dfrac{n}{m}$, i.e. a must be greater than the angle whose cosine is $\dfrac{n}{m}$, or in other words the ratio of the height of the cone to length of slant side must be less than $\dfrac{n}{m}$.

PROBLEM 132.   *From a given cone to cut a conic of given eccentricity and having a given distance FX between focus and directrix* (Fig. 135).

As in the last problem, draw some one plane of section of the required eccentricity, as geq, and determine its focus f and the trace (x) of its directrix.

Draw $v'x$, $v'f$ to the vertex of the cone; on xf make $xf_1 =$ the given distance FX, and through f_1 draw $f_1 F$ parallel to xv' meeting fv' in F.   Through F draw a line parallel to gq meeting the slant sides of the cone in A and A_1 and xv' in X.   This will be the trace of the required plane of section, A and A_1 being the vertices, F a focus, and X the trace of one of the directrices.

DEF.   If a straight line move so as to pass through the circumference of a given circle, and to be perpendicular to the plane of the circle, it traces out a surface called a *Right Circular Cylinder*.   The straight line drawn through the centre of the circle perpendicular to its plane is the *axis* of the cylinder.

The cylinder may evidently be regarded as a particular case of the cone, the vertex being at an infinite distance from the base so that the generators are ultimately parallel.

As with the right circular cone, it is evident that a section of the surface by any plane perpendicular to the axis is a circle, and that a section by any plane parallel to the axis (i.e. passing through the infinitely distant vertex) consists of two parallel lines.

PROBLEM 133. *To determine the section of a right circular cylinder by a plane inclined at any given angle (θ) to the axis* (Fig. 136).

Let *lm* be the line of intersection of the given plane of section with the horizontal plane of the base of the cylinder, i.e. the

Fig. 136.

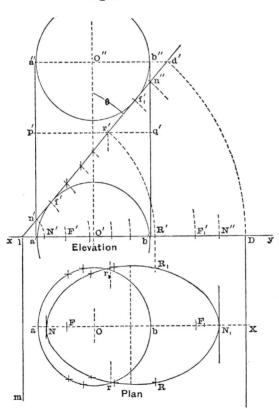

horizontal trace of the plane of section. Draw any ground line *xly* perpendicular to *lm*, and through *l* draw *ld'* making the angle

$d'ly$ equal to the complement of the given angle θ.   Let o be the plan of the axis of the cone, and through o draw $oo'o''$ perpendicular to xy; $o'o''$ will be the elevation of the axis of the cone on the vertical plane of projection, and ld' will be the trace on the same plane of the given section plane.

With centre o and radius equal to that of the cylinder describe a circle ab, and draw aob perpendicular to lm; through a and b draw $aa'a''$, $bb'b''$ perpendicular to xy, meeting it in a' and b', and the rectangle $a''a'b'b''$ will be the elevation of the cylinder.   Let ld' cut $a'a''$ in n' and $b'b''$ in n''.

Imagine a horizontal plane to cut the solid at any height between n' and n'', as at $p'q'$; it will evidently cut the cylinder in a circle of diameter $p'q'$, and which would in plan have o for its centre, and it will cut the section plane in a horizontal line the elevation of which is the point r', in which $p'q'$ cuts ld' and the plan of which is the line rr_1r' perpendicular to xy.   The points of intersection of the circle and line will evidently be points on the desired curve of intersection, and therefore if r, r_1 are the points in which the plan of the line cuts the circle ab (which is of course the *plan* of the circle $p'q'$) these will be the *plans* of the points in which the horizontal plane at the height $a'p'$ above the base of the cylinder cuts the required curve of intersection.

Now imagine the plane of section to be rotated round its horizontal trace lm until it coincides with the horizontal plane of projection.   In elevation the point r' would travel over the circular arc $r'R'$ struck with l as centre, meeting the ground line in R', while on plan the points r and r_1 would travel along lines rR, r_1R_1 perpendicular to lm. reaching the horizontal plane of projection in the points R, R_1 found by drawing $R'R_1R$ perpendicular to xy.

Similarly any number of additional points can be found by drawing a series of planes parallel to $p'q'$, all of which will of course cut the cylinder in circles, the plans of which are the circle ab.

The point n' travels in elevation over the arc $n'N'$, and the plan of N' is simultaneously on ab and on $N'N$ perpendicular to xy; and the point n'', the plan of which is b, similarly reaches the horizontal plane at N_1.

The required curve of intersection is *an ellipse* having NN_1 for major axis, and for minor axis a length equal to the diameter of the cylinder.

The minor axes of all ellipses which can be cut from the same cylinder are consequently of equal length, but the length of the major axis depends jointly on the diameter of the cylinder and the inclination of the cutting plane to its axis, since

$$n'n'' = a'b' \operatorname{cosec} \theta.$$

Just as in the case of the cone, if spheres be inscribed in the cylinder touching the plane of section they will do so in the foci of the curve of intersection. The elevations of these spheres are the circles shewn in the figure touching the line ld' in the points f' and f_1', and also touching $a'a''$, $b'b''$. f' travels over the circular arc $f'F'$, and $F'F$ perpendicular to xy, meeting ab in F, determines F, one of the foci.

The horizontal planes through the circles of contact of the spheres and cylinder intersect the plane of section in the directrices of the curve. d' is therefore the elevation of one of them, which after rotation of the section plane round lm comes into the position DX.

Proof. The line whose elevation is $f_1'r'$ is a tangent to the inscribed sphere, since it lies in a tangent plane to that sphere (the given section plane) and passes through the point f_1' in which the sphere touches the plane. It is therefore equal in length to any other tangent to the sphere drawn from the point whose elevation is r', and since r' is really on the surface of the cylinder, the length of the tangents drawn from it to the sphere must be $r'k'$, where $r'k'$ is parallel to the axis of the cylinder, and k' is on the circle of contact of sphere and cylinder. But $r'k' : r'd'$ in a constant ratio $= \cos \theta$, and $r'k' = F_1R$; $r'd' = RM$, where RM is perpendicular to DX meeting it in M, therefore $F_1R : RM$ in a constant ratio, or the locus of R is an ellipse.

THE OBLIQUE CYLINDER.

DEF. If a straight line, which is not perpendicular to the plane of a given circle, move parallel to itself, and always pass through the circumference of the circle, the surface generated is called an oblique cylinder.

The line through the centre of the circular base parallel to the generating lines is the axis of the cylinder.

The section of the cylinder made by a plane containing the axis and perpendicular to the base is called the *principal section*.

The section of the cylinder by a plane perpendicular to the principal section, and inclined to the axis at the same angle as the base, is called a *sub-contrary section*.

It is evident that any section by a plane parallel to the axis consists of two parallel lines, and that any section by a plane parallel to the base is a circle.

PROBLEM 134. *To determine the sub-contrary section of an oblique cylinder.*

Let o (fig. 137) be the centre of the circular base, and the circle on ab as diameter the base of the cylinder; let ob be the plan of the axis. Draw xy parallel to ab, so that the elevation on xy as ground line will be parallel to the principal section of the cylinder; draw aa', oo', bb' perpendicular to xy meeting it in a', o', b', which will be the elevations of the corresponding points of the base. Since the elevation is parallel to the principal section, the angle which the elevation of the axis (i.e. the line $o'c'$) makes with the ground line will be the real angle which the axis itself makes with the horizontal plane. Draw $a'a_1'$, $b'b_1'$ parallel to $o'c'$, these lines are the elevations of the bounding lines of the solid projected on the vertical plane standing on xy. Draw any line $a_1'b_1'l$ making the same angle θ with $o'c'$ as $o'c'$ makes with xy, meeting xy in l, and draw lm perpendicular to xy.

lm will be the horizontal trace and la_1' the vertical trace of a plane of sub-contrary section; and if this plane be rotated round lm till it coincides with the horizontal plane, every point on the

surface of the cylinder between a_1' and b_1' will evidently reach a point on the circle on ab as diameter, i.e. the true form of the sub-contrary section is a circle.

The horizontal projection of the sub-contrary section is the ellipse having cc_1 projected from c', the point in which $a_1'b_1'$ intersects the axis of the cylinder as major axis, and a_1b_1 the projection of $a_1'b_1'$ as minor.

PROBLEM 135.   *To determine the section of an oblique cylinder by a plane not parallel to the axis, to the base, or to a sub-contrary section.*

Case I.   Let the plane of section be perpendicular to the principal section (fig. 137).

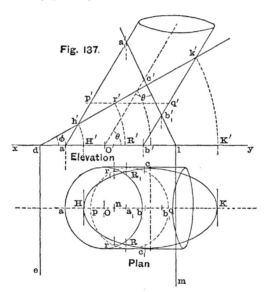

The horizontal trace (de) of the plane of section must be drawn perpendicular to ab, the plan of the axis.   If the plane of section makes an angle (ϕ) with the horizontal plane, the vertical trace must be drawn through d making this angle with xy.   Let it meet $a'a_1'$ in h' and $b'b_1'$ in k'.

Draw any circular section, as $p'q'$, between h' and k' meeting dk' in r_1'; the plan is of course the circle on pq as diameter projected from p' and q' on ab, and if the projection of the point r' cuts this circle in r and r_1 these will be the *plans* of two points on the required curve.   If rr_1 meet pq in n we have $rn^2 = pn \cdot nq$. If now the plane of section be rotated round de till it coincides with the horizontal plane, h' travels in elevation to H' and in plan to H, k' travels in elevation to K' and in plan to K, and r and r_1 reach R and R_1 respectively.   Therefore if RR_1 meet ab in N, $$RN^2 = pn \cdot nq = p'r' \cdot r'q' \, ;$$

but $p'r' : h'r'$ in a constant ratio,

and $r'q' : r'k'$ in the same ratio,

$\therefore \; p'r' \cdot r'q' : h'r' \cdot r'k'$ in a constant ratio ;

but $h'r' \cdot r'k' = HN \cdot NK,$

$\therefore \; RN^2 : HN \cdot NK$ in a constant ratio,

or the locus of R is an ellipse (Prop. 4, p. 108).

Case II.   Let the plane cut the cylinder in any manner (fig. 138).

Let ab be the diameter of the base perpendicular to the horizontal trace of proposed section plane.

The circle on ab is the plan of the base of the cylinder, ov the plan, and $o'v'$ the elevation of its axis, the elevation being projected on a plane perpendicular to the proposed section plane.   Lines through a and b parallel to ov are of course the plans of the generators through a and b, and if a and b are projected on to the ground line at a' and b' lines through these points parallel to $o'v'$ will be the elevations of these generators and will be the bounding lines of the solid as seen in the proposed elevation.

lm is the horizontal trace, and ln_1' the vertical trace of the section plane ; let $a'n'$ parallel to $o'v'$ meet ln_1' in n', and $b'n_1'$ meet it in n_1' ; n' and n_1' are evidently points on the required curve of intersection, and their plans n and n_1 are found by projecting n' and n_1' on to the plans of the generators through a and b.   Take any horizontal section of the cylinder between n' and n_1', as $p'q'$; the plan is of course a circle of diameter $p'q'$, and its position can be determined by projecting p' and q' on to the plans of the generators through a and b, as at p, q. This horizontal section and the proposed section plane intersect in a line the

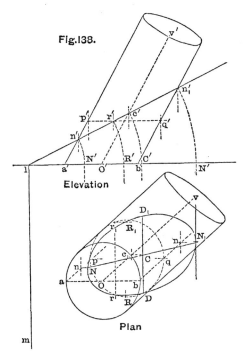

Fig.138.

Elevation

Plan

elevation of which is r', the point in which $p'q'$ cuts ln_1', and the plan of this line cuts the circle pq in points r and r_1 projected from r', which are *plans* of points on the required curve of intersection.

Now rotate the section plane round lm, its horizontal trace, till it coincides with the horizontal plane: in elevation the points n', r', n_1' travel over circular arcs to N', R', N_1'; in plan n, r, r_1, n_1 travel over lines perpendicular to lm to N, R, R_1, N_1, obtained by projecting N', R' and N_1'.

These are points situated on the true outline of the curve of intersection, and any additional number of points can be obtained in precisely the same manner. The curve is an ellipse having NN_1 as a diameter and RR_1 as a corresponding double ordinate, so that DD_1, the diameter conjugate to NN_1, can at once be drawn by bisecting NN_1 in C, drawing through C a parallel to RR_1 or to lm, and making on it $CD = CD_1 = ao$ the radius of circular base of cylinder.   That the curve is an ellipse may be proved similarly to Case I.

THE OBLIQUE CONE.

DEF.   If a straight line pass always through a fixed point and the circumference of a fixed circle, and if the fixed point be not in the straight line through the centre of the circle at right angles to its plane, the surface generated is called an *oblique cone*.

The fixed point is called the *vertex* and the line joining the vertex to the centre of the circle the *axis* of the cone.

The section of the cone made by a plane containing this axis and perpendicular to the circular base, is called the *principal section*.

The section made by a plane not parallel to the base, but perpendicular to the principal section, and inclined to the generating lines in that section at the same angles as the base, is called a *sub-contrary section*.

PROBLEM 136.   *To determine the sub-contrary section of an oblique cone* (Fig. 139).

Let o be the centre and oa the radius of the circular base, and let ov be the plan of the axis.   Draw a ground line xy parallel to ov, and let v' be the elevation of the vertex on a vertical plane standing on xy.   Project o to o', and the circular base to $a'b'$, so that $o'v'$ will be the elevation of the axis, and $a'v'b'$ the outline of the cone; $a'v'b'$ is evidently also identical with the principal section.

Draw any line $e'd'l$ making the angle $a'e'l =$ the angle $v'b'y$, and meeting $v'b'$ in d' and xy in l; the angle $e'd'v'$ is evidently equal to the angle $v'a'b'$, so that $e'l$ may be taken as the vertical trace of the plane of a sub-contrary section, the horizontal trace of which must be the line lm perpendicular to xy.

E.   17

Take any horizontal section as $p'q'$ between d' and e', the plan of which will be a circle on pq as diameter, p and q being

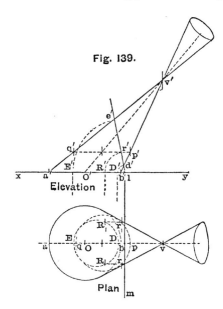

Fig. 139.

the projections of p' and q' on the plan of the axis or central plane of the cone. The plane of this section intersects the plane of sub-contrary section in a straight line, the elevation of which is the point r' in which $p'q'$ intersects le', and the plan of which is rr_1 projected from r'. If rr_1 meet the circle on pq in r and r_1, these will be plans of two points on the required curve of sub-contrary section, and if rr_1 meet pq in n,

$$rn^2 = np \cdot nq = r'q' \cdot r'p' = r'd' \cdot r'e';$$

since a circle can be described round $e'q'd'p'$.

Rotate the plane of section round its horizontal trace till it coincides with the horizontal plane of projection, and e', r' and d' travel to E', R' and D' the corresponding positions in plan being E, R and R_1 and D their projections. These are of course points on the real outline of the required curve, and if RR_1 meet ED in N, since

$$RN = rn, \quad EN = e'r', \quad ND = r'd',$$

we have $$RN^2 = EN \cdot ND,$$
or the locus of R is a circle on ED as diameter,

i. e. the sub-contrary section of an oblique cone is a circle.

It is evident that all sections parallel to the base or to the plane $e'lm$ are also circles.

Planes parallel to the base, or to a sub-contrary section, are called also *Cyclic Planes*.

PROBLEM 137.   *To determine the section of an oblique cone by a plane not parallel to a cyclic plane and not passing through the vertex* (Fig. 140).

Case I.   Let the plane be parallel to a tangent plane of the

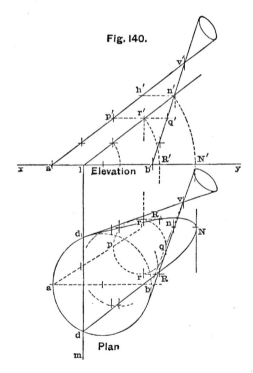

Fig. 140.

cone, i. e. let it be parallel to a generator and perpendicular to the plane containing that generator and the axis.

17—2

Let $a'v'b'$ be the elevation of the cone, v the plan of the vertex the elevation of which is v', and ab the diameter of the circular base parallel to the plane of the elevation.

It is convenient to take the plane of section perpendicular to the plane of the elevation; so that its horizontal trace lm may be drawn perpendicular to xy, and its vertical trace must then be drawn parallel either to $a'v'$ or to $b'v'$, since the plane itself must be parallel to one or other of these generators—let ln' parallel to $a'v'$ be its vertical trace. If lm cuts the circle on ab as diameter in d and d_1, these will be points on the required curve of intersection, and if ln' meets $b'v'$ in n', n' will be the elevation of another point, the plan of which will be n, the intersection of bv and the projection of n'.

Draw any horizontal plane as $p'q'$ between l and n', meeting $a'v'$ in p', $b'v'$ in q' and ln' in r'; this plane cuts the cone in a circle the elevation of which is $p'q'$, and the plan of which is a circle on pq as diameter obtained by projecting p' and q' on av and bv respectively. It meets the section plane in a line the elevation of which is the point r', and the plan of which is the line rr_1 projected from r'; if this line meets the circle on pq in r and r_1, these are the *plans* of two points on the required curve of intersection and similarly the plans of any additional number of points can be obtained.

Rotate the section plane round its horizontal trace till it coincides with the horizontal plane of projection; the point n' travels in elevation to N' and the point r' to R'; in plan n, r, and r_1 travel along nN, rR and r_1R_1 perpendicular to lm till they meet the projections of N' and R' respectively, and d, R, N, R_1 and d_1 will be points on the real outline of the required curve of intersection. It is a parabola having the tangent at N parallel to RR_1.

Proof. If K bisects RR_1, $KR^2 = p'r' \cdot r'q'$.

Through n' draw $h'n'$ parallel to $p'q'$ meeting $a'v'$ in h', then $h'n' = p'r'$,

$$r'q' : r'n' :: h'n' : h'v';$$

$$\therefore\ p'r' \cdot r'q'\ :\ h'n' \cdot r'n'\ ::\ h'n'\ :\ h'v',$$

$$\therefore\ KR^2\ :\ h'n' \cdot r'n'\ \text{in a constant ratio,}$$

but $r'n' = KN \cos\theta$, where θ is the angle between KN and pq, and is constant;

$\therefore\ KR^2 = KN$ multiplied by some constant, or the locus of K is a parabola.

Case II. Let the plane of section meet all the generating lines on the same side of the vertex (Fig. 141).

Let $a'v'b'$ be the elevation of the cone, v the plan of v' the vertex, and ab the diameter of the circular base parallel to the

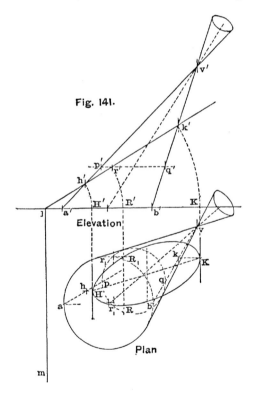

Fig. 141.

ground line and therefore the plan of $a'b'$. Let the plane of section be perpendicular to the vertical plane of projection, and draw its horizontal trace lm perpendicular to xy and its vertical trace cutting $a'v'$ in h', and $b'v'$ in k'. Project h' to h on av and k' to k on bv, then h and k are the *plans* of the points in which the generators through a and b meet the section plane, i. e. are the plans of two points on the required curve of intersection.

Imagine the cone cut by any horizontal plane as $p'q'$ between h' and k', the elevation of the curve of intersection will be the line $p'q'$, meeting $a'v'$ in p' and $b'v'$ in q' and lk' in r'; and the plan will be the circle on pq as diameter, obtained by projecting p' on av and q' on bv. The required plane of section cuts this plane of circular section in a line the elevation of which is r', and the plan of which is rr_1 projected from r'. If rr_1 meets the circle on pq in the points r and r_1, these are the plans of two points of the required curve of intersection. Similarly the plans of any additional number of points can be obtained.

Rotate the plane of section round its horizontal trace till it coincides with the horizontal plane of projection; in elevation h', r' and k' travel to H', R', and K', and on plan h, r, r_1 and k travel along hH, rR, r_1R_1, kK, perpendicular to lm till they meet the projections of H', R' and K'. The points H, R, K, R_1 are points on the real outline of the required curve of intersection. It is an ellipse having HK as a diameter, and RR_1 as corresponding double ordinate.

Case III. Let the section plane cut both sheets of the cone (Fig. 142).

Let $a'v'b'$ be the elevation of the cone, v the plan of v' the vertex, and ab the diameter of the circular base parallel to the ground line, and therefore the plan of $a'b'$. Let the plane of section be perpendicular to the vertical plane of projection, and draw its horizontal trace lm perpendicular to xy, and its vertical trace lk' cutting $b'v'$ in h', and $a'v'$ in k'. Project h' to h on bv, and k' to k on av, then h and k are the *plans* of the points in which the generators through a and b meet the section plane, i.e. are the plans of two points on the required curve of intersection. Imagine the cone cut by any horizontal plane as $p'q'$; the elevation of the circle in which this plane meets the cone will be

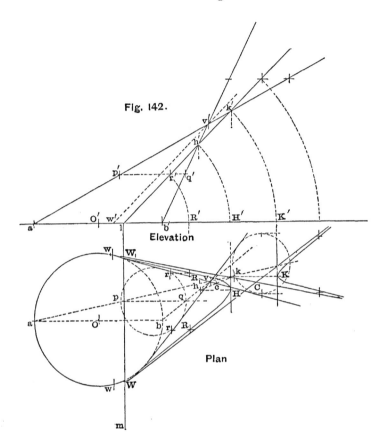

Fig. 142.

Elevation

Plan

the line $p'q'$ meeting $a'v'$ in p', $b'v'$ in q', and lk' in r', and the plan will be the circle on pq as diameter obtained by projecting p' and q' on av and bv respectively. The required plane of section cuts this plane of circular section in a line, the elevation of which is r', and the plan of which is rr_1 projected from r'. If rr_1 meets the circle on pq in the points r and r_1, these are the plans of two points of the required curve of intersection. Similarly the plans of any additional number of points can be obtained.

Rotate the plane of section round its horizontal trace lm till it coincides with the horizontal plane of projection ; in elevation h', r' and k' travel to H', R' and K', and on plan h, r, r_1 and k travel along hH, rR, r_1R_1, kK perpendicular to lm till they meet the projections of H', R' and K'. The points H, R, R_1 and K are points on the real outline of the required curve of intersection. It is an hyperbola having HK as a diameter, and RR_1 as corresponding double ordinate of the branch through H.

The asymptotes are parallel to the generators of the cone which are parallel to the plane of section. If therefore $v'w'$ be drawn parallel to lk' meeting xy in w', and w' be projected to meet the circular base ab in w and w_1, the *plans* of the asymptotes will be parallel to vw, vw_1. Bisect hk in c, and draw cW, cW_1 parallel respectively to vw and vw_1, and meeting lm in W, W_1 which will be points on the asymptotes, and they can therefore be drawn through C the point of bisection of HK.

Examples on Chapter IX.

1. AVA_1, an isosceles triangle, obtuse angled at V, is the elevation of a cone. Shew that if VB be drawn meeting AA_1 in B, and such that $\overline{VB}|^2 = AB . BA_1$ (Ex. 15, Chap. II.) and any plane be drawn having its vertical trace parallel to VB, and horizontal trace perpendicular to AA_1, it will cut the cone in a rectangular hyperbola.

2. Given a cone and a point inside it determine the conics which have the given point as focus.

[Draw an elevation $a'v'b'$ on a plane parallel to the plane containing the axis of the cone and the given point, and let f' be the elevation of the given point. The vertical traces of the required planes of section must be tangents at f' to the circles touching $a'v$ and $b'v'$, and passing through f'. Two solutions are generally possible.]

3. Shew that all sections of a right cone, made by planes parallel to tangent planes of the cone, are parabolas, and that the foci lie on a cone having with the first a common vertex and axis.

[Shew that the foci of parallel sections lie on a straight line through the vertex.]

4. Find the least angle of a cone from which it is possible to cut an hyperbola, whose eccentricity shall be the ratio of two to one.

5. Cut from a right cylinder an ellipse whose eccentricity shall be the ratio of the side of a square to its diagonal.

[In the cylinder inscribe a sphere, centre C; determine a point X in the horizontal plane through the centre such that $\dfrac{r}{CX} = $ the above ratio, where r is the radius of the sphere. The required plane of section must be a tangent plane to the sphere through the point X.]

6. Shew how to cut from a given cone a hyperbola whose asymptotes shall contain the greatest possible angle.

[The plane of section must be parallel to the axis, pp. 246 and 241.]

7. Cut from a given cone the hyperbola of greatest eccentricity.

[The plane of section must be parallel to the axis, p. 248.]

8. Different elliptic sections of a right cone are taken having equal major axes; shew that the locus of the centres of the sections is a spheroid, oblate or prolate, according as the vertical angle of the cone is greater or less than 90°.

[Consider a series of sections perpendicular to a principal section of the cone. The centre is a fixed point on a line of constant length (the major axis), sliding between two fixed lines (the two generators of that section). It therefore traces out an ellipse which by revolution round the axis of the cone generates a spheroid.]

9. Different elliptic sections of a right cone are taken such that their minor axes are equal; shew that the locus of their centres is the surface formed by the revolution of an hyperbola about the axis of the cone.

[Consider a series of sections perpendicular to a principal section of the cone. Take any section parallel to the base and divide the diameter of that section, so that the product of the two parts $= b^2$ where b is the semi-length of the constant minor axis; the corresponding elliptic section must pass through this point of division, and all these points lie on a hyperbola, the asymptotes of which are the generators of the principal section taken (Prop. 1, p. 160).]

10. Shew how to cut a right cone so that the section may be an ellipse whose axes are of given lengths.

[The centre of the section made by the plane perpendicular to any principal section must be the intersection of the ellipse and hyperbola in which such principal section cuts the surfaces referred to in examples 8 and 9.]

11. Shew how to cut from a right cone a section of given latus rectum.

[Any point F on a hyperbola described as in Ex. 9 may be taken as focus, and the plane of section must be a tangent plane at F to the sphere inscribed in the cone, and passing through F.]

CHAPTER X.

WHEN one curve rolls without sliding upon another, any point invariably connected with the rolling curve describes another curve, called a *roulette*. The curve which rolls is called the generating curve, and the curve on which it rolls is called the directing curve, or the *base*.

Only a few of the simpler examples of roulettes are here given, the first being the most simple of all, viz. the cycloid.

DEF. The cycloid is the path described by a point on the circumference of a circle, rolling upon a fixed right line, in one plane passing through the line.

In the construction this plane coincides with the plane of the paper.

PROBLEM 138. *To describe a cycloid, the diameter of the circle being given* (Fig. 143).

Let AB be the diameter of the given circle, C its centre, and suppose that the tracing point is the point B, and that at the moment A is the point of contact of the circle with the directing line. Draw the directing line XAY a tangent at A to the circle. The tracing point B will evidently reach the guiding line at points X and Y on opposite sides of A such that $AX = AY =$ the semi-circumference AB, since each point of the semi-circumference comes down successively on a corresponding point of the line.

The following geometrical construction gives an exceedingly close approximation to the length of the circumference of a circle:—From C, the centre, draw a radius CH making an angle of $30°$ with the radius CB, and draw HK perpendicular to AB meeting it in K. At A, the extremity of the diameter through B, draw a tangent to the circle and on it make $AL = 3 \cdot AB$. KL will be

Fig. 143.

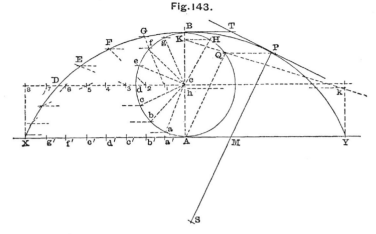

very nearly the circumference of the circle and its semi-length
may be taken for the length AX or AY.

[In the figure L does not fall within the limits of the paper,
but if AK is bisected in h and hk on a parallel to the tangent at A
be made $= 3$ times the radius of the circle, Kk may be taken as the
semi-circumference.]

Divide up AX into any number of equal parts (say 8) as at
a', b', c',... and divide the semi-circumference AB into the same
number as at a, b, c,...   Draw a line through C parallel to XAY,
which will evidently be the path of the centre of the circle, i.e. as
the circle rolls along AX the centre will always be on this line;
and draw $a'1$, $b'2$, $c'3$... perpendicular to AX, the points 1, 2, 3, &c.,
being on the path of the centre.   The point a will evidently come
down to a', b to b', and so on; and when a has come to a', the
centre of the circle will be at 1 and the tracing point will be on a
line making an angle with $a'1$ equal to the angle aCB, which is of
course equal to ACg, since $Aa = gB$.   Draw $1G$ parallel to Cg and
make $1G = Cg$, the radius of the rolling circle. G will be a point
on the required curve.

Similarly, when b has rolled down to b', the centre of the circle
will be at 2 vertically above b', the tracing point will be on a line
making with $b'2$ an angle $=$ the angle bCB, i.e. $=$ the angle ACf, or

it will be on a line $2F$ parallel to Cf and at a distance from 2 equal to the radius of the circle.

Similarly for the remaining points c', d', &c.

It will be noticed that the lengths $1G$, $2F$, &c., may be determined without actual measurement by drawing through g, f, &c., parallels to AX meeting the corresponding lines through 1, 2, &c., in the points G, F, &c., the figures $1CgG$, $2CfF$ are parallelograms and therefore in each case $1G = Cg$, $2F = Cf$, and so on.

The curve should be drawn free-hand through the series of points thus found, and the half loop corresponding to the circle rolling on AY may be found by the same construction or may be put in by symmetry. The line $X8$ is a tangent to the curve at the point X.

The length AX may be determined arithmetically by multiplying the length of the radius AC by $3.14...$ and may then be laid down by scale : the diagonal scales usually supplied with cases of mathematical instruments can conveniently be used for the purpose. In many works on geometry the length AX is determined by dividing up the semi-circle into any number of equal parts (say n) and laying off along AX the length of the chord of one of the parts repeated n times. This method is radically bad and should never be adopted : if the number of equal parts into which the semi-circle is divided is small it gives only a very rough approximation to the truth, while if the number is increased it is almost impossible to measure the length of the chord so accurately but that in repeating it n times an appreciable error will be introduced. A long length should in fact never be determined as the sum of a series of short ones.

To draw the normal at any point of a cycloid.

In all roulettes the normal at any point passes through the corresponding point of contact of the rolling and guiding curves. This point is called the *Instantaneous Centre*. The *direction of motion* of the tracing point will evidently at any moment be perpendicular to the line between it and the point about which the rolling curve is turning, i.e. the corresponding instantaneous centre, and since the direction of motion at any point must co-incide with the tangent at that point, the normal must pass through the instantaneous centre.

In the figure, when the tracing point is at E the centre is at 3 and c' is the instantaneous centre, so that Ec' is the normal at E; this is evidently parallel to eA, e being the point in which a parallel to AX through E meets the circle on AB as diameter, so that the normal at any point P may be thus constructed :—

Through P draw a parallel to the directing line AY meeting the circle on AB in the point Q. The normal at P will be parallel to AQ, and since the angle AQB is a right angle the tangent at P will be parallel to QB.

If the normal at P meet the directing line in M and PM be produced to S so that $PS = 2PM$, S will be the centre of curvature at the point P. The evolute of the cycloid is two equal semi-cycloids, the vertices being at X and Y and the cusp on BA produced at a distance from $A = AB$.

Let the tangent at P meet the tangent at the vertex in T, then the length of the arc BP of the cycloid is double the intercept TP of the tangent, i.e. double the chord BQ of the circle. Hence the whole length of the cycloid is 4 times the diameter of the generating circle.

DEF. If, as in the cycloid, a circle rolls along a straight line, any point in the plane of the circle but not on its circumference traces out a curve called a *Trochoid*.

PROBLEM 139. *To describe a trochoid, the diameter of the circle and the distance of the tracing point from its centre being given* (Fig. 144).

Let AB be the diameter of the given circle, C its centre, and CP the distance of the tracing point from the centre.

Draw XAY a tangent to the circle, and as in the last problem determine the length AX or AY equal to the semi-circumference of the circle AB. Draw $C8$, the path of the centre, through C parallel to XAY, and through X draw $X8$ perpendicular to XA.

Divide $C8$ into any number of equal parts (8 in the fig.), and with centre C and radius CP draw a circle. The point P in which this

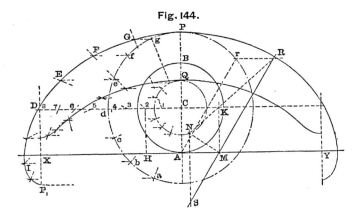

Fig. 144.

circle cuts AB produced will be the vertex of the required curve. Divide the semi-circumference of the circle into the same number of equal parts Pg, gf, &c., as has been chosen for the division of the path of the centre.

Draw $1G$ parallel to Cg and gG parallel to AX: their intersection G will be a point on the required curve. Similarly $2F$ parallel to Cf and fF parallel to AX will intersect in a point on the curve, and so on in succession. When B has come down to X the tracing point will evidently be at P_1 vertically below X on $8X$ produced so that $8P_1 = CP$; the tangent at P_1 is parallel to AX.

The construction is obvious from that of the cycloid.

In the figure a second trochoid is drawn generated by a point Q inside the rolling circle, to which the foregoing description applies exactly by the substitution of Q for P.

To draw the normal at any point of a trochoid.

Consider for a moment the point F. When the tracing point is at F the centre of the rolling circle will be at 2 and the point of contact of the rolling circle and directing line will be H on AX vertically below 2; i.e. H will be the instantaneous centre, and therefore FH will be the normal at F, since the direction of motion of F must be perpendicular to FH. But FH is parallel to fA, since the triangles $F2H, fCA$ are in all respects equal and are similarly situated, and therefore the normal at any point R may be thus constructed :—

Through R draw a parallel to the directing line meeting the circle described with C as centre and CP as radius in the point r, and the normal RM will be parallel to the line joining r to A, the lowest point of the rolling circle when its centre is C.

To find the centre of curvature at any point R^*.

Find K, the position of the centre of the rolling circle corresponding to R. (K will of course be vertically above M.) Join RK and draw MN perpendicular to RM meeting RK in N. Draw NS perpendicular to the guiding line meeting RM in S. S will be the required centre of curvature.

DEF. The Epicycloid is the path described by a fixed point on the circumference of a circle rolling on the convex side of a fixed circle, both circles lying in the same plane.

PROBLEM 140. *To describe an epicycloid, the radii of the rolling and directing circles being given* (Fig. 145).

Let O be the centre of the directing circle, OA its radius, AC the radius of the rolling circle, C, on OA produced, its centre, and let B be the other extremity of the diameter through A. Suppose B to be one position of the tracing point. As the one circle rolls round the other let the point B come down to X on the one side of A and to Y on the other, X and Y being on the directing circle. The arc AX will necessarily be equal to the arc AY, and equal to the semi-circumference of the rolling circle.

These points may be thus determined :—

Let the length of the semi-circumference AB be S, then

$$S = \pi \,.\, AC,$$

π being the circular measure of two right angles.

---

* The construction for the centre of curvature of this and the following roulettes was given by M. Savary in his *Leçons des Machines à l'École Polytechnique*, and is quoted by Williamson, *Differential Calculus*, 3rd ed., p. 345, where its proof is given.

Let θ be the circular measure of the angle subtended by the

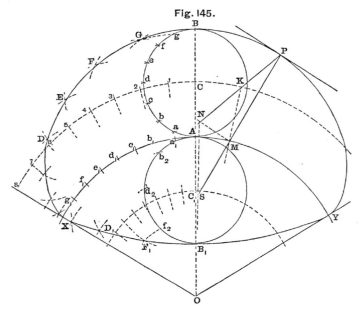

Fig. 145.

arc AX (the length of which is S), at the centre of the directing circle ; then

$$S = \theta \cdot AO = \pi \cdot AC \,;$$

$$\therefore \quad \theta : \pi :: AC : AO,$$

or if n is the number of degrees in the angle AOX,

$$n : 180^{\circ} :: AC : AO,$$

$$\text{or} \quad n = 180^{\circ}\frac{AC}{AO},$$

which determines n.

[In the figure $AO = 3AC$ so that the angle AOX contains 60°.]

Draw the path of the centre of the rolling circle, i.e. an arc with centre O, and radius OC, and let OX produced meet it in 8. Divide up the arc $C8$ into any convenient number of equal parts (8 in the fig.) and draw the radii $O1$, $O2$... cutting the directing circle in a' b'.... Divide up the semi-circumference of the rolling circle into the same number of equal parts Aa, ab....

E.   18

As the one circle rolls on the other, the point a will evidently come down to the point a', b to b' and so on : when a has come to a', the centre of the rolling circle will be at the point 1, and the tracing point will evidently be on a line making with $a'1$ an angle equal to the angle aCB which is equal to the angle ACg. Hence an arc described with centre 1, and radius CB, will intersect an arc described with centre O, and radius Og, in a point G of the required curve, for the triangles $G1O$ and gCO are equal in all respects :—i.e. G is the position of the tracing point corresponding to a', being the point of contact of the rolling and directing circles.

Similarly an arc described with centre 2, and radius CB will intersect an arc described with centre O, and radius Of in a point F of the required curve, and so on in succession for the points 3, 4, &c.

The arcs gG, fF, &c. will cut the corresponding arcs described with the successive centres 1, 2, &c. in two points, but it is evident by inspection which of the points must be taken, viz. that on the side of the corresponding radius $O1$, $O2$, &c. remote from OA.

The radius $OX8$ is a tangent to the curve at the point X.

To draw the normal at any point P of an epi-cycloid. From P with the radius AC of the rolling circle describe an arc cutting the path of the centre in K. [It will do so in two points but the one lying within the angle POB must be taken.] This will be the position of the centre of the rolling circle when the tracing point is at P. Draw KO cutting the directing circle in M, the point of contact between the circles when the tracing point is at P: i.e. M is the *instantaneous centre* corresponding to P.

Therefore PM is the normal at P.

To find the centre and radius of curvature at any point P. From M *the instantaneous centre* draw MN perpendicular to PM meeting PK, the radius of the rolling circle when the tracing point is at P, in N. Then NO (O being the centre of the guiding circle) will cut PM produced in S the required centre of curvature.

DEF. The Hypo-cycloid is the path described by a fixed point on the circumference of a circle rolling on the concave side of a fixed circle, both circles lying in the same plane.

PROBLEM 141. *To describe a hypo-cycloid the radii of the rolling and directing circles being given* (Fig. 145).

OA is the radius of the directing circle, and O its centre, AC' is the radius of the rolling circle, and B' the tracing point when the centre is at C'. The construction is identical with that for the epi-cycloid. In the figure the radius AC' is equal to AC the radius of the epi-cycloid, and B' of course reaches the directing line at X and Y—the points F' and D' are the positions of the tracing point when the points b_2 and d_2 are the points of contact of the rolling and directing circles.

DEF. When, as in the epi-cycloid, a circle rolls on the convex side of another, any point in the plane of the rolling circle, but not on its circumference traces out a curve called an *Epitrochoid*.

PROBLEM 142. *To describe an epi-trochoid, the rolling and guiding circles, and the position of the tracing point being given* (Fig. 146).

[In the figure the tracing point is assumed outside the rolling circle; it might be inside it.]

Let O be the centre of the directing circle, OA its radius, AC the radius of the rolling circle; C, on OA produced, its centre; let B be the other extremity of the diameter through A, and P on CB produced be one position of the tracing point. As in the epi-cycloid determine an arc AX or AY of the guiding circle equal in length to the semi-circumference of the rolling circle, so that B comes down to X and Y as the circle rolls round: i.e. construct angles AOX and AOY each containing n degrees where

$$n = 180^0 \frac{AC}{AO}.$$

[In the figure $AO = 3AC$ so that $n = 60$.]

Draw the path of the centre of the rolling circle, i.e. the circular arc with centre O, and radius OC, and produce the

Fig. 146.

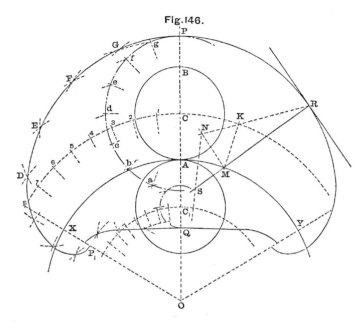

radius OX to meet it in 8. Divide up $C8$ into any convenient number of equal parts $C1$, 12, &c.—(8 in the figure), and divide up the semi-circle drawn through P, with centre C, into the same number Pg, gf, &c. With centre 1, and radius equal to CP, describe an arc, and with centre O, and radius Og, describe a second arc cutting it in G. G will be a point on the curve. Similarly with centre 2, and radius equal to CP, describe an arc, and with centre O, and radius Of, describe a second arc cutting it in F. F will be a point on the curve, and so on in succession for the points 3, 4, &c.

The arcs gG, fF, &c. will cut the corresponding arcs described with the successive centres 1, 2, &c. in two points, but it is evident by inspection which of the points must be taken, viz. that on the side of the corresponding radius $O1$, $O2$, &c. remote from OA.

The radius $OX8$ is a normal to the curve at the point P_1.

To draw the normal at any point R of an epi-trochoid.

Find *K* the corresponding position of the centre of the rolling circle, i.e. with centre *R*, and radius equal to *CP*, describe an arc cutting the path of the centre in *K*. [It will do so in two points, but the one must be taken lying within the angle *ROB*.]

Draw *KO* cutting the directing circle in *M*. *M* will be the *instantaneous centre* corresponding to *R*. Therefore *RM* is the normal at *R*.

To find the centre and radius of curvature at any point R.

From *M* the *instantaneous centre* draw *MN* perpendicular to *RM* meeting *RK* (*K* being as above) in *N*. Then, if *O* is the centre of the directing circle, *ON* will cut the normal *RM* produced in *S*, the required centre of curvature.

DEF. The *Hypo-trochoid* is the curve traced out by any point in the plane, but not on the circumference of a circle, rolling on the concave side of a fixed circle, both circles lying in the same plane.

PROBLEM 143. *To describe a hypo-trochoid, the directing and rolling circles, and the position of the tracing point being given* (Fig. 146).

[In the figure the tracing point is inside the rolling circle, but by the above definition this is not a necessary condition.]

OA is the radius of the directing circle, and *O* its centre, *AC'* is the radius of the rolling circle, and *Q* the tracing point when the centre is at *C'*. The construction is identical with that for the epi-trochoid.

Companion to the cycloid.

DEF. If a line *NE* (Fig. 147) be drawn perpendicular to a fixed diameter *AB* of a circle, meeting it in *N*, and the circle itself in *e*, and if *NE* be made equal to the arc *Be*, the locus of the point *E* is called the *Companion to the Cycloid*.

PROBLEM 144. *To describe the companion to the cycloid, the generating circle being given* (Fig. 147).

C is the centre, and *AB* a diameter of the given circle. Through

A draw XAY a tangent to the given circle, and on it make $AX = AY =$ the semi-circumference. (Prob. 138.) Divide AY

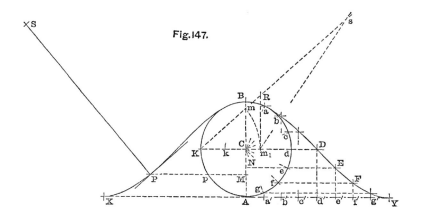

Fig. 147.

into any convenient number of equal parts as at $a', b', c' \ldots$ and divide the semi-circumference AB into the same number of equal parts as at $a, b, c \ldots$

It will be observed that the lettering proceeds from A in the one case, and from B in the other.

Through $a', b', c' \ldots$ rule perpendiculars to AY, and through $a, b, c \ldots$ rule parallels to AY. The intersections of corresponding lines as $D, E, F \ldots$ are points on the required curve.

The construction is obvious.

To draw the tangent at any point P.

Draw PM parallel to AX meeting the circle in p, and the diameter AB in M. Make Cm on $CB = Mp$, and join m to K the extremity of the diameter perpendicular to AC. The tangent at P is parallel to mK. The curve has parallel tangents at points equi-distant from CK.

To find the radius of curvature at any point P.

It is easily proved analytically that $\rho = \dfrac{\overline{mK}\,|^3}{a \cdot CM}$, where ρ is the radius of curvature, m and M are points corresponding to P as above, and a is the radius of the generating circle.

Make Km_1 on $KC = Km$, and draw m_1R perpendicular to KC meeting Km in R, also make Kk on $KC = CM$. Through m_1 draw m_1s parallel to kR meeting KR in s, and Ks will be the length of the required radius of curvature. Make PS on the normal at $P = Ks$, and S will be the centre of curvature at P.

Evidently $\qquad Ks : KR :: Km_1 : Kk,$

or $\qquad\qquad Ks = \dfrac{KR \cdot mK}{CM},$

but $\qquad KR : Km :: Km_1 : CK,$ or $KR = \dfrac{mK^2}{a}$;

$$\therefore\ Ks = \frac{\overline{mK}|^3}{a \cdot CM} = \rho.$$

EXAMPLES ON CHAPTER X.

1. Shew that if the diameter of the rolling circle be half that of the directing circle, the hypo-cycloid becomes a straight line.

2. Shew that if the diameter of the rolling circle be half that of the directing circle any hypo-trochoid becomes an ellipse.

3. Shew that if AOB be a diameter of the guiding circle, and P any point on it, the hypo-cycloids described by the circles having AP and BP as diameters, and P as tracing point, are identical.

4. A is a fixed point on the circumference of a circle of radius R. The points L and M are taken on the same side of A such that arc $AL = m \cdot$ arc AM, where m is a constant. Shew that LM will always touch the epi-cycloid described with a circle of radius $r\left(= \dfrac{R}{m+1} \right)$ rolling on a circle of radius $\rho = R - 2r$, the point A being the centre of the loop, and the centre of the guiding circle coinciding with that of the given one.

[As a numerical example take $R = 3\frac{3}{4}$, $m = 4$.]

5. A is a fixed point on the circumference of a circle of radius R. The points L and M are taken on opposite sides of A, such that arc $AL = m$. arc AM, where m is a constant. Shew that LM will always touch the hypo-cycloid described with a circle of radius $r = \dfrac{R}{m-1}$ rolling under a circle of radius $\rho = R + 2r$, the point A being the centre of the loop and the centre of the guiding circle coinciding with that of the given one.

6. Shew that the radius of curvature of an epi-cycloid at any point varies as the perpendicular on the tangent at the point, from the centre of the fixed circle.

7. Shew that the evolute of the epi-cycloid described with guiding circle of radius a and rolling circle of radius b is a similar figure, the radii of the fixed and generating circles being $\dfrac{a^2}{a-2b}$ and $\dfrac{ab}{a+2b}$ respectively.

8. Shew that the evolute of the hypo-cycloid is a similar figure, the radii of the fixed and generating circles being $\dfrac{a^2}{a-2b}$ and $\dfrac{ab}{a-2b}$ respectively.

[To make a practicable figure b must be much smaller than a.]

9. If a parabola rolls on another equal parabola shew that the locus of the focus of the rolling one is the directrix of the other.

CHAPTER XI.

WHEN a line rotates in a plane about a fixed point of its length, and a point travels continuously in the same direction along the line according to some fixed law, the path of the moving point is called a spiral. The fixed point is called the *pole;* a fixed line in the plane passing through the pole from which the position angle of the moving line may be measured is called the *initial line*, and the line drawn from the pole to any point of the curve is called the *radius vector* of that point.

After rotating through four right angles the revolving line comes back to the position it occupied at starting, but there is of course a different value for the length of the radius vector, and since the position angle may increase without limit, so too does the value of the radius vector. Spirals consequently extend to an infinite distance from the pole, and consist of a series of convolutions round it.

Cases of mathematical instruments usually contain a diagonal scale, the unit of which is half-an-inch, and on which lengths can be read to two places of decimals. In the numerical examples which follow, this scale is intended to be used.

DEF. In the *Spiral of Archimedes* the length of the radius vector is directly proportional to its position angle.

Let r be the length of the radius vector of any point, θ the angle which it makes with the initial line; the above definition is expressed symbolically by the equation $r = a\theta$, where a is any numerical constant.

In this equation θ is the circular measure of the position angle, and therefore $r = a$ when θ is unity, i.e. when the number of degrees in the position angle is $57\cdot2957\ldots$ i.e. corresponding to this angle measured from the initial line, the tracing point is at a distance of a units (inch or any other that may be chosen) from the pole; when $r = 0$, $\theta = 0$, or the initial line is the position of the revolving line when the travelling point is at the pole.

PROBLEM 145. *To describe the spiral of Archimedes, the pole, two points on the curve, and the unit of the curve being given* (Fig. 148).

Let O be the pole, P and Q the two points on the curve which we will suppose to be on the same convolution; and let OQ be

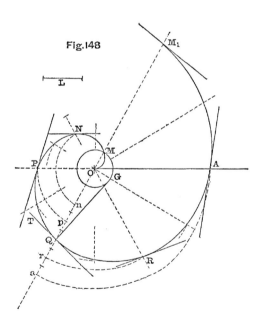

Fig. 148

greater than OP; let θ be the angle between OP and the initial line, and the length L the given unit.

$$OP = a\theta$$
$$OQ = a\left(\theta + QOP\right);$$

therefore $\qquad OQ - OP = a \times$ circ. meas. of QOP

or $\qquad a = \dfrac{OQ - OP}{\text{circ. meas. of } QOP}.$

$OQ - OP$ can be measured by scale, the number of degrees in the angle QOP can be measured by a protractor and its circular measure can be obtained from a table of the circular measures of angles, and the numerical value of a thus calculated: then $\theta = \dfrac{OP}{a}$, the length OP being of course measured on the same scale as that used for determining $OQ - OP$, which gives the circular measure of the angle between OP and the initial line, and the corresponding number of degrees can be obtained from the table.

To take a numerical example:

Let the unit of length be $\frac{1}{2}$ an inch. Suppose

$$OQ = 2,$$
$$OP = 1\cdot 5,$$

and the angle $QOP = 60^{\circ}$, the circular measure of which is

$$\frac{3\cdot 14159\ldots}{3} = 1\cdot 0472\ldots$$

$$a = \frac{2 - 1\cdot 5}{1\cdot 0472} = \frac{\cdot 5}{1\cdot 0472} = \cdot 477\ldots$$

then $\qquad\qquad \theta = \dfrac{1\cdot 5}{\cdot 477\ldots} = 3\cdot 14$

the number of degrees corresponding to which may be taken 180°.

The initial line will therefore be the line OA. If the tracing point after one complete revolution of the generating line cuts OP again in P' we have

$$OP = a\theta$$

and $\qquad\qquad OP' = a\,(\theta + 2\pi),$

therefore $\qquad\qquad OP' - OP = 2\pi a.$

Successive points on the curve may at once be found thus :— Construct an angle $QOR =$ angle QOP; with centre O and radius OP describe an arc cutting OQ in p; on OQ produced make

$= Qp$ and with centre O and radius Or describe an arc cutting R in R a point of the curve.

Similarly if $R\hat{O}S = P\hat{O}Q$, and Qs on OQ produced $= 2Qp$, an arc scribed with centre O and radius Os will cut OS in S a point of the curve. (In the figure S coincides with A on the initial line.)

In like manner points can be found nearer the pole than P by constructing angles on the side of OP remote from Q equal respectively to POQ, $2POQ$, $3POQ$, &c., and diminishing the radii vectores by the constant difference pQ.

To draw the tangent at any point of the curve.

A known expression for the angle which the tangent at any point makes with the radius vector is $\phi = \tan^{-1}\dfrac{r}{a}$, i.e. the tangent of the angle is the radius vector divided by the given constant of the curve.

Therefore to draw the normal at any point Q, on the radius G at right angles to OQ measure a length $OG = a$, the constant of the curve, and QG will be the normal at Q, for evidently

$$\tan OGQ = \frac{OQ}{OG} = \frac{r}{a} = \tan \phi.$$

Hence if a circle be drawn with centre O, and radius $= a$, normals at all the points on the curve can at once be drawn by merely joining them to the corresponding points in which such circle cuts the perpendicular radii.

The initial line is a tangent at the pole.

If ρ is the radius of curvature at any point

$$\rho \ : \ \sqrt{a^2 + r^2} \ :: \ a^2 + r^2 \ : \ 2a^2 + r^2,$$

so that ρ can be calculated without much difficulty.

PROBLEM 146. *To describe the spiral of Archimedes, the pole, the initial line and the constant of the curve being given* (Fig. 149).

Here a is given in the equation $r = a\theta$. Let O be the pole, and OA the initial line. In the figure, the unit being the length $, a = \cdot 239.$

Determine some convenient length of radius corresponding to a multiple (n) of 4 right angles; say the greatest distance to which

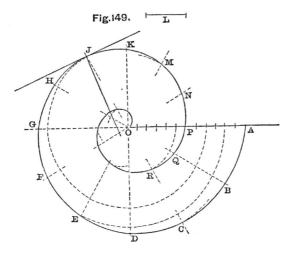

Fig. 149.

it is proposed to draw the curve. In the figure e.g. A is taken at angular distances of 8 right angles from the initial line (i.e. $n = 2$), so that

$$OA = \cdot 239 \times 4\pi$$
$$= \cdot 239 \times 4 \times 3\cdot 14159\ldots$$
$$= 3\cdot 60 \text{ units.}$$

Draw OD at right angles to OA and divide up the quadrants formed at O into any number (m) of equal parts (in the figure $m = 3$) and draw the radii OB, OC, &c. through the points of division. Divide OA into $4 . m . n$ equal parts. In the figure therefore OA is divided into 24 equal parts. Then arcs drawn through the successive points on OA with centre O will intersect the corresponding radii in points on the curve. The point P in the figure of course bisects OA, and after one complete convolution has been found the curve can be completed by measuring from B, C, &c. on the successive radii a constant distance BQ, CR, &c. $= AP$.

THE RECIPROCAL OR HYPERBOLIC SPIRAL.

DEF. In this curve the length of the radius vector is inversely proportional to its position angle.

The equation to the curve may therefore be written $\dfrac{1}{r} = a\theta$, where r is the length of any radius vector, θ the circular measure of the angle it makes with the initial line, and a a numerical constant.

When $\theta = 0$, r is therefore infinite, and r diminishes as θ increases, but the curve does not reach the pole for any finite value of θ. Corresponding to the value $\theta = 1$, $r = \dfrac{1}{a}$; i.e. the radius vector making 57·2957... degrees with the initial line is $\dfrac{1}{a}$ units long.

A line parallel to the initial line and $\dfrac{1}{a}$ units distant from it, is an *asymptote* to the curve.

PROBLEM 147.　*To draw the reciprocal spiral, the pole, the initial line and the unit and constant of the curve being given* (Fig. 150).

Let O be the pole and OA the initial line.　In the figure $a = \dfrac{1}{6}$ the unit being the length L.

Fig.150.

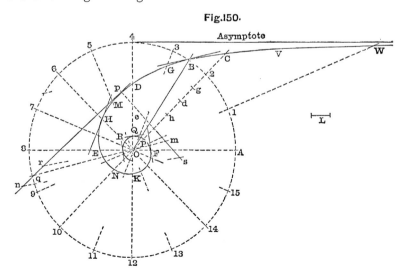

Draw $O4$ perpendicular to OA and with O as centre, and $\dfrac{1}{a}$ as radius describe a circle 4, 8, 12,... and divide it up into any number of equal parts, as at 1, 2, 3...

Draw the line OB making 57·2957... degrees with OA and cutting the circle in B; B will be a point on the curve.

Determine the length of radius vector corresponding to any convenient division of the circle—say the radius making 45° with the initial line—i.e. determine

$$r = \frac{1}{a} \cdot \frac{4}{\pi} = \frac{24}{3 \cdot 14159} = 7 \cdot 63...$$

Draw the line $O2$, and produce it to C making $OC = 7 \cdot 63$ units. C will be a point on the curve. As the angle doubles the radius diminishes one half; so that if OC is bisected in d, the length Od will be the length of radius vector making a right angle with the initial line, i.e. D on the line $O4$, OD being equal to Od, is another point on the curve.

Bisect OD in e and make OE on $O8 = Oe$; E will be a point on the curve.

OE is also of course $= \frac{1}{4}OC$.

Similarly OF the radius corresponding to $\theta = 2\pi$ is $\frac{1}{2}OE$ or $\frac{1}{8}OC$.

G the point on the curve corresponding to $\theta = \frac{3}{2} \cdot \dfrac{\pi}{4}$ is at a distance $\frac{2}{3}$ of OC from O. OH the radius corresponding to $\theta = 3 \cdot \dfrac{\pi}{4}$ is of course $\frac{1}{2}OG$ or $\frac{1}{3}$ of OC. OK the radius corresponding to $\theta = 6 \cdot \dfrac{\pi}{4}$ is $\frac{1}{2}OH$.

OM the radius corresponding to $\theta = \frac{5}{2} \cdot \dfrac{\pi}{4}$ is $\frac{2}{5}OC$, and ON the radius corresponding to $\theta = 5 \cdot \dfrac{\pi}{4}$ is $\frac{1}{2}OM$ or $\frac{1}{5}OC$.

In the second convolution

OP on OC, i.e. corresponding to $\theta = 9 \cdot \dfrac{\pi}{4}$ is $\frac{1}{9}OC$,

OQ on OD ,, ,, ,, $= 10 \cdot \dfrac{\pi}{4}$ is $\frac{1}{10}OC$,

OR on OH ,, ,, ,, $= 11 \cdot \dfrac{\pi}{4}$ is $\frac{1}{11}OC$,

OS on OE ,, ,, ,, $= 12 \cdot \dfrac{\pi}{4}$ is $\frac{1}{12}OC$,

and so on, and similarly any additional number of points can be obtained.

In the figure OV bisects the angle AOG and therefore
$$OV = 2 \cdot OG,$$
OW bisects the angle AOC and $OW = 2 \cdot OC$.

To draw the tangent at any point p.

Draw the radius Oq of the circle described with centre O and radius $\dfrac{1}{a}$ perpendicular to Op. pq will be the tangent at p.

To determine the centre and radius of curvature at any point p.

Draw the normal pm perpendicular to the tangent pq and meeting qO in m. On pq make $pr = Oq = \dfrac{1}{a}$, and $pn' = mq$. Then ns drawn through n parallel to rm, meeting pm in s, determines s the required centre.

THE LITUUS.

In this curve the radius is inversely proportional to the square-root of the angle through which it has revolved. Its equation is therefore
$$\frac{1}{r} = a \sqrt{\theta},$$
or as it may also be written
$$\frac{1}{r^2} = a^2\theta.$$

The radius therefore diminishes as the angle increases and is of infinite length when $\theta = 0$: it never vanishes however large θ may be, so that the spiral never reaches the pole, but makes an infinite series of convolutions round it.

PROBLEM 148. *To draw the Lituus, the pole, the initial line and the unit and constant of the curve being given* (Fig. 151).

Let O be the pole, and OA the initial line. In the figure $a = \frac{1}{3}$, the unit being the length L. Draw OC perpendicular to OA, and determine the value of r corresponding to $\theta = \frac{\pi}{2}$, i.e. to θ being the circular measure of a right angle.

In the figure

$$\frac{1}{\overline{OC}|^2} = \frac{1}{9} \cdot \frac{\pi}{2},$$

or
$$\overline{OC}|^2 = 9 \times \frac{2}{3 \cdot 14159 \ldots} = 5 \cdot 72.$$

Make Oc on OA equal to this length, and make OB on AO produced equal to unity on the scale adopted. A mean proportional between OB and Oc will evidently be the required length OC, i.e. a semi-circle on Bc will cut OC in C, a point on the curve.

Draw radii OG, OH bisecting the quadrants COD, DOE.

Trisect Oc in e and g, and take two parts measured from O as Og. A mean proportional between OB and Og will be equal to the length OG at which the curve cuts the bisector OG of the right angle COB.

Bisect Oc in d. A mean proportional between OB and Od will give the length of the radius vector OD corresponding to $\theta = \pi$.

Divide Oc into five equal parts, and take two of them from O as Oh. A mean proportional between OB and Oh will give the length OH of the radius vector corresponding to

$$\theta = \frac{5\pi}{4}.$$

E. 19

A mean proportional between OB and Oe ($\frac{1}{3}$rd of Oc) gives OE the length corresponding to $\theta = \dfrac{3\pi}{2}$.

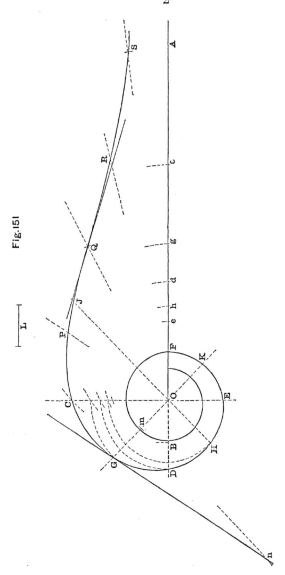

Fig.151

Similarly a mean proportional between OB and $\frac{2}{7}Oc$ would give OK the radius corresponding to $\theta = \frac{7}{4}\pi$, and a mean proportional between OB and $\frac{1}{4}Oc$ would give OF corresponding to $\theta = 2\pi$, but this is more easily determined by making it equal $\frac{1}{2}OC$, for since the square of the radius is inversely proportional to the angle, the radius diminishes $\frac{1}{2}$ as the angle increases four times.

For the same reason the length OJ on HO produced will be $2OD$ since the angle $AOJ = \frac{1}{4}$ of two right angles.

Draw the angle AOP to contain 57.29... degrees; the arc subtending this angle is equal to the radius, i.e. corresponding to it, $\theta = 1$, and therefore OP the corresponding radius must contain $\dfrac{1}{a}$ units (in the figure $OP = 3$).

Bisect the angle AOP by OQ, and make $OQ^2 = \dfrac{2}{a^2}$ (in the figure $OQ = \sqrt{18} = 4\cdot24...$).

Q is a point of contrary flexure in the curve, i.e. at that point it becomes convex towards the initial line, the radius of curvature being infinite.

Bisect the angle AOQ by OR, and make $OR =$ twice OP; R will be a point on the curve.

Bisect AOR by OS, and make $OS =$ twice OQ; S will be a point on the curve.

In the second convolution the following table gives the values of r corresponding to successive values of θ differing by $45°$, and similarly for the third convolution.

If 2 be taken as the numerator of all the fractions the successive denominators evidently differ by unity.

The values of r may of course all be calculated arithmetically, instead of being obtained geometrically from the calculated value of one of them.

θ	r^2			
$2\pi + \dfrac{\pi}{4}$	$\dfrac{2}{9} Oc$	i.e. r must be a mean proportional between OB and $\dfrac{2}{9} Oc$		
$2\pi + \dfrac{\pi}{2}$	$\dfrac{1}{5} Oc$	,,	,, ,,	$\dfrac{1}{5} Oc$
$2\pi + \dfrac{3\pi}{4}$	$\dfrac{2}{11} Oc$	,,	,, ,,	$\dfrac{2}{11} Oc$
3π	$\dfrac{1}{6} Oc$	,,	,, ,,	$\dfrac{1}{6} Oc$
$2\pi + \dfrac{5\pi}{4}$	$\dfrac{2}{13} Oc$	,,	,, ,,	$\dfrac{2}{13} Oc$
$2\pi + \dfrac{3\pi}{2}$	$\dfrac{1}{7} Oc$	,,	,, ,,	$\dfrac{1}{7} Oc$
$2\pi + \dfrac{7\pi}{4}$	$\dfrac{2}{15} Oc$	,,	,, ,,	$\dfrac{2}{15} Oc$
4π	$\dfrac{1}{8} Oc$	,,	,, ,,	$\dfrac{1}{8} Oc$

To draw the tangent at any point.

A known expression for the angle which the tangent at any point makes with the radius vector is

$$\phi = \tan^{-1}\left(-\frac{2}{r^2 a^2}\right);$$

$$\therefore \quad \tan\phi = -\frac{2}{r^2 a^2} = -2\theta.$$

The value of $\tan\phi$ for any point can therefore easily be calculated numerically, and the corresponding number of degrees obtained from a set of tables; the angle then being plotted by means of a protractor. The minus sign in the above expressions denotes that ϕ is always greater than a right angle when measured on the θ side of the radius. It becomes more and more nearly a right angle as the angle increases. At the point Q corresponding to

$$\theta = \tfrac{1}{2}, \quad \phi = 135^\circ.$$

The tangent may be constructed geometrically, though not very conveniently, thus :—

we have
$$\tan\phi = -\frac{2}{r^2 a^2} = -\frac{2OP^2}{r^2},$$

where OP is the radius corresponding to unit angle. Determine a length l such that

$$OB : OP :: 2OP : l,$$

so that $l = 2OP^2$, since OB is unity on the scale adopted ;

$$\therefore \quad \tan \phi = -\frac{l}{r^2} .$$

The value of r^2 is known, because it is some definite fraction of Ac. At G on the curve for example it is the length Og. From the point at which the tangent is required measure any convenient fraction of the length r^2 along the radius vector, from the extremity draw a line perpendicular to the radius, and measure on it the same fraction of the length l, and the required tangent will pass through the point thus obtained.

In the figure Gm is $\frac{1}{4}Og$, and mn is $\frac{1}{4}l$, then Gn is the tangent.

Owing to the rapid diminution of r^2 as the angle increases the method very soon becomes impracticable.

If ρ is the radius of curvature at any point, and r the corresponding radius vector,

$$\rho : \sqrt{4 + a^4 r^4} :: r\,(4 + a^4 r^4) : 2\,(4 - a^4 r^4).$$

The Logarithmic or Equiangular Spiral.

In this spiral the radius increases in a geometric while the angle increases in an arithmetic ratio. The angle of revolution is therefore proportional to the *logarithm* of the length of the radius vector, whence it derives its first name; it is called equiangular because in it the tangent at any point makes a constant angle with the radius vector.

This constant angle is called the angle of the spiral.

The equation to the curve is generally expressed in the form

$$r = a^{\theta},$$

where a is some constant on which the form of the curve depends. From it evidently

$$\log r = \theta \log a ;$$

and since the logarithm of 1 is 0, r must evidently be of unit length when $\theta = 0$, i.e. the curve must cut the initial line at unit distance from the origin.

If this condition is not fulfilled the equation to the curve is of the form $r = ba^\theta$ where b is another constant, and in this form the initial line must be taken so that it cuts the curve at a distance b from the origin.

The known constant value ϕ of the angle which the tangent at any point makes with the radius vector is

$$\phi = \tan^{-1} \frac{1}{\log_e a},$$

where e is the base of Napierian logarithms, i.e. ϕ is an angle such that

$$\tan \phi = \frac{1}{\log_e a}$$

$$= \frac{\log_{10} e}{\log_{10} a}.$$

The value of $\log_{10} e$ is $0\cdot 43429448$.

From the definition of the curve it follows that any radius vector is a mean proportional between the two at equal angular distances from it on opposite sides. This property gives the best method of constructing the curve geometrically when the pole and two points are given or determined.

PROBLEM 149. *To draw a logarithmic spiral, the value of the constant in the equation, and the unit of the curve being given* (Fig. 152).

Let the equation be $r = \overline{1\cdot 15}\,|^\theta$, the unit being the length L.

Take O the pole, and OA the initial line—the curve will cut this line in the point M at unit distance from O.

Suppose the revolving line to have made one complete revolution, so that it again coincides with OA; the corresponding value of θ will be the circular measure of four right angles ;—

i.e. 2π or $2(3\cdot 14159...) = 6\cdot 28318$.

The corresponding value of r is given by

$$\cdot \log r = 6 \cdot 28318 \log (1 \cdot 15)$$
$$= 6 \cdot 28318 \times \cdot 0606978$$
$$= \cdot 381376 ;$$
$$\therefore \quad r = 2 \cdot 41 \text{ very nearly} - = ON,$$

and N is a second point on the curve.

Fig. 152.

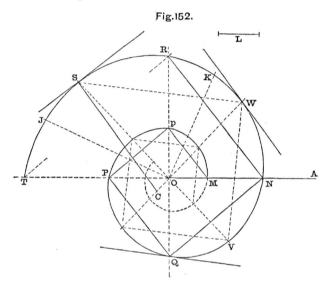

Make OP on MO produced a mean proportional between OM and ON, and P will be a third point on the curve. Through O draw QOp at right angles to OM, make OQ a mean proportional between OP and ON, and Q will be a point on the curve.

Similarly if the curve cuts QO again in R, $OR : ON :: ON : OQ$ which determines R. To do so evidently all that is necessary is to draw NR parallel to PQ or perpendicular to QN, and thus a series of points lying on two lines perpendicular to each other, and passing through the pole can be determined.

It is of course easy to interpolate points between those of the original series; for bisect the angle TOR by the line OS, and make OS a mean proportional between OT and OR, and on SO produced make OV a mean proportional between ON and OQ.

S and V will be points on the curve.

Draw OW at right angles to OS, and make OW a mean proportional between OS and OV (i.e. on SV describe a semi-circle cutting OW in W), and W will be a point on the curve. Then a series of points on the lines OS and OW can be obtained by drawing, as shewn by the dotted lines, parallels to SW and WV alternately.

The angle between any tangent and its radius vector is given by the equation

$$\phi = \tan^{-1} \frac{\cdot 43429448}{\log (1 \cdot 15)} \, ,$$

i.e. $\tan \phi = \dfrac{\cdot 43429448}{\cdot 0606978}$

$$= 7 \cdot 155,$$

whence $\phi = 82^{\circ}$ nearly (more exactly $81^{\circ}.58'$).

The tangents can therefore be drawn at all the points found by drawing lines through them making this angle with the radii.

The dotted part of the curve arises from negative values of the angle of rotation; it never reaches the pole.

Centre of Curvature.

The centre of curvature at any point S can easily be determined when the angle between the radius and tangent is known. Draw the normal SC, and from O the pole draw OC perpendicular to OS the radius vector ; C will be the required centre.

PROBLEM 150. *To describe an equiangular spiral, the pole O and two points S and K on the curve being given* (Fig. 152).

Let $OS = r_1$, $OK = r_2$, and the angle $KOS = a$. (In the figure $OS = 3\cdot3$, $OK = 2\cdot78$, and $KOS = 1\cdot22173... =$ the c.m. of 70°.)

The angle of the spiral may be determined from the following equation—

$$\tan \phi = \frac{a \log_{10} \epsilon}{\log r_1 - \log r_2} = \frac{1\cdot22173 \times \cdot43429}{\cdot5185139 - \cdot4440448} = 7\cdot124,$$

whence $\phi = 82^{\circ}$ nearly.

The constant a of the curve is then given by

$$\log_{10} a = \frac{\log_{10} \epsilon}{\tan \phi} = \frac{\cdot 43429}{7 \cdot 124} = \cdot 0609,$$

$\therefore a = 1 \cdot 15$ very approximately.

Taking OK as the initial line the equation to the curve may be written
$$r = r_2 a^\theta.$$

Draw OJ at right angles to OK and on it take a length OJ equal to $r_2 a^{\frac{\pi}{2}}$, i.e. determined from the equation

$$\log OJ = \log r_2 + \frac{\pi}{2} \log a$$
$$= \cdot 4440448 + 1 \cdot 5707 \times \cdot 0609 = 3 \cdot 47.$$

We have now two points on radii at right angles to each other, and other points can at once be found by the preceding problem.

Any number of *points* on the curve can be found without determining either a or ϕ by making each radius a mean proportional between the two at equal angular distances from it. Thus the radius bisecting the angle KOS must be a mean proportional between OK and OS, and the radius making an angle $2a$ with OK must be a third proportional to OK and OS.

Points at equal angular distances can easily be found by Problem 8, when the lengths of two radii separated by that angular distance are known.

In practice ϕ should always be determined, and tangents drawn at all the points found, because these tangents are of great assistance in tracing the curve through the points.

PROBLEM 151. *To inscribe a Logarithmic Spiral in a given parallelogram* (Fig. 153).

Let $ABCD$ be the given parallelogram, a the circular measure of its acute angle. [In the figure $AB = 3$, $AD = 4$, the unit being the length L, and the angle BAD contains $75°$, so that its circular measure is $1 \cdot 309 \dots$]

Let p and q be the perpendicular distances between the opposite pairs of sides, p being greater than q.

In the fig. $p = 3\cdot86$, and $q = 2\cdot89$.

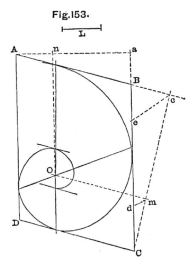

Fig.153.

If ϕ be the angle of the spiral, it can be determined from the equation

$$\tan\phi = \frac{a\,\log_{10} e}{\log p - \log q},$$

or with the above dimensions

$$\tan\phi = \frac{1\cdot309 \times \cdot43429}{\cdot5865873 - \cdot4608978}$$

$$= \frac{\cdot5385}{\cdot1257} = 4\cdot284,$$

∴ ϕ contains 77° very nearly.

Next determine the number (N suppose), the log. of which

$$= \frac{\pi\,\log e}{\tan\phi},$$

i.e. in the present case $\log N = \dfrac{3\cdot1416 \times \cdot43429}{4\cdot284}$

$$= \cdot3185,$$

∴ from a table of logs $N = 2\cdot08.$

Divide the perpendiculars p and q so that one portion shall be to the other :: $1 : N$, and lines drawn through these points of

division parallel to the sides of the given parallelogram will intersect in O the pole of the required spiral. In the figure the perpendicular Cc is divided by making Cd on $CB =$ unity on any
convenient scale, and $de = 2\cdot08$ on the same scale, then dm parallel
to ec divides Cc at the point m in the required ratio. Similarly
Aa is divided in n, and nO and mO perpendicular to Aa and Cc
respectively intersect in O the required pole.

The Involute of the Circle. The Evolute of a Curve has already
(p. 91) been defined as the locus of the centres of curvature, and
considered with respect to its Evolute the curve is called the
Involute of its Evolute. If an inextensible string be imagined to
lie in contact with the evolute and to be kept stretched while
gradually unwound from it, a certain fixed point on the string will
describe the corresponding involute. The free portion of the
string will be a tangent to the evolute at the point it quits it, and
a normal to the involute at the point reached at the moment by
the tracing point.

PROBLEM 152. *To draw the Involute of a given circle to pass
through a given point* (Fig. 154).

1st. Let the given point be on the circle. Let C be the
centre and AB a diameter of the given circle, and let A be a point

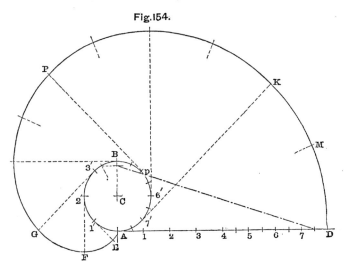

Fig.154.

on the involute.   Draw the tangent at A, and on it determine a length AD equal to the circumference (see p. 267).   Divide AD into any convenient number of equal parts $A1$, 1.2,...&c., and the circumference into the same number $A1'$, $1'2'$....   Draw tangents to the circle at $1'$, $2'$...

If we imagine a string unwound from the circle starting from A,—when its point of contact is $1'$, i.e. when the free portion of the string is a tangent to the circle at $1'$, the length of the free portion will of course be equal to the arc $A1'$, or to the length $A1$ of the straight line AD.   Make $1'E$ on the tangent at $1'$ equal to $A1$, and E will therefore be a point on the curve.   Similarly make $2'F$ on the tangent at $2'$ equal to $A2$, and F will be a point on the curve, and so on in succession.

2nd.   Let the given point be P.   Through P draw a tangent to the given circle meeting it in p.   If A is the point where the required involute through P would meet the circle and θ be the circular measure of the angle subtended at the centre by the arc Ap we have $\theta = \dfrac{\text{arc } Ap}{AC}$; but the length of the arc Ap must be the line Pp so that if the lengths Pp and AC be measured on any scale the numerical value of θ can be calculated, and the corresponding number of degrees obtained from a table.   This of course determines A and the construction reduces to the first case.

As the distance from the pole increases and the points found on the curve get further and further apart, others can be determined between those of the original series by bisecting the corresponding arcs of the circle and divisions of the straight line AD, as shewn at M.

Tangents to the circle are of course normals to the involute, and the centre of curvature at any point is the point of contact of the tangent drawn from that point to the circle.

The involute of the circle is the locus of the intersection of tangents drawn at the points where any ordinate meets a circle and the corresponding cycloid.

Examples on Chapter XI.

1. Draw a spiral of Archimedes to touch a given line, the pole O and the constant (a), and unit of the curve being given.

[If r is the length of rad. vector to the point of contact of the given tangent, and p the length of the perpendicular on it from the pole

$$r^2 - \frac{p^2}{2} = \pm p \, \sqrt{\left. a^2 + \frac{\overline{p}}{2} \right|^2}.$$

Construct therefore a rectangle equal to the sum of the two rectangles

$$p \times \frac{p}{2}, \text{ and } p \times \sqrt{\left. a^2 + \frac{\overline{p}}{2} \right|^2}. \qquad \text{(Prob. 18.)}$$

The last expression is of course the length of the hypotenuse of a right-angled triangle, the sides of which are a and $\dfrac{p}{2}$, and is consequently always greater than $\dfrac{p}{2}$. The negative sign in the above equation therefore gives an imaginary result. A mean proportional between the sides of the rectangle constructed as above is the required length r.]

2. Draw a spiral of Archimedes to touch a given line PT at a given point P, and to have a given pole O.

[Through P draw Pa perpendicular to PT, and through O draw Oa perpendicular to OP meeting Pa in a. The length Oa is the unit of, and is proportional to, the constant of the curve, and the initial line is at an angle POA from OP given by

circular measure of $POA = \dfrac{OP}{Oa}$.]

3. Draw a reciprocal spiral, the pole O, and two points P, Q on the curve being given.

[Compare problem 145. Let $OP = r$, $OQ = r_1$ of which let r be the greater; the angle $POQ = a$, and the angle between the initial line and $OP = \theta$, then

$$\frac{1}{r} = a\theta,$$

$$\frac{1}{r_1} = a\,(\theta + a),$$

$\therefore$ $$\frac{1}{r_1} - \frac{1}{r} = a\alpha, \text{ or } a = \frac{1}{\alpha} \cdot \frac{r - r_1}{r r_1}.$$

The value of a can be obtained from a table of the circular measures of angles, and if a fourth proportional l be determined to $r - r_1$, r and r_1

$$\frac{1}{a} = al,$$

which determines a. Any convenient scale can be used for measuring l and the unit of that scale will then be the unit of the curve ; then $\theta = \frac{1}{a} \times \frac{1}{r}$, the length of r being measured on the same scale. The initial line can then be drawn.]

4.   Draw a reciprocal spiral, the pole O, a point P on the curve and the tangent at that point being given.

[Draw OT perpendicular to OP meeting the tangent at P in T. $OT = \frac{1}{a}$, so that the constant of the curve is known.   If the circular measure of the angle between the initial line and OP is θ

$$\frac{1}{OP} = \frac{1}{OT} \cdot \theta, \text{ or } \theta = \frac{OT}{OP},$$

and the initial line can be drawn.]

5.   Draw the Lituus, the pole O and two points P and Q on the curve being given.

[Let $OP = r$, $OQ = r_1$, r being greater than r_1; the angle $POQ = a$, and the angle between the initial line and $OP = \theta$.

Then $$\frac{1}{r} = a\sqrt{\theta},$$

$$\frac{1}{r} = a\sqrt{\theta + a},$$

$$\therefore \qquad r^2\theta = r_1{}^2\left(\theta + a\right),$$

or
$$\theta = a\,\frac{r_1{}^2}{r^2 - r_1{}^2}\,.$$

Take a fourth proportional l to

$$r_1,\ \ r + r_1\ \text{and}\ \ r - r_1,$$

then
$$\theta = a\,\frac{r_1}{l}\,,$$

and can be calculated, the lengths r_1 and l being measured on any convenient scale.]

6.   Draw an equiangular spiral to touch three given lines AB, BC, CA in three given points P, Q, R respectively.

[On PR as chord describe a segment of a circle containing an angle equal to the external angle between the tangents AB and CA. This is a locus of the pole. Similarly on PQ as chord describe a segment of a circle containing an angle equal to the external angle between the tangents AB and BC which will be a second locus. The pole is thus determined.]

7.   Draw an equiangular spiral of given angle (ϕ) to touch three given lines AB, BC, CA.

[Suppose the spiral is to touch BA and BC produced. Through B draw a line dividing the angle ABC so that the perpendicular (p_1) dropped from any point on it on AB is to the perpendicular (p_2) dropped from the same point on BC as $1 : a^\alpha$, where a is the constant of the required curve, and α is the circular measure of the supplement of the angle ABC, i.e. $\dfrac{p_2}{p_1} = a^\alpha$.

a is of course the number whose logarithm is

$$0\cdot43429448 \times \cot\phi,$$

and can therefore be obtained from a table of logarithms. The line so drawn is a locus of the pole. Similarly draw a line through A dividing the angle between BA produced and AC, so that

$\frac{q_2}{q_1} = a^\beta$, where q_1 and q_2 are perpendiculars on AB, AC respectively, and B is the circular measure of the angle BAC. This line will be a second locus of the pole which is therefore known.]

8. Draw an equiangular spiral, the pole O, and two tangents TP, TQ being given.

[Draw perpendiculars p_1, p_2 on TP, TQ from O of which let p_2 be the greater; then

$$\log a = \frac{\log p_2 - \log p_1}{a} = \log_{10} e \cdot \cot \phi,$$

where a is the constant of the curve, a the circular measure of the angle between the tangents alternate with that in which O lies, and ϕ the constant angle between the tangent and radius vector. ϕ can therefore be determined from a table of logarithms.]

CHAPTER XII.

MISCELLANEOUS CURVES.

The Harmonic Curve or Curve of Sines.

In this curve the ordinates are proportional to the sines of angles which are the same fractions of four right angles as the corresponding abscissæ are of some given length. It is the curve in which a musical string vibrates when sounded.

PROBLEM 153. *To draw the Harmonic Curve, the length and amplitude of a vibration being given* (Fig. 155).

Let AB be the given length, AO the given amplitude. With centre O on BA produced describe a semi-circle $4A4'$, and divide it up into any convenient number of equal parts. Bisect AB in C, and divide up AC and CB into the same number of equal parts chosen for the semi-circle. Draw the successive ordinates $1a$, $1b$, &c., and from the corresponding points on the semi-circle draw parallels to AB meeting the ordinates in a, b,... &c., which will be points on the curve. The length from A to C is half a wave length which will be repeated from C to B on the other side of AB. C is a point of inflection on the curve, the radius of curvature there becoming infinite.

To draw the tangent at any point P.

Through P draw pPM parallel to AB, cutting the semi-circle in p; and make $PM = AC$. Draw pm perpendicular to OA cutting it in m, and make Mm' on $MP = Om$. Through M draw MN perpendicular to PM or AB, and on it make $Mg = 3.14...$ on any convenient scale. On MP make $Mk = $ unity on the same

E.   20

scale, and draw $m'N$ parallel to kg cutting MN in N. N will be a
point on the tangent at P.

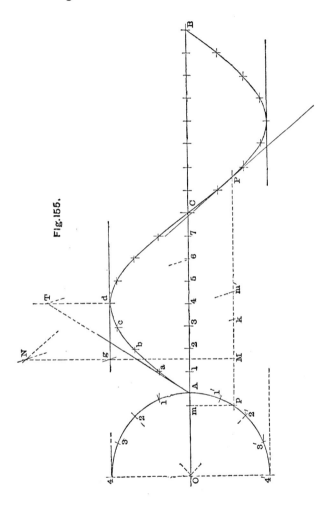

Fig. 155.

The lines corresponding to $m'N$ will of course be parallel for
all points on the curve, so that the points k and g need only be
found once.

A parallel to kg through the point 6 (the quadrisection of CA)
cutting $4T$ in T determines AT and CT, the tangents at A
and C.

Ovals of Cassini.

When a point moves in a plane so that the product of its distances from two fixed points in the plane is constant, it traces out one of Cassini's ovals. The fixed points are called the foci. The equation of the curve is therefore $rr_1 = k^2$, where r and r_1 are the distances of any point on the curve from the foci and k is a constant.

Corresponding to any given foci an infinite number of ovals may of course be drawn by varying k.

PROBLEM 154. *To describe an oval of Cassini, the foci F and F_1 and the constant k of the curve being given* (Fig. 156).

Draw a line through F and F_1 and bisect FF_1 in C: through C draw BCB_1 perpendicular to FF_1, and with F as centre and

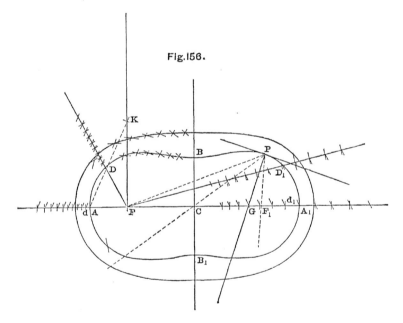

Fig.156.

radius $= k$ describe an arc cutting BCB_1 in B and B_1. B and B_1 will evidently be points on the curve.

Draw FK perpendicular to FF_1 and make $FK = k$, and on CF make CA and CA_1 each $= CK$. A and A_1 will be points on the

curve, for
$$CA^2 = CK^2 = CF^2 + FK^2,$$
$$\therefore \; CA^2 - CF^2 = k^2 = (CA + CF)(CA - CF);$$
but
$$CA + CF = F_1A \text{ and } CA - CF = FA,$$
$$\therefore \; FA \cdot F_1A = k^2.$$

With centre F and any radius greater than FA and less than FA_1 describe an arc dD cutting FA in d. Through K draw Kd_1 perpendicular to dK and cutting FF_1 in d_1. A circle described with centre F_1 and radius Fd_1 will cut the arc dD in D, a point on the curve.

Evidently by symmetry D_1, the intersection of arcs of the same radii as the above but struck from the opposite foci as centres, will also be on the curve, and so also will be the intersections on the other side of AA_1. Similarly any number of points may be found.

An alternative method may be adopted as soon as two points such as A and D, not very far apart, and the two corresponding points A_1 and D_1 are found. If two series of terms in geometrical progression are found, FA and FD being successive terms of the one and FA_1 and FD_1 successive terms of the other (Problem 8), circles struck with the corresponding terms of each as radii and with the opposite foci as centres intersect in points of the curve, the radii increasing from the one focus and diminishing from the other. This is shewn in the figure, and this construction moreover enables at once any number of ovals to be drawn, the intersection of any two circles of opposite series being taken as a starting point, and the successive intersections giving succeeding points. The second curve drawn in the figure is an example of this.

It may be noticed that a circular arc with centre at the focus coincides very closely with the oval at the vertices A and A_1.

To draw the tangent at any point P.

The angle FPG which the normal at any point P makes with the focal chord FP is equal to the angle which the other focal chord F_1P makes with the chord CP drawn from P to the centre.

The Cissoid of Diocles.

This curve, named after Diocles, a Greek mathematician, who is supposed to have lived about the sixth century of our era, was invented by him for the purpose of constructing the solution of the problem of finding two mean proportionals. The curve is generated in the following manner:—

In the diameter ACB of the circle $ADBE$ (fig. 157) make $AN = BM$, and draw MQ and NR perpendicular to AB, and let MQ meet the circle in Q, then AQ and NR intersect in a point on the curve, i.e. the locus of this intersection is the Cissoid.

By similar triangles $\dfrac{RN}{AN} = \dfrac{QM}{AM} = \dfrac{\sqrt{AM \cdot MB}}{AM}$, since AQB is a right angle; or if we call $RN = y$, $AN = x$, and the radius of the circle a,

$$\frac{y}{x} = \frac{\sqrt{(2a-x)\,x}}{2a-x} = \sqrt{\frac{x}{2a-x}}\,,$$

which is the equation to the curve referred to rectangular axes with A as origin and AB as axis of x.

PROBLEM 155. *To describe the Cissoid corresponding to a circle of given diameter* (Fig. 157).

Of course the above description is really a construction for the curve, since by it any number of points can be determined. The curve may also be described by continuous motion thus :

Draw a diameter AB of the circle, and the tangent at B. If A is a point on the curve, this tangent will be an asymptote. Through C, the centre of the circle, draw a parallel to the tangent at B of indefinite length, and make AO on CA produced equal to AC. Cut a piece of paper to a right angle as abc, and on one side of it mark off from the angle the points d, c, making $bd = dc = AC$, the radius of the given circle. If the paper be now placed so that the edge ba passes through O, and the point c is always on ECD, the point d will be on the curve, and by moving it the positions of any number of points can easily be marked off on the paper. The curve is evidently symmetrical about AB,

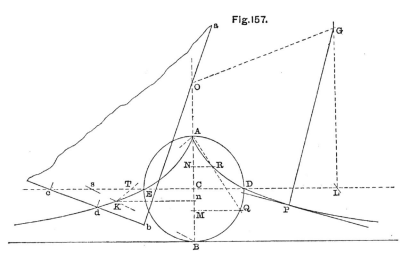

Fig. 157.

there is a cusp at A, and D and E, the extremities of the diameter perpendicular to AB, are points on the curve.

To draw the tangent at any point P.

From P, with radius AC, mark off L on the diameter ECD. Through L draw LG parallel to AB, and through O draw OG parallel to PL, meeting LG in G. G will be a point on the normal at P, and the tangent is therefore perpendicular to PG.

It may be noted that the area included between the curve and the asymptote is three times the area of the generating circle.

The problem of finding two mean proportionals between two given quantities a and b is, to find two quantities m and n such that

$$m^2 = an \quad \text{and} \quad n^2 = mb,$$

or that $$m^3 = a^2b \quad \text{and} \quad n^3 = ab^2.$$

By means of the cissoid corresponding to the circle, the radius of which is equal to a, the smaller of the given quantities a and b, the first term m can easily be found thus:

Make CS on the diameter $DCE = b$. By hypothesis S will always fall beyond E. Draw BS cutting the cissoid in K. Then AK will cut CS in a point T at a distance from C equal to the required quantity m, i.e. $CT^3 = m^3 = a^2b$. For draw the ordinate Kn. By similar triangles

$$\frac{CT}{Kn} = \frac{AC}{An}, \text{ or } CT^3 = \frac{Kn^3}{An^3}a^3,$$

and

$$\frac{CS}{Kn} = \frac{BC}{Bn} = \frac{BC}{2a - An},$$

$$\therefore CS = \frac{Kn}{2a - An}a;$$

but An is the x and Kn is the y of the point K, and it has been therefore already proved that

$$Kn^2 = \frac{An^3}{2a - An};$$

$$\therefore CT^3 = \frac{\overline{An}|^3}{2a - An} \cdot \frac{Kn}{\overline{An}|^3}a^3$$

$$= \frac{Kn}{2a - An}a^3 = CSa^2$$

$$= a^2b.$$

When m is found the second mean proportional n can be found by similar triangles, for

$$a : m :: n : b.$$

If CS or b be made equal to $2a$, m will be the length of the side of a cube, the volume of which is twice that of a cube of side a, since in this case $m^3 = 2a^3$.

The Conchoid of Nicomedes.

If through a fixed point O a straight line POp be drawn meeting a fixed right line LM in R, and RP, Rp be taken each of the same constant length, the locus of P and p is called the conchoid.

If OD be drawn perpendicular to LM meeting it in A, and $OA = a$, $RP = b$, and $AOR = \theta$,

$$OP = OR + RP = \frac{a}{\cos\theta} + b.$$

Also $Op = OR - Rp$, since we go in the positive direction from O to R, and in the negative from R to p;

$$\therefore \quad Op = \frac{a}{\cos \theta} - b,$$

so that the polar equation of the curve, O being the pole and AD the initial line, will be

$$(r \pm b) \cos \theta = a.$$

PROBLEM 156. *To draw the Conchoid, the constants a and b being given* (Fig. 158.)

Draw the line OD, and make OA on it $= a$, and AD, Ad each $= b$.

Fig. 158.

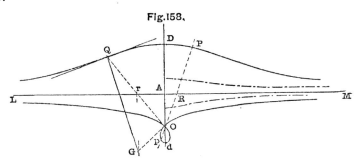

Through A draw LAM perpendicular to OA ; LM will be an asymptote of the curve. Draw any line OP through O meeting LM in R, and on it make $RP = Rp = b$.

By definition P and p will be points on the curve, and similarly any additional number of points may be determined.

The curve is evidently symmetrical about OD.

If b is less than a, the form of the curve is that shewn by the dotted lines.

When $b = a$ the point O is a cusp on the curve.

To draw the normal at any point Q.

Let OQ meet LM in r; draw rG perpendicular to LM and OG perpendicular to OQ intersecting in G, which will be a point on the required normal; for the line OQ is moving so that it always passes through O while a fixed point on it is travelling along

LM ; i.e. at the moment the line is moving along OQ (or turning about some point on OG), and also along LM (or turning about some point in rG), i.e. G is the centre of instantaneous rotation.

The Witch of Agnesi.

Let AB (fig. 159) be a diameter of a circle, NM a line perpendicular to AB meeting it in N and the circle in M. If P be taken on NM produced so that

$$\frac{PN}{AB} = \frac{MN}{AN},$$

the locus of the point P is the curve called the Witch.

If a be the radius of the circle we have from the above

$$\frac{PN^2}{4a^2} = \frac{MN^2}{AN^2} = \frac{BN}{AN} = \frac{2a - AN}{AN},$$

or putting $AN = x$, and $PN = y$,

$$xy^2 = 4a^2 (2a - x),$$

which is the equation to the curve referred to rectangular axes with A as origin and AB axis of x.

PROBLEM 157. *To describe the Witch of Agnesi corresponding to a circle of given diameter* (Fig. 159).

Let AB be the given diameter, C its centre; draw the tangent at B, and through A draw any number of lines AE, AF,...&c., cutting the circle in E, F, &c., and the tangent at B in $e, f,...$ &c. Lines drawn through E and e respectively parallel and perpendicular to the tangent will intersect in Q, a point on the curve; similarly lines through F and f intersect in R, and so any number of points can be determined.

The construction is obvious from the definition of the curve.

The curve is symmetrical about AB and cuts the diameter perpendicular to AB at distances from the centre equal to the diameter; the tangents at these points pass through B.

If CB be bisected in D and DK be drawn perpendicular to AB meeting the curve in K, K is a point of inflection on the curve. The tangent to the circle at A is an asymptote to the curve.

To draw the tangent at any point T.

Through T draw tTv parallel to AB meeting the tangent at B in t and the asymptote in v. Draw Aw perpendicular to At meet-

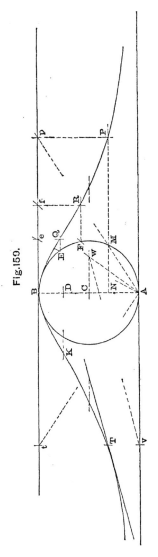

Fig.159.

ing the ordinate through C, the centre of the circle in w. The tangent at T is parallel to vw.

THE CATENARY.

The curve in which a heavy inextensible string, freely suspended from two points, hangs under the action of gravity, is called the Catenary. If the mass of a unit length of the string is everywhere constant, i.e. if the string is of uniform density and thickness, the curve in which the string hangs is called the Common Catenary.

Investigation of the conditions of the statical equilibrium of the string gives for the curve of the common catenary the well-known equation

$$y = \frac{c}{2} \left\{ e^{\frac{x}{c}} + e^{-\frac{x}{c}} \right\},$$

the axis of y being a vertical line through the lowest point of the curve, and the axis of x a horizontal line in the plane of the string at a distance c below the lowest point. c is the length of string, the weight of which measures the tension at the lowest point, and e is the base of Napierian logarithms.

At a distance c from the origin measured along the axis of x, the corresponding value of y is

$$\frac{c}{2} \{ e^1 + e^{-1} \},$$

at a distance $2c$ it is

$$\frac{c}{2} \{ e^2 + e^{-2} \},$$

and so on; and if we make c the unit of length the corresponding values of y are
$$\tfrac{1}{2} \{ e^1 + e^{-1} \},$$
$$\tfrac{1}{2} \{ e^2 + e^{-2} \},$$
and so on.

The third column of the following table gives the value of $\frac{y}{c}$ at the corresponding points along the axis of x as shewn by the first column

$$e = 2 \cdot 718281828 \ldots \qquad \log_e 10 = \cdot 43429448 \ldots$$

Abscissæ	$\frac{1}{2}\{e^{\frac{x}{c}} + e^{-\frac{x}{c}}\}$	$\dfrac{y}{c}$
$x = \dfrac{c}{4}$	$\frac{1}{2}\,(1\cdot28405 + \cdot77880)$	$1\cdot03142$
$x = \dfrac{c}{2}$	$\frac{1}{2}\,(1\cdot6487\ \ + \cdot60653)$	$1\cdot1276$
$x = \dfrac{3c}{4}$	$\frac{1}{2}\,(2\cdot117\ \ \ + \cdot47144)$	$1\cdot294422$
$x = c$	$\frac{1}{2}\,(2\cdot71828 + \cdot36788)$	$1\cdot54308$
$x = 2c$	$\frac{1}{2}\,(7\cdot389\ \ \ + \cdot13534)$	$3\cdot76217$
$x = 3c$	$\frac{1}{2}\,(20\cdot0855 + \cdot049787)$	$10\cdot0676\ldots$
$x = 4c$	$\frac{1}{2}\,(54\cdot598\ \ + \cdot018316)$	$27\cdot308\ldots$

PROBLEM 158. *To draw the common catenary, the unit c being given.*

Example 1. ($c = OA$) fig. 160.

Draw the horizontal line Ox and the vertical line Oy. On Oy measure $OA = c$. A will be the lowest point of the curve. Set off from O along Ox lengths $Oa = ab = bd = c$, and draw the ordinates through a, b, d... parallel to Oy.

On the ordinate through a measure from a a length $ap_1 =$ (the number in third column of above table opposite $x = c$) $\times\, c$, i.e. $1\cdot54308 \times c$ (e.g. if c is $\frac{1}{2}''$ it is only necessary to measure off on a diagonal scale of half inches a length $1\cdot54$). p_1 will be a point on the curve. Similarly on the ordinate through b measure $bp_2 =$ (number in column 3 opposite $x = 2c$) $\times\, c$, i.e. $3\cdot76217 \times c$. p_2 will be a point on the curve. Similarly for ordinate through d.

Points can of course be found between A and p_1 by using the fractions of c given in the table.

Example 2. ($c = OA$) fig. 161.

The points p_1, p_2, p_3, p_4 on the ordinates through a, b, d, e, where
$$Oa = ab = bd = de = \tfrac{1}{4}c,$$
are given by the table: the next point furnished by the table would be on the ordinate through f, where $ef = Oe$. Points on

ordinates between e and f may be found without calculation as follows :

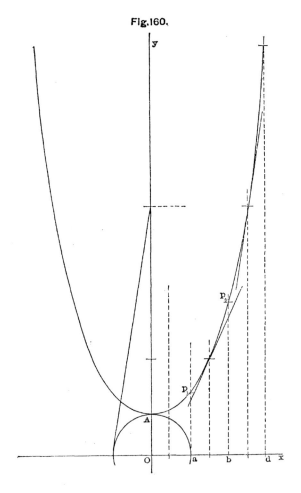

Fig. 160.

Any three equidistant ordinates $(y_{n-1},\ y_n,\ y_{n+1})$ are connected by the relation

$$y_{n-1} \times y_{n+1} = y_n^2 + k^2,$$

where k is some constant, i.e. if $eg = de$

$$gp_5 = \frac{\overline{ep_4}^2 + k^2}{dp_3}.$$

Construct the right-angled triangle AOm, with hypotenuse $Am = ap_1$, the ordinate at distance $Oa = de = eg$ from origin : the length Om is the value of the constant k.

If p_4q_4 be drawn parallel to Ox and meeting Oy in q_4,

$$\overline{mq_4}|^2 = \overline{ep_4}|^2 + k^2,$$

so that the required length gp_5 can be determined by taking a third proportional to dp_3 and mq_4.

Similarly, if $gh = eg = Oa$,

$$ep_4 : mq_5 :: mq_5 : hp_6;$$

or, since $eh = be$, hp_6 may be determined from

$$bp_2 : m_1q_4 :: m_1q_4 : hp_6,$$

where m_1 is a point on Ox such that $Am_1 = bp_2$.

To draw the tangent at any point (p_5 *say*).

With centre O and radius OA describe a circle; through p_5 draw p_5q_5 parallel to Ox and meeting Oy in q_5. The tangent at p_5 will be parallel to one of the tangents which can be drawn from q_5 to the above circle.

From g, the foot of the ordinate at p_5, draw gt perpendicular to the tangent at p_5 meeting it in t. $gt = OA$, the c of the curve, and p_5t is the length of the arc of the curve between p_5 and the lowest point, i.e. $p_5t =$ arc Ap_5.

To determine the centre and radius of curvature at any point (*as p_3*).

Draw the normal at p_3 meeting the horizontal axis Ox in G. On the normal make $p_3S = p_3G$. S will be the required centre, and Sp_3 the radius of curvature.

PROBLEM 159. *To draw a catenary, the vertex A, the axis Ay and a point Q being given* (Fig. 161).

The following method is approximate only, but gives tolerably close results provided the depth of A below Q does not exceed two-thirds of the distance of Q from Ay.

Find on Ay the centre (F) of the circle passing through A and Q, and determine the length of the circular arc AQ, i.e. from a table of the circular measure of angles get the circular measure corresponding to the number of degrees in the angle AFQ and

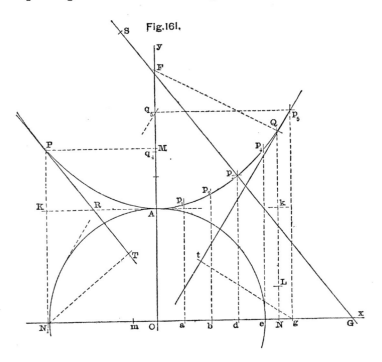

Fig. 161.

multiply this number by the length FA measured on any convenient scale. [In the figure AFQ contains $64°$, the circular measure of which is 1.117, and $FA = 5$, the unit being $\frac{1}{4}$ inch; the length of the circular arc AQ is therefore 5.585 units.] From Q set off downwards on a parallel to Ay drawn through Q the length $QL =$ the circular arc AQ as above determined, and let the horizontal through A meet QL in k, and make LN on Q produced through L a third proportional to twice Qk and kL; i.e. take

$$LN : kL :: kL : 2 . Qk.$$

N will be a point on the axis Ox of the required catenary, i.e. c is determined for the required curve.

[N is easily determined by inflecting from L to Ak produced a length $Lk_1 =$ twice Qk; produce k_1L to n making $Ln = kL$.

n will be a point on the required axis of Ox; for by the similar triangles Lkk_1, LNn,

$$LN : Lk :: Ln : Lk_1 :: Lk : 2.Qk.]$$

The construction is based on the assumption that the length of the arc of a catenary near the vertex does not sensibly differ from the circular arc passing through its centre and extremities; and the point N is determined so that the tangent from it to a circle with centre Q and radius QL shall be equal to Nk.

PROBLEM 160. *To draw a catenary, a point of suspension P, the tangent PT at that point, and the depth PK of the loop being given* (Fig. 161).

Draw the horizontal through K meeting PT in R.

On PR produced make $RT = RK$, and draw TN_1 perpendicular to PT meeting PK in N_1.

$KN_1 = $ the unit c for the required curve. PT is the length of the arc between P and the lowest point, and a known expression for its length is

$$PT = \frac{c}{2} \left(e^{\frac{x}{c}} - e^{-\frac{x}{c}} \right),$$

where $x = AK$.   Also

$$PN_1 = \frac{c}{2} \left(e^{\frac{x}{c}} + e^{-\frac{x}{c}} \right),$$

$$\therefore \quad \frac{PN_1 + PT}{c} = e^{\frac{x}{c}};$$

or

$$\frac{x}{c} \log e = \log \overline{PN_1 + PT} - \log c,$$

i.e.

$$x = KN_1 \left\{ \frac{\log \overline{PN_1 + PT} - \log KN_1}{\log e} \right\},$$

which determines the vertex A.

PROBLEM 161. *To draw a catenary, the axis Oy, a point P on the curve, and the tangent PT being given* (Fig. 161).

Through P draw PN_1 parallel to Oy, and PM perpendicular to Oy meeting it in M.   Let the angle $TPN_1 = \theta$, and if PT is

= length of arc between P and A the vertex, we have if TN_1 is perpendicular to PT,

$$PT = PN_1 \cos \theta = \frac{c}{2} \left\{ \epsilon^{\frac{PM}{c}} - \epsilon^{-\frac{PM}{c}} \right\},$$

and

$$PN_1 = \frac{c}{2} \left\{ \epsilon^{\frac{PM}{c}} + \epsilon^{-\frac{PM}{c}} \right\},$$

$$\therefore \; PN_1 (1 + \cos \theta) = c \cdot \epsilon^{\frac{PM}{c}},$$

but

$$c = TN_1 = PN_1 \sin \theta,$$

$$\therefore \; \cos \frac{\theta}{2} = \sin \frac{\theta}{2} \epsilon^{\frac{PM}{c}} \text{ or } \epsilon^{\frac{PM}{c}} = \cot \frac{\theta}{2},$$

$$\therefore \; \frac{PM}{c} \log \epsilon = \log \cot \frac{\theta}{2},$$

or

$$c = PM \left\{ \frac{\log \epsilon}{\log \cot \dfrac{\theta}{2}} \right\}.$$

By means of a table of logarithms, the value of c can be calculated, and when the length N_1T is known, the points N_1 and T are of course easily determined.

THE TRACTORY OR ANTI-FRICTION CURVE.

The involute of the Catenary is called the Tractrix or Tractory. Since in the catenary (fig. 161) gt drawn from the foot of the ordinate at any point P, perpendicular to the tangent at P, meets it in a point t such that $Pt =$ arc of catenary measured from the lowest point, t is evidently a point on the involute of the catenary and tg is a tangent to the involute. Also tg is constant (p. 318) and equal to OA, and therefore the Tractory is a curve such that the intercept on its tangent between the point of contact and a fixed right line is constant. This fixed length is called the *constant of the curve*.

E.

The equation of the tractory may be written

$$t \log \frac{t - \sqrt{t^2 - y^2}}{y} + x + \sqrt{t^2 - y^2} = 0,$$

where OA (fig. 162) is the axis of y, ON the axis of x and $OA = t$ the constant of the curve.

PROBLEM 162.   *To draw a Tractory the constant t being given* (Fig. 162).

Describe the catenary corresponding to the unit $t = OA$ (Problem 158).

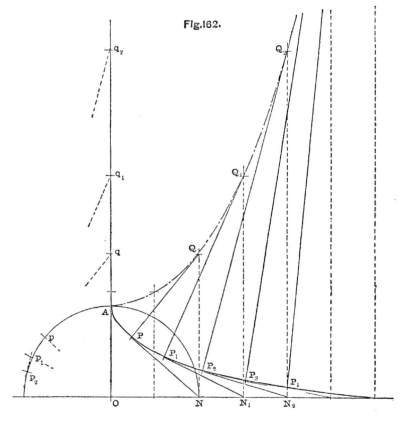

Fig.162.

In the figure since $ON = OA$, QN the ordinate of the catenary $= 1\cdot543\ldots \times OA$, and so for other points.

Draw QP the tangent at Q (p. 318) and NP perpendicular to QP and therefore parallel to Op. P is a point on the tractrix as already shewn, and similarly other points can be determined.

The centre of curvature at P is of course the point Q.

The line ON is an asymptote to the curve, and by the revolution of the curve round ON a solid is generated, the form of which has been adopted for the foot of a vertical shaft working in a socket or step. This pivot is known as Schiele's Anti-Friction Pivot. The theoretical advantage of the adoption of the form in this case is that the vertical wear of the pivot and step is everywhere equal.

INVERSE CURVES.

DEF. If on any radius vector OP drawn from a fixed origin O, a point P' be taken such that the rectangle $OP \cdot OP'$ is constant, the point P' is called the inverse of the point P; and if P describe any curve, P' describes another curve called the inverse of the former, with respect to the pole O.

Let O be the pole and P, Q two points on any curve, and let P_1, Q_1 be the inverse points, then by definition

$$OP \cdot OP_1 = OQ \cdot OQ_1 = k^2 \text{ suppose.}$$

A circle can therefore be described round PQQ_1P_1 and hence the triangles OQP and OP_1Q_1 are equiangular. (Euc. III. 22.)

$$\therefore \frac{PQ}{P_1Q_1} = \frac{OP}{OQ_1} = \frac{OP \cdot OQ}{OQ \cdot OQ_1} = \frac{OP \cdot OQ}{k^2}.$$

Since the angle $OQ_1P_1 =$ the angle OPQ, it follows that when Q moves up to and coincides with P so that PQ becomes the tangent at P, Q_1 moves up to and coincides with P_1, and Q_1P_1 becomes the tangent at P_1, and the angle OP_1T_1 between OP_1 and Q_1P_1 produced is equal to the angle OPQ, so that the tangents to a curve and its inverse at corresponding points make equal angles with the radius vector but on opposite sides of it.

The Limaçon. The inverse of an ellipse or hyperbola with respect to a focus is called a limaçon. The polar equation to an ellipse or hyperbola, the focus being the pole and the major axis the initial line, is $r = \dfrac{b^2}{a} \cdot \dfrac{1}{1 + e \cos \theta}$, where a and b are the major and minor axes of the ellipse or the transverse and conjugate axes of the hyperbola, and e is the eccentricity of the curve (pp. 99 and 154).

If r be produced to a length r' such that $rr' = k^2$ (Def. p. 323), the above equation becomes

$$\frac{k^2}{r'} = \frac{b^2}{a} \frac{1}{1 + e \cos \theta} \text{ or } r' = \frac{ak^2}{b^2}(1 + e \cos \theta),$$

which is of the form $r' = A \cos \theta + B$ the equation to the Limaçon.

$$A = \frac{ak^2}{b^2} e = \frac{ak^2}{b^2} \cdot \frac{\sqrt{a^2 \pm b^2}}{a} = \frac{k^2}{b^2} \sqrt{a^2 \pm b^2},$$

the positive sign being taken for an hyperbola, negative for an ellipse, and $B = \dfrac{ak^2}{b^2}$ so that $\dfrac{A}{B} = e$ the eccentricity of the conic.

Hence the constant for the Inverse being given, the values of A and B for the limaçon corresponding to any particular conic can be calculated—and conversely the equation to the Limaçon being given, and also the constant k, the particular conic of which it is the inverse may be determined by solving the above two equations for a and b.

Evidently A is less than B in the inverse of the ellipse, and greater in the inverse of the hyperbola.

PROBLEM 163. *To describe a Limaçon, the equation to the curve being given* (Fig. 163).

Let the given equation be $r = A \cos \theta + B$.

Draw a circle of diameter $OD = A$, and on DO set off from D on each side of D lengths DM, Dm each equal to B. M and m are evidently the points corresponding to the values of θ, zero and 180°, O being the pole; i.e. OD must be the initial line.

Through O draw any line whatever cutting the circle in Q.

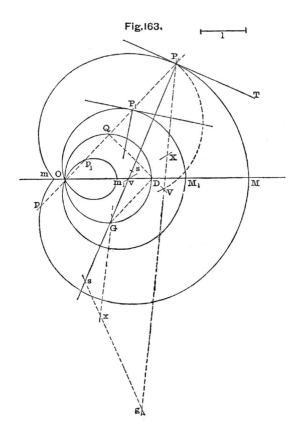

Fig.163.

On it from Q on each side of Q set off lengths QP, Qp each equal to B. P and p will be points on the curve;

for $\qquad OP = OQ + QP = OD \cos DOQ + QP$

$$= A \cos \theta + B,$$

and $\qquad Op = QP - OQ = QP - OD \cos DOQ$

$$= QP + OD \cos (180 + DOQ)$$

$$= A \cos \theta + B,$$

the θ in this case of course corresponding to the radius Op.

Similarly, by drawing a series of lines through O and setting off on them from the points where they cut the circle, the constant length B any number of points can be determined.

In the figure the outer curve with plain letters is the inverse of an ellipse, and the inner one with suffixed letters the inverse of an hyperbola.

The values of the constants are $A = 2\cdot1$,

B for the outer curve $= 2\cdot4$,

B ,,   inner   ,, $= \cdot84$, the unit being the length l.

Hence corresponding to the value $k^2 = 1\cdot7$ we have

$$2\cdot1 = \frac{1\cdot7}{b^2}\sqrt{a^2 - b^2},$$

and
$$2\cdot4 = \frac{1\cdot7}{b^2}\,a,$$

whence $a = 3$ and $b = 1\cdot46$ the semi-axes of the ellipse of which the figure is the inverse; and corresponding to the value $k^2 = 9$ we have

$$2\cdot1 = \frac{9}{b^2}\sqrt{a^2 + b^2},$$

$$\cdot84 = \frac{9a}{b^2},$$

whence
$$a = 2\cdot03,$$
$$b = 4\cdot66,$$

the semi-axes of the hyperbola of which the inner curve is the inverse.

To draw the normal at any point P of a Limaçon.

Through D draw DG parallel to OP, meeting the circle on OD as diameter again in G, which will be a point on the required normal.

To find the centre of curvature at any point P.

On OP as diameter describe a semicircle, and draw QV perpendicular to OP meeting it in V. On PG, the normal at P, make

$Pv = PV$ and draw vX parallel to GV meeting PV in X. On PV make $Pg = 2 \cdot PG$ and draw Gx through G parallel to Pg and $= PX$. gx will intersect PG in s, the other extremity of the diameter of curvature at P, so that S the required centre is the point of bisection of Ps.

Proof. It is easily shewn analytically that if ρ is the radius of curvature at P,

$$\rho = \frac{\{A^2 + 2AB \cos \theta + B^2\}^{\frac{3}{2}}}{2A^2 + 3AB \cos \theta + B^2},$$

where A and B are the constants of the curve and θ is the angle DOP.

But $\qquad A^2 + 2AB \cos \theta + B^2 = PG^2,$

and $\qquad \therefore\ A^2 + AB \cos \theta = PG^2 - (B^2 + AB \cos \theta),$

$$\therefore\ \rho = \frac{PG^3}{2 \cdot PG^2 - (B^2 + AB \cos \theta)}.$$

But $\qquad QV^2 = OQ \cdot QP = AB \cos \theta,$

and $\qquad PV^2 = PQ^2 + QV^2 = B^2 + AB \cos \theta,$

$$\therefore\ \rho = \frac{PG^3}{2PG^2 - PV^2}.$$

By construction $\qquad PX : PV :: Pv : PG,$

and $\qquad Pv = PV,\ \therefore\ PX \cdot PG = PV^2,$

$$\therefore\ \rho = \frac{PG^2}{2PG - PX},$$

i.e. $2\rho : PG :: 2PG : 2PG - PX,$

or $2\rho : 2\rho - PG :: 2PG : PX,$

but $Ps : Gs :: Pg : GX,$

i.e. $Ps : Ps - PG :: 2PG : PX,$

$$\therefore\ Ps = 2\rho.$$

The limaçon is an epi-trochoid, the diameters of the directing and rolling circles being equal.

The Inverse of a Parabola is called a Cardioid, i.e. a Cardioid is a Limaçon in the equation of which the constants A and B are equal.

Its equation is therefore $r = A \ (1 + \cos \theta)$.

The inner loop disappears in this case, and the origin is a cusp on the curve.

PROBLEM 164. *To describe a Cardioid, the equation to the curve being given* (Fig. 164).

Let the given equation be

$$r = A \ (1 + \cos \theta).$$

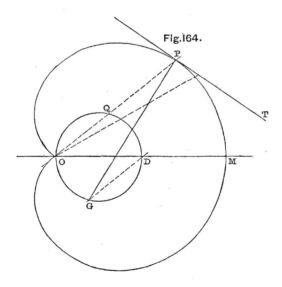

Fig.164.

Draw a circle of diameter $OD = A$ and on OD produced set off

$$DM = A.$$

M is evidently the point on the curve corresponding to zero value of θ, O being the pole; i.e. OD must be the initial line.

Through O draw any line whatever cutting the circle in Q, and on OQ produced make $QP = OD = A$. P will be a point on the curve, for

$$OP = OQ + QP = OD \cos DOQ + QP = A\,(1 + \cos \theta).$$

Similarly, any number of points on the curve can be obtained.

To draw the normal at any point P.

Through D draw DG parallel to OP meeting the circle again in G. G is a point on the required normal.

THE LEMNISCATE OF BERNOULLI.

The inverse curve of the Rectangular Hyperbola with respect to its centre is called a Lemniscate.

The polar equation to the rectangular hyperbola, the centre being the pole, and one of the axes the initial line, is

$$r^2 \cos 2\theta = a^2.$$

If any radius vector OP, O being the centre, is produced to P' so that $OP \cdot OP' = k^2$, where k is any constant, P will by definition be a point on the inverse.

If $OP = r$, $OP' = r'$, this may be written

$$r^2 r'^2 = k^4 \quad \text{or} \quad r'^2 = \frac{k^4}{a^2} \cos 2\theta\,;$$

the polar equation to the lemniscate may therefore be written

$$r^2 = K^2 \cos 2\theta.$$

The lemniscate is a particular case of the ovals of Cassini, the distance between the foci being $\sqrt{2}K$ and the product of the focal distances of any point of the curve being $\dfrac{K^2}{2}$.

PROBLEM 165. *To describe a lemniscate, the constant of the curve being given* (Fig. 165).

Draw any two lines OB, Ob at right angles to each other. On OB make $OA = OA_1 =$ the constant K of the curve. A and A_1

are evidently points on the curve corresponding to the values of

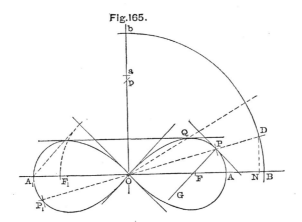

Fig.165.

θ, zero and 180°. On Ob make $Oa = OA$, and with O as centre, and Aa as radius, describe a quadrant of a circle Bb.

Draw any line OD through O meeting the circle in D, and draw DN perpendicular to OA meeting it in N. With A as centre, and ON as radius describe an arc cutting Ob in p, and make OP, OP_1 on OD each $= Op$. P and P_1 will be points on the curve.

Similarly any additional number can be determined.

The curve passes through the origin for $r = O$ when $2\theta = 90°$, and lines drawn through O making 45° with OA (the initial line) are tangents to the curve at O.

Proof. The equation to the curve may be written

$$r^2 = K^2 (2 \cos^2 \theta - 1) \text{ or } \frac{r^2 + K^2}{2K^2} = \cos^2 \theta,$$

but

$$\cos^2 DON = \overline{\frac{ON}{OL}}\Big|^2 = \frac{\overline{ON}\Big|^2}{2K^2} ;$$

$$\therefore r^2 = \overline{ON^2}\Big| - K^2,$$

which by construction it does since

$$AP = ON \text{ and } OA = K.$$

Between the values $90°$ and $270°$ for 2θ, $\cos 2\theta$ is negative, and consequently no real values for r exist.

The length OQ corresponding to an angle $AOQ = 30°$ is $\frac{1}{2}OB$, and the tangent at Q is parallel to OB.

To draw the tangent and normal at any point.

The angle OPG between the radius vector OP and the normal PG is twice the angle POA. Considered as one of Cassini's ovals the foci are at F and F_1 where $OF = OF_1 = \frac{1}{2}OB$, and the normal may of course be drawn in the manner given for those curves, i.e. by making the angle $F_1PG = $ angle OPF.

PROBLEM 166. *Given two points A and O, and a line OB through one of them, to determine the locus of a point P moving so that the angles which OP makes with PA and with a parallel to OB through P, shall be equal* (Fig. 166).

On OA as diameter describe a circle, and through O draw a perpendicular to OB.

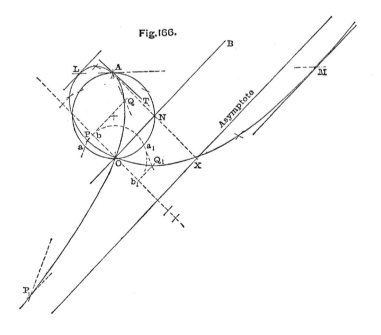

Fig.166.

With O as centre and any radius less than OA, describe a circle cutting the circle on OA in a and a_1, and the perpendicular through O in b and b_1.

Draw Aa meeting parallels to OB through b and b_1 in P and P_1, and draw Aa_1 meeting the same parallels in Q and Q_1. P, Q, P_1 and Q_1 will be points on the required locus, for the triangles ObQ, Oa_1Q, e.g. are equal in all respects.

Similarly any additional number of points can be determined as shewn.

The curve extends to an infinite distance on both sides of O, and has an asymptote parallel to OB on the opposite side to A and at the same distance from OB as A; or if AN be drawn perpendicular to OB and NX on it be made equal to AN, the asymptote passes through X.

The internal and external bisectors of the angle AOB are tangents at O to the two branches of the curve passing through that point. The tangent at A is inclined to OA at an angle OAT = angle AOB, and parallels to OB at distances from it = OA are tangents to the curve. The points of contact L and M of these last are determined by drawing LAM perpendicular to OA. At some point beyond M the curve becomes convex to the asymptote.

This problem is a solution of the question :—to find the point on a spherical mirror, on which a ray from any point A must impinge in order that it may be reflected parallel to a given direction.

For if O be the centre of the mirror, the circular arc representing the section of the mirror by the plane passing through A, O, and the line OB through O parallel to the given direction, will of course cut the curve in points such that the incident and reflected rays make equal angles with the normals at those points. In other words the problem is to find the point P on a given circle at which the lines AP, PB, A being a given point and PB being parallel to a given line make equal angles with the normal at P.

The whole curve in such a case need not be drawn, since it

is easy to find points on the curve in the neighbourhood of the part of the mirror required and to draw an arc of the curve through them.

PROBLEM 167. *Given three points A, B, C, to determine the locus of a point P moving so that the angles which PC makes with PA and PB are always equal* (Fig. 167).

Let AC be greater than BC. On AC and BC as diameters describe circles, and with centre C and any radius not greater than

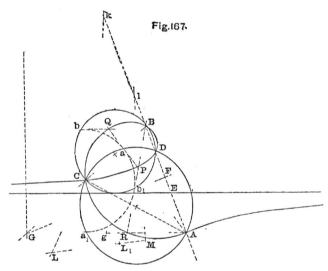

Fig. 167.

BC describe an arc cutting the circle on AC in a and a_1, and the circle on BC in b and b_1. The lines Aa, Aa_1 will intersect both the lines Bb and Bb_1 in points on the required locus. Only three of the intersections are shewn in the figure, viz. the points P, Q and R, the fourth not falling within the limits of the paper. Similarly any additional number of points can be determined as shewn.

The curve extends to an infinite distance on both sides of the line AB, and has an asymptote parallel to the line joining C to the centre point of AB, and which cuts AB between A and D the foot of the perpendicular from C on AB at a distance DE from D, which may be thus determined.

Let $BC = a$, $AC = b$, $AD = m$, $BD = n$ and $CD = h$.

It can be shewn analytically that the length

$$DE = \overline{m - n} \frac{a^2 + b^2}{\overline{m - n}|^2 + \overline{2h}|^2} \cdot$$

On DA make $DF = DB$, therefore $AF = \overline{m - n}$.

Draw FG perpendicular to AB meeting BC in G, so that

$$FG = 2DC = 2h ;$$

$$\therefore \quad \overline{AG}|^2 = \overline{AF}|^2 + \overline{FG}|^2 = \overline{m-n}|^2 + \overline{2h}|^2.$$

Draw GK perpendicular to AG meeting AB in K, so that by similar triangles

$$AF : AG :: AG : AK ;$$

$$\therefore \quad \overline{AG}|^2 = AF . AK.$$

In the figure K is beyond the limits of the paper, but if AG is bisected in g, and gk is drawn perpendicular to AG meeting AB in k, $Ak = \frac{1}{2}AK$ and therefore $\overline{AG}|^2 = 2 . AF . Ak.$

The above expression for DE therefore becomes

$$DE = \frac{a^2 + b^2}{AK} \cdot$$

Draw CL perpendicular to AC and make $CL = CB$ so that

$$AL^2 = a^2 + b^2.$$

On AB make $Al = AL$, and through l draw lM parallel to KL meeting AL in M. (In the figure AL is bisected in L_1 so that kL_1 is parallel to KL.)   By similar triangles

$$AM : Al :: AL : AK \text{ or } AM = \frac{Al . AL}{AK} = \frac{\overline{AL}|^2}{AK}$$

$$= \frac{a^2 + b^2}{AK} ,$$

i.e. AM will be the required length DE.   The asymptote can then be drawn through E parallel to the line joining C to the middle point of AB.

The internal and external bisectors of the angle ACB are tangents at C to the two branches of the curve passing through that point.

The tangents AT, BT_1 at A and B make angles CAT, CBT_1 with CA and CB equal respectively to the angles CAB, CBA.

This problem is a solution of the question :—to find the point on a spherical mirror on which a ray from A must impinge in order that it may be reflected to B;—for if C be the centre of the mirror, the circular arc representing the section of the mirror by the plane passing through A, B and C will of course cut the curve in points such that the rays from A and B make equal angles with the normals at the points. In other words the problem is to find the point P on a given circle at which the lines AP, BP, A and B being given points make equal angles with the normal at P.

The whole curve in such a case need not be drawn, since it is easy to find points on the curve in the neighbourhood of the point required and to draw an arc of the curve through them.

Magnetic curves.

The locus of the vertex of a triangle described on a given base and having the sum of the cosines of the base angles constant, is called a magnetic curve.

If AB be the given base, and P a point on the locus, we must therefore have $\cos PAB + \cos PBA = k$, and corresponding to different values of k, we get a series of curves passing through A and B. These represent the *lines of force* in the plane of the paper due to a magnet whose poles are the points A and B.

The greatest value of k is 2, since the numerical value of the cosine of an angle is never > 1, and k may have any value between 0 and 2.

PROBLEM 168. *To draw a magnetic curve, the base AB and the constant k being given* (Fig. 168).

On AB as diameter describe a circle $ARQB$, and on AB take a point M such that
$$AM = k \cdot AB.$$

Draw any line through A cutting the circle in Q, and make Aq on $AM = AQ$.

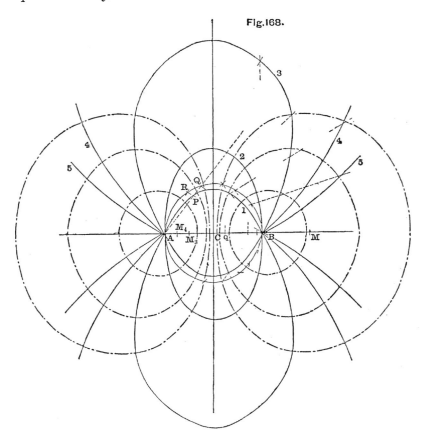

Fig.168.

With centre B, and radius $BR = Mq$ describe an arc cutting the circle in R.

BR will intersect AQ in P a point on the required curve, for

$$\cos BAP = \frac{AQ}{AB} \quad \text{and} \quad \cos ABP = \frac{BR}{AB};$$

$$\therefore \quad \cos BAP + \cos ABP = \frac{AQ + BR}{AB} = \frac{Aq + qM}{AB} = k.$$

Similarly, any additional number of points can be obtained.

The tangents at A and B may be determined by considering that when P moves down to B the angle BAP becomes zero, and its cosine $=$ unity ;

$$\therefore \quad \cos ABT = k - 1.$$

In the curve marked 1 in the figure $k = \frac{3}{2}$,

$$\quad ,, \quad\quad ,, \quad\quad 2 \quad\quad ,, \quad\quad k = 1,$$
$$\quad ,, \quad\quad ,, \quad\quad 3 \quad\quad ,, \quad\quad k = \frac{1}{2},$$
$$\quad ,, \quad\quad ,, \quad\quad 4 \quad\quad ,, \quad\quad k = \frac{1}{4},$$
$$\quad ,, \quad\quad ,, \quad\quad 5 \quad\quad ,, \quad\quad k = \frac{1}{8}.$$

For curve number 2 therefore M coincides with B,

$$\quad ,, \quad\quad 3 \quad ,, \quad M \quad\quad ,, \quad\quad C, \text{ the centre}$$

of the circle on AB.

For curves Nos. 4 and 5 M is at M_3 and M_4 respectively bisecting and quadrisecting AC.

Corresponding to the value 2 of k we get the diameter AB itself for the locus, and corresponding to the value zero we get the productions of the diameter to the right and left of AB.

Each curve cuts the diameter of the circle perpendicular to AB at a distance from A or $B = \dfrac{AB}{k}$.

The chain-dotted curves in the figure are *equi-potential* curves (see next problem) and cut all the lines of force or magnetic curves at right angles.

Equi-potential Curves.

If the lines of force due to a magnet, in any plane passing through its poles, are cut normally by a series of curves, these are known as equi-potential curves, and by revolution round the line joining the poles they generate equi-potential surfaces.

If A and B are the poles of the magnet, and the length $AB = c$, the distances of any point P on one of the curves, from A and B are known to be connected by the relation

$$\frac{1}{AP} - \frac{1}{BP} = \frac{k}{c}$$

where k is constant throughout the particular curve considered, i.e. the equation to the series of curves may be written

$$\frac{1}{r} - \frac{1}{r_1} = \frac{k}{c},$$

where r and r_1 denote the distances of a point from A and B.

The value of k of course varies from curve to curve of the series.

PROBLEM 169. *To draw an equi-potential curve, the poles A and B and the constant k being given* (Fig. 169).

First determine the points in which the curve cuts the line AB.

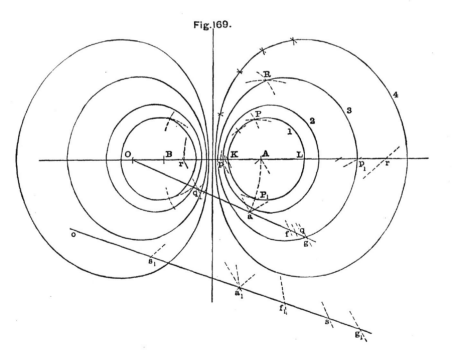

Fig. 169.

At the point K we evidently have

$$AK + BK = c, \text{ i.e. } r + r_1 = c \text{ or } r_1 = c - r$$

which, combined with the equation

$$\frac{1}{r} - \frac{1}{r_1} = \frac{k}{c},$$

determines the value of r and r_1.

We evidently have

$$\frac{1}{r} - \frac{k}{c} = \frac{1}{r_1} = \frac{1}{c - r},$$

or

$$\frac{c - kr}{cr} = \frac{1}{c - r},$$

or

$$c^2 - (\overline{2 + k}) cr + kr^2 = 0$$

a quadratic to determine r or AK, but the smallest of the two roots is the only admissible solution.

At the point L we have $BL - AL = c$,

i.e. $r_1 - r = c$ or $r_1 = c + r$.

The equation $\dfrac{1}{r} - \dfrac{1}{r_1} = \dfrac{k}{c}$ becomes therefore in this case

$$\frac{1}{r} - \frac{k}{c} = \frac{1}{c + r} \quad \text{or} \quad \frac{c - kr}{cr} = \frac{1}{c + r},$$

or

$$r^2 + cr = \frac{c^2}{k},$$

and one of the roots of this equation is the length AL.

To find any points on the curve ; on AB determine a length AO such that $AO = \dfrac{2c}{k}$, i.e. take

$$AO \ : \ AB \ :: \ 2 \ : \ k.$$

Through O draw any line Oa and on it make $Oa = OA$; set off on aO on each side of a equal lengths aq, aq_1 ; and through a draw ap parallel to Aq meeting AB in p and also draw ap_1 parallel to Aq_1 meeting AB in p_1. Then Ap and Ap_1 are corresponding values of r and r_1 for a point on the curve and therefore a circle described with centre A and radius Ap will intersect a circle described with centre B and radius $= Ap_1$ in points P and P_1 on the curve.

The distances aq, aq_1 must be taken within certain limits, since the length Ap which depends on aq cannot be greater than AL or less than AK. These limits can evidently be determined by drawing through A a parallel to Ka meeting aO in f, and similarly drawing Ag parallel to a line through a and point l on AB such that $Al = AL$. The points q must then be taken between f and g.

In the figure, the value of k for the curve marked 1 is $\frac{3}{2}$,

,,	,,	,,	,,	2 ,, 1,
,,	,,	,,	,,	3 ,, $\frac{1}{2}$,
,,	,,	,,	,,	4 ,, $\frac{1}{4}$,

and the corresponding values of AK and AL are

$$\text{for 1,} \quad AK = \frac{c}{3}, \qquad\qquad AL = c \cdot \frac{\sqrt{33} - 3}{6},$$

$$\text{,, 2,} \quad AK = \frac{c}{2}(3 - \sqrt{5}), \quad AL = \frac{c}{2}(\sqrt{5} - 1),$$

$$\text{,, 3,} \quad AK = \frac{c}{2}(5 - \sqrt{17}), \quad AL = c,$$

$$\text{,, 4,} \quad AK = \frac{c}{2}\{9 - \sqrt{65}\}, \quad AL = \frac{c}{2}(\sqrt{17} - 1).$$

These values can of course be determined arithmetically, or graphic methods may be employed.

Proof. From the similar triangles Opa, OAq

$$\frac{Ap}{aq} = \frac{OA}{Oq} = \frac{l}{l + aq} \quad \text{if } OA = l \quad \text{or} \quad \frac{1}{Ap} = \frac{l + aq}{l \cdot aq},$$

from the similar triangles Oap_1, Oq_1A

$$\frac{Ap_1}{aq_1} = \frac{OA}{Oq_1} = \frac{l}{l - aq_1} \quad \text{or} \quad \frac{1}{Ap_1} = \frac{l - aq_1}{l \cdot aq_1};$$

$$\therefore \quad \frac{1}{Ap} - \frac{1}{Ap_1} = \frac{2}{l} \quad \text{since } aq_1 = aq,$$

but l by construction $= \dfrac{2c}{k}$;

$$\therefore \quad \frac{1}{Ap} - \frac{1}{Ap_1} = \frac{k}{c}$$

or Ap and Ap_1 are corresponding values of r and r_1.

It may be noticed that the line corresponding to Oa of curve 1, is, for No. 3 the line oa_1, the distance between A and the intersection of AB and oa_1 being $4 \cdot AB$; that the limits, between which points corresponding to q must be taken are f_1 and g_1, and that the point R on the curve corresponds to s and s_1 on oa_1, $a_1 r$ being parallel to As and $a_1 r_1$ to As_1; so that

$$AR = Ar \quad \text{and} \quad BR = Ar_1.$$

The equi-potential curve corresponding to zero value of k, is the perpendicular to AB through its centre point.

THE CARTESIAN OVAL.

This curve owes its name to Descartes who first discussed its properties. M. Chasles, Mr Cayley, Mr Casey and others have since devoted a good deal of attention to it. A short discussion of the curve, treated geometrically, will be found in Chap. xx. of Williamson's *Differential Calculus*, 4th Edition, from which the following is mainly taken.

DEF. The locus of a point moving so that the sum or difference of its distances each multiplied by some constant from two fixed points, called the foci, is constant, is called a Cartesian oval.

If F, F_1 are the two fixed points, P the moving point, and $FP = r$, $FP_1 = r_1$ and $FF_1 = c$, the equation of the curve may be written in either of the forms

$$nr \pm lr_1 = mc \quad \dots\dots\dots\dots\dots\dots(1),$$

or $$\qquad r \pm Mr_1 = K \quad \dots\dots\dots\dots\dots\dots(2),$$

where K is some given length and M may be assumed to be less than unity.

PROBLEM 170. *To draw a Cartesian oval, the foci and constants of the curve being given* (Fig. 170).

Let F_1 and F_3 be the given foci, and the length $F_1F_3 = c_2$. The line joining F_1, F_3 is called the axis.

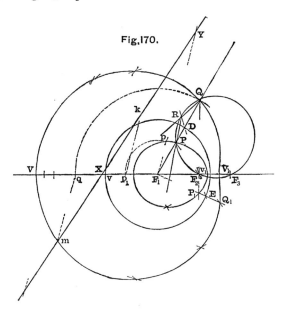

Fig. 170.

Let the distance of any point P on the curve from F_1 be denoted by r_1, and from F_3 by r_3, and suppose the equation of the curve to be written in the second of the above forms, i.e.

$$r_1 \pm Mr_3 = K.$$

On the line joining the foci, make $F_1X = K$, and through X draw a line XY making any convenient angle with the axis. On XY determine a length XY such that

$$XY : F_1X :: 1 : M.$$

With centre F_1 and any convenient radius less than F_1X describe an arc pp_1 cutting the axis in p_1; draw p_1k parallel to F_1Y meeting XY in k, and with centre F_3 and radius $= Xk$ describe an arc cutting the former in p; p will be a point on the curve, for

$$r_1 + Mr_3 = K;$$

$$\therefore \ r_3 = \frac{K - r_1}{M},$$

but $$p_1X = K - r_1,$$

and $$Xk : p_1X :: XY : F_1X :: 1 : M,$$

i.e. $$Xk \text{ or } r_3 = \frac{K - r_1}{M}.$$

Similarly any additional number of points may be determined.

Again with centre F_1 and any convenient radius greater than F_1X describe an arc Qq cutting the axis in q. Draw qm parallel to F_1Y cutting YX in m, and with centre F_3 and radius $= Xm$ describe an arc cutting the former in Q. Q will be a point on the curve, for

$$r_1 - Mr_3 = K,$$

$$\therefore \ r_3 = \frac{r_1 - K}{M};$$

but $$Xq = r_1 - K,$$

and $$Xm : Xq :: XY : F_1X :: 1 : M,$$

i.e. $$Xm \text{ or } r_3 = \frac{r_1 - K}{M}.$$

The curve consists of two ovals one lying wholly inside the other, the point p belonging to the inner, and Q to the outer.

The radii F_1p, F_1Q must be taken within certain limits which may be determined thus :—

To find the points in which the curve cuts the axis.

Let the inner curve cut the axis in v and v_1, and the outer in V and V_1.

We have

$$r_1 \pm Mr_3 = K, \quad \therefore \ r_3 = \frac{K - r_1}{M},$$

or $$r_3 = \frac{r_1 - K}{M},$$

the positive sign referring to the inner curve, and the negative sign to the outer.

At v and V we have

$$r_1 + c_2 = r_3,$$

i.e.
$$F_1 v + c_2 = F_3 v = \frac{K - F_1 v}{M},$$

or
$$F_1 v \left(1 + M\right) = K - M \cdot c_2,$$

which determines $F_1 v$, and

$$F_1 V + c_2 = F_3 V = \frac{F_1 V - K}{M},$$

or
$$F_1 V \left(1 - M\right) = K + M \cdot c_2,$$

which determines $F_1 V$.

Again at v_1 and V_1 we have

$$r_1 + r_3 = c_2,$$

i.e.
$$F_1 v_1 + F_3 v_1 = c_2 = F_1 v_1 + \frac{K - F_1 v_1}{M},$$

or
$$F_1 v_1 \left(1 - M\right) = K - M \cdot c_2,$$

which determines $F_1 v_1$, and

$$F_1 V_1 + F_3 V_1 = c_2 = F_1 V_1 + \frac{F_1 V_1 - K}{M},$$

or
$$F_1 V_1 \left(1 + M\right) = K + M \cdot c_2,$$

which determines $F_1 V_1$.

The radii for points on the inner oval must be greater than $F_1 v$ and less than $F_1 v_1$, and for points on the outer greater than $F_1 V_1$ and less than $F_1 V$.

Geometrical properties of the Curve.

The curve is evidently symmetrical about the axis.

Draw any line through F_1 cutting the curve in P and Q (on the same side of F_1); describe a circle round the triangle PQF_3 cutting the axis again in F_2, then $F_1 P \cdot F_1 Q = F_1 F_2 \cdot F_1 F_3$; but $F_1 P \cdot F_1 Q$ is constant, for

$$\overline{F_3 P}\big|^2 = \overline{F_1 P}\big|^2 + c_2{}^2 - 2 F_1 P \cdot c_2 \cdot \cos F_3 F_1 P = \overline{\frac{\overline{F_1 P - K}}{M}}\bigg|^2,$$

or $\quad \overline{F_1P}\rvert^2(1-M^2)-2\left(K-c_2M^2\cos F_3F_1P\right)F_1P-M^2.c_2{}^2+K^2=0,$

and F_1P and F_1Q are the roots of this equation, so that their product $=\dfrac{K^2-M^2c_2{}^2}{1-M^2}$ and is constant. Hence F_2 is a fixed point and it possesses the same properties relative to the curve as F_1 and F_3; in other words F_2 is a third focus. This may most conveniently be shewn from the equation of the curve in the form

$$nr_1 \pm lr_3 = mc_2,$$

where r_1 is the distance of any point on it from F_1, r_3 its distance from F_3 and $F_1F_3=c_2$, and $n>m>l$. Let $F_1F_2=c_3$ and denote the distance of a point from F_2 by r_2.

It is easily seen that the triangles F_1PF_2 and F_1F_3Q are equiangular;

$$\therefore \frac{F_1Q}{F_1F_3}=\frac{F_1F_2}{F_1P} \text{ and } \frac{F_3Q}{F_1F_3}=\frac{F_2P}{F_1P};$$

$\therefore$ the equation $\qquad nF_1Q - l.F_3Q = m.F_1F_3$

may be written

$$n.F_1F_2 - l.F_2P = m.F_1P,$$
$$\text{i.e. } \quad m.r_1 + l.r_2 = n.c_3 \quad \dots\dots\dots\dots\dots\dots(3),$$

which shows that the distances of any point on the inner oval from F_1 and F_2 are connected by an equation similar in form to (1) and consequently F_2 is a third focus of the curve.

In like manner since the triangles F_1QF_2 and F_1F_3P are equiangular, the equation

$$n.F_1P + l.F_3P = mF_1F_3$$

gives $\qquad n.F_1F_2 + l.F_2Q = m.F_1Q,$

or $\qquad mr_1 - l.r_2 = n.c_3 \quad \dots\dots\dots\dots\dots\dots(4),$

or the same holds for the outer oval.

Combined with the previous result, this shews that the conjugate ovals of a Cartesian referred to the two internal foci are represented by the equation

$$mr_1 \pm lr_2 = n.c_3 \quad \dots\dots\dots \dots\dots\dots\dots(5),$$

and referred to the two extreme foci by

$$nr_1 \pm lr_3 = mc_2.$$

Similarly it is easily seen that referred to the middle and external foci, they are represented by

$$nr_2 - mr_3 = \pm lc_1 \dots\dots\dots\dots\dots\dots\dots (6),$$

where $c_1 = F_2 F_3.$

Taking the equation (5) referred to the two internal foci, it may be written

$$r_1 \pm \frac{l}{m} r_2 = \frac{n}{m} c_3,$$

or $r_1 \pm A \cdot r_2 = B$ where A and B are constants.

With centre F_1 and radius $= B$ describe a circle DE.

[Evidently comparing equations (1) and (2) we may take

$$n = 1, \quad l = M, \quad m = \frac{K}{F_1 F_3},$$

so that B or $\dfrac{n}{m} c_3 = \dfrac{F_1 F_3}{K} \cdot F_1 F_2,$

i.e. $B : F_1 F_3 :: F_1 F_2 : K.$]

Let any line through F_1 meet it in D and the curve in P and Q. Let DF_2 meet the circle again in E.

Now $PD = B - PF_1 = A \cdot PF_2,$

$$QD = F_1 Q - B = A \cdot F_2 Q;$$

$$\therefore \quad F_2 Q : F_2 P :: QD : DP,$$

so that $F_2 D$ bisects the angle $PF_2 Q$.

Produce PF_2 and QF_2 to intersect $F_1 E$ in Q_1 and P_1. The triangles $PF_2 D$ and $P_1 F_2 E$ are similar and

$$\therefore \quad \frac{P_1 E}{F_2 P_1} = \frac{PD}{F_2 P} = A;$$

and consequently the point P_1 lies on the inner oval. So also the point Q_1 lies on the outer.

Again, since F_2D bisects the angle PF_2Q,

$$F_2P \cdot F_2Q = PD \cdot DQ + \overline{F_2D}|^2$$

$$= A^2 \cdot F_2P \cdot F_2Q + \overline{F_2D}|^2,$$

or $\qquad (1 - A^2)\, F_2P \cdot F_2Q = \overline{F_2D}|^2,$

and by similar triangles $\dfrac{F_2P}{F_2P_1} = \dfrac{F_2D}{F_2E}$;

$$\therefore (1 - A^2)\, F_2Q \cdot F_2P_1 = F_2D \cdot F_2E,$$

i. e. the rectangle under F_2Q and F_2P_1 is constant; a theorem due to M. Quetelet.

If the curve has been constructed from the two internal foci, the external focus can easily be determined, for the angle $F_1P_1F_2$ = the angle $F_1PF_2 = F_1F_3Q$, i. e. the angle F_1P_1Q = the angle F_1F_3Q or a circle through F_1P_1Q passes also through F_3.

To draw the tangent and normal at any point P.

Let F_1P meet the circle DE (of radius as previously described) in D and let F_2D meet the circle through PQF_2F_3 in R. Then R is a point on the normal at P and also on the normal at Q.

They may also easily be drawn without using the circle DE.

The equation of the curve referred to the extreme foci has been shewn to be

$$nr_1 \pm lr_3 = mc_2.$$

On PF_1, PF_3 measure lengths PL, PM proportional to n and l respectively, i. e. make $PL : PM :: n : l$.

Bisect LM in G and G will be a point on the normal at P.

The normal at Q may be constructed in exactly the same way, one of the two lengths being measured on the corresponding focal radius produced.

Similarly lengths on PF_1, PF_2 proportional to m and l determine the normal at P from vectors drawn from the internal foci.

ELASTIC CURVES.

In the widest sense of the term, an elastic curve is the figure assumed by the longitudinal axis of an originally straight bar under any system of bending forces. It is here restricted to the figure taken by a slender flat spring of uniform section when acted upon by a pair of equal and opposite forces.

The essential property of the curve under these conditions is that the *radius of curvature at any point is inversely proportional to the perpendicular distance of that point from the line of action of the forces*. Its equation may therefore be written

$$\rho y = a^2,$$

where ρ is the radius of curvature at any point, y the distance of that point from a fixed line in the plane of the curve and a constant.

A very close approximation to the form of the curve can be easily drawn by considering it as formed of a series of circular arcs—the appropriate radius for each being determined.

PROBLEM 171. *To draw an elastic curve the constant of the curve and the distance of the extreme point of the loop from the line of action of the forces being given.*

1st. A bent bow (Fig. 171).

Let AB be the line of action of the given forces, CD the maximum ordinate of the curve from AB. From any point D in AB draw DC perpendicular to AB and on it make $DC =$ the given maximum ordinate. From C inflect to AB a length $CE =$ the given constant of the curve and draw EO_1 perpendicular to CE meeting CD in O_1. Evidently $CD : CE :: CE : O_1C$, so that O_1 is the required centre of curvature at C and may be taken as the centre of a circular arc extending to a reasonably short distance on either side of C, draw it say to F and since FO_1 is the normal at F the centre for the adjacent arc must be taken on FO_1. Draw FG parallel to AB meeting CD in G and on DA make $DH = CE$ = the given constant of the curve. HK perpendicular to GH

meets CO_1 in a point K such that

$$GD : DH :: DH : DK;$$

Fig.171.

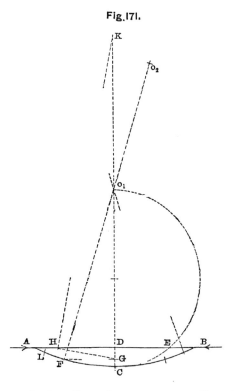

i.e. DK is the required radius of curvature at F, and therefore if FO_2 on FO_1 be made equal to DK, O_2 may be taken as the centre of a circular arc extending to a reasonably short distance from F as to L. Any number of successive centres may similarly be determined.

2nd. An undulating figure crossing AB at any number of intermediate points.

a. Let the given constant of the curve be greater than the maximum ordinate (Fig. 172).

Divide the given length AB into a number of equal parts corresponding to the number of required undulations and at the centre of one such segment of the line draw CD perpendicular to AB and equal to the given maximum ordinate, from C inflect to

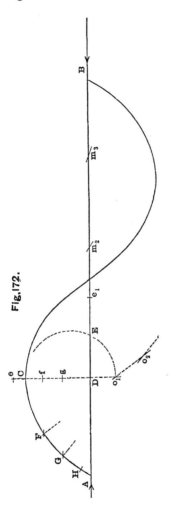

Fig. 172.

AB a length CE equal to the given constant and draw EO_1 perpendicular to CE meeting CD in O_1. O_1 will be the required centre of curvature at C for evidently $CD : CE :: CE : CO_1$; and a circular arc may be drawn through C with centre O_1 and extending to a reasonably short distance on either side of C as to F. The centre of the adjacent arc must lie on FO_1. Draw Ff

parallel to AB meeting CD in f and on DC, DB respectively make $De = De_1 = CE$. Through e draw em_2 parallel to fe_1, meeting AB in m_2 and Dm_2 will be the required radius of curvature at F for evidently $Df : De_1 :: De : Dm_2$, i.e. $\rho y = a^2$ where y is the ordinate of F. On FO_1 make $FO_2 = Dm_2$ and O_2 may be taken as the centre of the arc adjacent to CF. Similarly any number of additional centres may be determined—supposing the second arc extends to G, draw Gg parallel to AB, em_3 parallel to ge_1 and on GO_2 make GO_3 equal to Dm_3, O_3 will be the centre of curvature at G. As the radius of curvature at A is infinite the portion AH may be drawn tangential to the adjacent arc.

β. Let the given constant be less than the maximum ordinate (Fig. 173).

Divide up AB and draw CD the maximum ordinate as before. On CD describe a semicircle and in it make CE equal to the

Fig. 173.

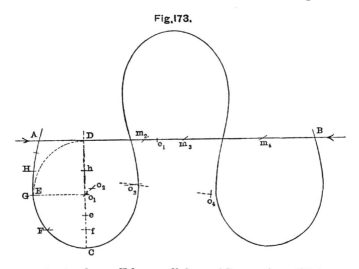

given constant: draw EO_1 parallel to AB meeting CD in O_1 the required centre of curvature at C. The rest of the construction is exactly similar to the above. $De = De_1 = CE$. Ff is parallel to AB and em_2 parallel to fe_1 determines Dm_2 the radius at F. In the figure G is taken on EO_1 so that g coincides with O_1 and em_3 parallel to O_1e_1 determines Dm_3 the radius of curvature at G.

3rd. The points A and B coinciding, which may give, with an endless spring, a figure of 8 (Fig. 174).

On CD describe a semi-circle; in it make CD equal to the given constant and draw EO_1 perpendicular to CD meeting it in

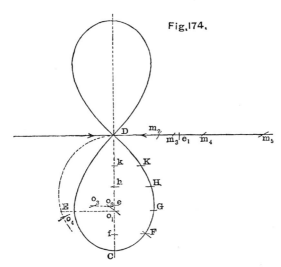

Fig.174.

O_1 which will be the required centre of curvature at C. Make $De = De_1 = CE$, De_1 being perpendicular to DC, and successive

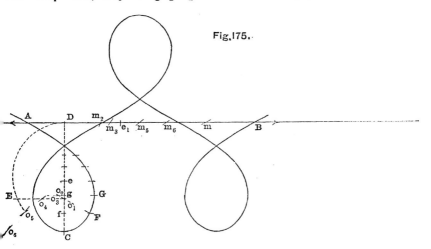

Fig.175.

centres may be determined precisely as before, the curve at D being drawn tangential to the adjacent arc.

4th. In figs. 171 to 174 inclusive the forces are directed *towards* each other. When they act in directions *from* each other the spring may form one or more loops, with the ends and intermediate portions meeting or crossing AB, as shewn in fig. 175,

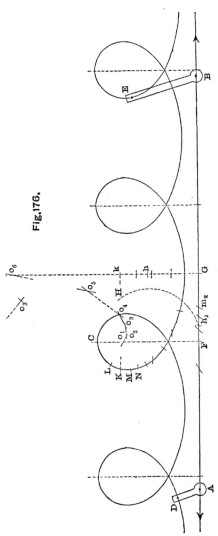

Fig.176.

the construction for which is exactly similar to the preceding and which is lettered to correspond.

5th. If the forces are directed from each other at the points A, B, in two rigid levers AD, BE to which the spring is fixed at D and E, the spring forms one or more looped coils lying altogether at one side of the line of action AB (fig. 176).

The general method of construction is the same as before, but the radius of each arc corresponding to its central portion instead of to one extremity has been determined.

Let CF be a maximum ordinate; on it describe a semi-circle and in the semi-circle make CH equal to the given constant: draw HO_1 perpendicular to CF meeting it in O_1 the centre of curvature at C. Draw GO_6 parallel to CF and at a distance from it equal to one-half the desired length of the loop of the curve, and on it make $Gh = CH$ the given constant: make Gh_1 on AB equal to Gh. Take any convenient point K at about the centre point of the intended second arc of the curve and draw Kk parallel to AB meeting GO_6 in k, then hm_2 drawn through h parallel to kh_1 determines Gm_2 the required radius of curvature at K. Take any convenient point L on the arc struck through C and join it to the centre O_1; make LO_2 on $LO_1 = Gm_2$, and O_2 will be the required second centre. Similarly any additional number of centres can be determined.

CURVES OF PURSUIT.

When a point A moves so that it is continually directed towards a second point B also in motion in some known curve, the locus of A is called a "*curve of pursuit.*"

The problem was first presented in the form—To find the path described by a dog which runs to overtake its master.

The velocities of the two moving points must of course be known, and the required locus can then be easily traced to any required degree of approximation by supposing the direction of motion to be constant for a short interval and then to be suddenly deflected.

PROBLEM 172. *A moves in a straight line from A to B with constant velocity, and C starts from C with constant velocity double that of A and is constantly directed on A. To find the curve of pursuit* (Fig. 177).

Set off from *A* along *AB* any convenient equal distances *A*1,

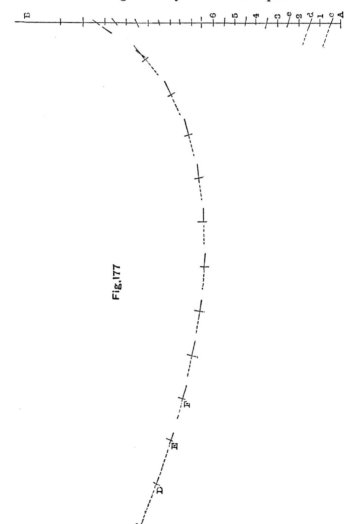

Fig. 177

12, 23,... While A advances from A to 1 suppose C's motion to be directed on c the centre point of $A1$. Then when A arrives at 1, C will be at the point D on Cc such that $CD =$ twice $A1$— while A advances from 1 to 2 suppose C's motion to be directed on d, the centre point of 12; then when A is at 2 C will be at the point E on Dd such that $DE =$ twice 12, and similarly any number of successive points can be determined.

EXAMPLES.

1.   Draw a Harmonic Curve given the length AB of a vibration and a point P on the curve.

[From P draw PN perpendicular to AB meeting it in N.   If a is the amplitude of the vibration $PN = a \sin \theta$,

and $\qquad\qquad \theta : 2\pi :: AN : AB$,

$$\therefore a = \frac{PN}{\sin \dfrac{2\pi \cdot AN}{AB}},$$

which determines a.

The expression $2\pi \cdot \dfrac{AN}{AB}$ is the circular measure of the angle, the sine of which can then be obtained from a trigonometrical table.]

As a numerical example take $AB = 10 \cdot 8$, $AN = 1 \cdot 75$, $PN = 1 \cdot 67$. a then equals $1 \cdot 96$ very approximately.

2.   Draw a Cassini's oval, the foci F, F_1, and a point P on the curve being given.

[Take a mean proportional (k) between the focal distances FP, F_1P. k is the constant of the curve.   Prob. 154.]

3.   Draw a Cassini's oval, the foci F, F_1 and a tangent PT being given.

[Bisect FF_1 in C and draw CT perpendicular to PT meeting it in T.   From one of the foci F draw a line meeting CT in Q

and on CF_1 describe a segment of a circle containing an angle equal to the angle CQF (Prob. 30) and cutting FQ in p. The locus of p will intersect the given tangent in its point of contact, and the question reduces to the preceding. The line FQ must be drawn within certain limiting positions in order that the circle may meet it in real points.]

4. Draw through a focus F of a lemniscate a line which shall cut the curve at a given angle a.

[Let C be the centre and F_1 the second focus. On CF_1 describe a segment of a circle containing an angle $\frac{\pi}{2} - a$, and meeting the curve in P. FP will be the required line.]

5. Given the centre C, direction of axis CA, and a point P, on a lemniscate, draw the tangent at the point.

[Draw CB perpendicular to CA, and CT (between CB and CP) making the angle BCT = angle ACP. Bisect CP in D and draw DT perpendicular to CP. T will be a point on the tangent at P.]

6. Describe a lemniscate with given centre C, given direction of axis CA, and to cut a given right line at a given angle.

[The direction of a tangent is obviously given. Through C draw a line parallel to this given direction, and the angle between this line and CB, perpendicular to CA, is three times the angle ACP, where P is the point in which the required tangent meets the given line.]

7. Describe a lemniscate, with given centre C, given direction of axis CA, and to pass through a given point P.

[Draw the tangent and normal at P. Ex. 5. Let the normal meet CA in G. Bisect the angle CPG by PD meeting CA in D. Through P draw lines making equal angles with PD and cutting off equal distances CF, CF_1 on CA. (Prob. 19.) F and F_1 are the foci of the required curve.]

8. *ab, a'ab'* are two lines at right angles to each other and
$a'a = ab' = \frac{1}{2}ab$. *ab* moves round in the plane of the two lines till
b comes to *b'* and *a* to *a'*, the centre point *c* of *ab* moving always
along *ca* and a certain point *d* of *ab* describing a circular arc
round *b'*. Determine the position of *d* and draw the loci of *b* and
a throughout the motion.

9. A pendulum 5" long vibrates uniformly in an arc of 40°.
A fly starting at the bottom crawls at a uniform speed to the
top, arriving there in the time taken by a forward and backward
swing of the pendulum. Trace the course of the fly.

10. A train is running in a straight line at 10 miles an
hour. The door (30" wide) of one of the carriages is opened
with uniform angular velocity till it stands at right angles to the
direction of motion in $\frac{1}{2}$ a second and closed again in the same
time. Draw the curve traced out by a point on the edge of the
door. Scale, $\frac{1}{2}$ = 1 foot (Harmonic Curve).

11. *BD* is a line $1\frac{3}{4}$" long. Draw *AB, DC* perpendicular to
BD and each 2" long, the points *A* and *C* being on opposite sides
of *BD*. Consider these lines as three bars jointed at *B* and *D*,
and free to turn in the plane of the paper about the points *A* and
C as centres. Trace the locus of the centre point of *BD*.

[The complete locus is a figure of 8, the central portion being
very nearly straight lines.]

12. *C* is the centre of a circle, *A* and *B* are points outside
the circle and in its plane. A double string is wrapped round
the circle and the free loop is led off so that one portion passes
round *A* and the other round *B*. Shew that any fixed point on
the loop describes an hyperbola as the string is unwound by the
rotation of the circle.

As a particular example take *CA* = 2", *CB* = 2", diameter of
circle $\frac{7}{8}$", and one position of the tracing point $1\frac{1}{4}$" from *A* and
$2\frac{1}{4}$" from *B*.

CHAPTER XIII.

SOLUTION OF EQUATIONS.

Graphic methods may be applied to the solution of algebraical and trigonometrical equations, and in certain cases the process is much simpler and more expeditious than the arithmetical or analytical one. This is particularly the case with certain statical questions in which a position of equilibrium is defined by two angles for which two equations are given. " The equation for either variable which results from eliminating the other may be one of high degree, the approximate solution of which by the methods of the Theory of Equations would be very troublesome. In such cases it is often possible to obtain a solution sufficiently accurate for practical purposes by constructing curves corresponding to the equations and taking their points of intersection*."

For example, to find θ from the equation

$$c \sin (2\theta - a) = a \sin \theta \dots\dots\dots\dots\dots\dots(1),$$

c, a and a being given constants.

If we trace the curves $r = a \sin \theta$,

$$r = c \sin (2\theta - a),$$

then at their points of intersection the equation (1) is satisfied—the same origin and initial line being of course taken in tracing both loci.

---

* Minchin's *Statics*, 3rd Edition, p. 49.

At first a rough tracing only is necessary, the object of this rough preliminary tracing being merely to find the places in the neighbourhood of which the curves really intersect. Then devote very special care to the tracing of the curves in these indicated neighbourhoods and in these alone. We shall thus get a value or values of the unknown variable accurate within certain narrow limits of error due to the draughtsmanship and possibility of measuring given quantities. This is as exact a solution as the graphic method pure and simple enables us to obtain, but by analysis a further step can be taken. We have obtained a near value (say ω) of θ, which does not quite satisfy (1), but $\omega + \delta$ does, where δ is a small unknown quantity. If we write $\omega + \delta$ for θ in (1) and then, δ being very small, put $\cos \delta = 1$, $\sin \delta = \delta$, we have

$$c \sin (2\omega - a) + 2c \cos (2\omega - a) \times \delta = a \sin \omega + a \cos \omega \times \delta,$$

$$\therefore \; \delta = \frac{a \sin \omega - c \sin (2\omega - a)}{2c \cos (2\omega - a) - a \cos \omega},$$

so that δ and therefore $\omega + \delta$, or a still nearer value of θ, is known.

In general, if we have to solve $F(\theta) = f(\theta)$, i.e. any given function of $\theta = $ to some other given function, we may trace the curves $\qquad r = F(\theta); \; r = f(\theta),$

and get an approximate value ω of θ from their points of intersection as above. Then the correction δ is given by the equation

$$F(\omega) + \delta F'(\omega) = f(\omega) + \delta f'(\omega),$$

or $\qquad\qquad \delta = \frac{f(\omega) - F(\omega)}{F'(\omega) - f'(\omega)};$

the dashes denoting the differential coefficients of the original functions.

Example:—Solve the equation $2^\theta = 5 \sin \theta$.

$r = 2^\theta$ represents an equiangular spiral, (Prob. 149),

$r = 5 \sin \theta$ represents a circle of diameter 5 units, passing through the origin and its centre on line through the origin perpendicular to the initial line.

Let ω be the circular measure of the angle between the initial line and the radius drawn from the origin to a point of intersection of these curves, then

$$\delta = \frac{2^\omega - 5 \sin \omega}{5 \cos \omega - 2^\omega \log_e 2},$$

ω will be an approximate solution of the original equation; and ω + δ a more exact one.

PROBLEM 173. *To solve the quadratic equation*

$$x^2 - 2Ax + B^2 = 0 \text{ (Fig. 178).}$$

Draw two lines Oa, Ob at right angles to each other, and on one of them make $Ob = B$.

With b as centre and A as radius describe an arc cutting Oa in a, so that $Oa = \sqrt{A^2 - B^2}$; and with centre a and radius ab

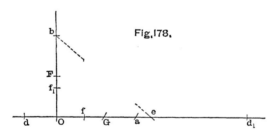

Fig. 178.

describe arcs cutting Oa in d and d_1. Od and Od_1 are lines representing the two values of x in the above equation. If the numerical values of the roots are required they must be measured of course on the same scale which has been used for laying off the lengths A and B.

If A is numerically less than B the roots become imaginary, and the graphic method is not applicable.

As a numerical example we may take the equation to determine the length AK in problem 169.

Here AK is one of the roots of $kr^2 - \overline{2 + k}|cr + c^2 = 0$,

or $\qquad r^2 - \dfrac{2 + k}{k} c . r + \dfrac{c^2}{k} = 0,$

which is of the above form if $A = \dfrac{(2+k)\,c}{2k}$ and $B = \dfrac{c}{\sqrt{k}}$.

Suppose $k = \dfrac{3}{2}$ then $A = \dfrac{7c}{6}$ and $B = \dfrac{\sqrt{2}}{\sqrt{3}}c$,

where c is a given length.

Make Oe in fig. $178 =$ this given length c.

On Oa, Ob, take $Of = Of_1$, then ff_1 represents $\sqrt{2}$ the length Of being the unit; make OF on $Ob = ff_1$.

With centre f_1 and radius $= 2$. Of describe an arc cutting Oa in G, then OG represents $\sqrt{3}$, the length Of being the unit. Through e draw a parallel to FG meeting Ob in b.

Since evidently $\qquad Ob : Oe :: \sqrt{2} : \sqrt{3}$,

$Ob =$ the constant B of the equation.

With centre b and radius $= \dfrac{7c}{6}$ describe an arc cutting Oa in a, and with centre a and radius ab describe arcs cutting Oa in d and d_1. Od, Od_1 represent the values of r in the equation, and the particular value of AK in Problem 169 is $Od = \dfrac{Oe}{3}$.

PROBLEM 174. *To solve the quadratic equation*

$$x^2 + 2Ax + B^2 = 0.$$

The solution is exactly the same as that of the last problem, but both roots are negative.

PROBLEM 175. *To solve the quadratic equation*

$$x^2 - 2Ax - B^2 = 0 \text{ (Fig. 179)}.$$

Draw 2 lines Oa, Ob at right angles to each other and on them make $Oa = A$, $Ob = B$:

then $\qquad\qquad ab = \sqrt{A^2 + B^2}$.

With centre a and radius ab describe an arc cutting Oa in d

and d_1. Od, Od_1 represent the roots of the equation, but the smaller one must be taken with negative sign.

A may be greater or less than B.

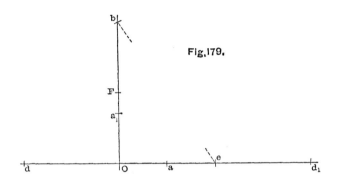

Fig. 179.

PROBLEM 176.   *To solve the quadratic equation*

$$x^2 + 2Ax - B^2 = 0.$$

The solution is identical with that of the last problem, but the greater root must be taken with negative sign.

As a numerical example take the equation to determine the length AL in Problem 169.

$$r^2 + cr - \left(\frac{c}{\sqrt{k}}\right)^2 = 0 \text{ so that } A = \frac{c}{2} \text{ and } B = \frac{c}{\sqrt{k}},$$

suppose $k = \frac{1}{2}$. $\therefore$ $Ob : c :: \sqrt{2} : 1.$

Make $Oe = c$; bisect Oe in a and make $Oa_1 = Oa$ so that

$$aa_1 : Oa :: \sqrt{2} : 1.$$

Make OF on $Ob = aa_1$ and through e draw eb parallel to aF;

then $Ob = B.$

With centre a and radius ab describe arcs cutting Oa in d and d_1. Od is the positive root of the equation, and is the length AL in curve No. 3 of Problem 169.

$a \cos \theta + b \sin \theta = c.$

PROBLEM 177.   *To solve graphically the equation*
$$a \cos \theta + b \sin \theta = c \text{ (Fig. 180).}$$

Draw 2 lines at right angles to each other as $AO, AB.$ Make
$AO = a$ and $AB = b$ on any convenient scale.   Describe a circle

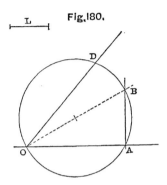

Fig. 180.

round OAB (its centre will of course be at the middle point of
OB) and with centre O and radius $OD = c$ describe an arc cutting
it in D, the angle AOD is the required angle θ.

[In the figure $a = 2\cdot5$, $b = 1\cdot3$, $c = 2\cdot65$, the unit being the
length L and $\theta = 47\cdot5°.$]

Proof. $\cos BOD = \dfrac{OD}{OB} = \dfrac{c}{OB},$

$$\cos (AOD - AOB) = \dfrac{c}{OB},$$

$$\cos AOD \cos AOB + \sin AOD \sin AOB = \dfrac{c}{OB},$$

$$\cos AOD \, \dfrac{a}{OB} + \sin AOD \, \dfrac{b}{OB} = \dfrac{c}{OB},$$

$$\therefore \ AOD = \theta.$$

The second point D_1 in which the arc described with centre O
and radius c would cut the circle gives when c is greater than a a
second solution, the angle AOD_1 being the value of θ in this case.

When c is less than a so that D_1 falls between O and A the
second solution corresponds to $a \cos \theta - b \sin \theta = c.$

PROBLEM 178. *A and B are two fixed points and P a variable point, the position of which is defined by the angles PAB (= θ) and PBA (= ϕ); draw the locus represented by the equation*

$$sin\ \theta + sin\ \phi = a,$$

where a is constant. [*a may be either positive or negative but its numerical value cannot be greater than* 2.] (Fig. 181.)

On AB make $BC = a \cdot AB$, and describe a semi-circle on AB. Draw a line Ap meeting the semi-circle in p and on BA make

Fig. 181.

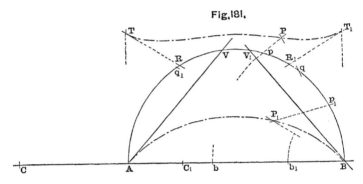

$Bb = Bp$. With centre A and radius $= bC$ describe an arc cutting the semi-circle in q, and draw Bq cutting Ap in P. P will be a point on the required locus. Similarly any number of points can be determined.

If a is greater than unity, i.e. if BC is greater than AB, the locus will meet AT, BT_1 drawn perpendicular to AB, in points T and T_1 determined by inflecting AR, BR in the semi-circle each equal to AC and drawing BR, AR_1 meeting AT, BT_1 in T and T_1 respectively. BT, AT_1 are tangents to the required locus at T and T_1. Lines drawn from A to points between R_1 and B do not intersect the locus in real points.

If a is less than unity, i.e. if BC_1 is less than AB, the curve passes through A and B and the tangents at those points can be drawn by inflecting BV, AV_1 in the semi-circle each equal to BC_1. AV, BV_1 are tangents to the required curve. In the figure the value of a for the upper curve is $\frac{3}{2}$ and for the lower $\frac{3}{4}$. There are similar branches on the other side of AB corresponding to negative values of the angles.

Proof. $\qquad$ $\sin PAB = \dfrac{pB}{AB}$, and $\sin PBA = \dfrac{Aq}{AB}$,

i.e. $\qquad$ $\sin \theta + \sin \phi = \dfrac{pB + Aq}{AB} = \dfrac{Bb + bC}{AB} = \dfrac{BC}{AB} = a.$

PROBLEM 179. *To determine values of r and θ which simultaneously satisfy the equations*

$$r^2 \cos 2\theta = a^2 \ldots (1), \ and \ r . \sin \overline{a - \theta} = b . \sin a \ldots (2),$$

where θ is the angle between the radius vector r and a fixed right line and a, b and a are constants.

Equation (2) may be written $\dfrac{r}{b} = \dfrac{\sin a}{\sin (a - \theta)}$, so that r and b are evidently sides of a triangle the opposite angles of which are a (or $\pi - a$) and $\overline{a - \theta}$.

Let OA (fig. 182) be the fixed straight line from which θ is measured, O the origin. On it make $OB = b$ and through B draw

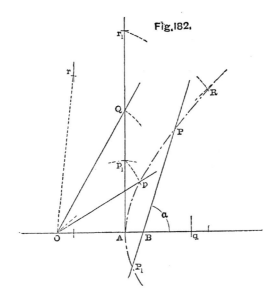

Fig.182.

BP making an angle α with the positive direction of the initial line. BP is the locus represented by (2), for P being any point on it $OP = r$ and $BOP = \theta$, so that

$$\frac{OP}{OB} = \frac{\sin OBP}{\sin BPO} = \frac{\sin \alpha}{\sin \alpha - \theta}.$$

To find points on the second locus. Make $OA = a$; when $\theta = O$, $r = \pm a$ so that the curve passes through A, and A_1 on the other side of O such that $OA_1 = a$ would be a second point on the locus. The curve is symmetrical about OA because negative values of θ give the same r as the corresponding positive values. Through O draw any line Op and make the angle $AOQ =$ twice the angle AOp. Draw AQ perpendicular to OA meeting OQ in Q, then $\cos 2 . AOp = \dfrac{OA}{OQ}$, and $\therefore$ if p is a point on the curve

$$Op^2 . \frac{OA}{OQ} = OA^2,$$

or
$$Op^2 = OA . OQ.$$

Make Oq on $OA = OQ$ and on Oq describe a semi-circle cutting AQ in p_1 and make $Op = Op_1$. Similarly any additional number of points on the curve may be determined, and at the points P and P_1 where the line BP intersects the curve the same values of θ and r hold for both.

As the angle AOp increases the line OQ will not intersect AQ within any reasonable distance; the length OQ may however be determined by bisecting or quadrisecting OA and taking the intersection of the ordinate through the point of division with the line corresponding to OQ—the distance of which from O will be the half or quarter of the diameter of the required semi-circle. The length Or, for example, corresponding to the radius vector OR is one-fourth the diameter of the semi-circle which determines r_1 on AQ and so the length OR.

The only portions of the second locus which it is necessary to trace, are of course those in the immediate neighbourhood of the points where it cuts the line, and a trial or two readily shews whereabouts the radii Op should be drawn.

The second locus is a rectangular hyperbola with centre O and transverse axis $2a$, and if this were recognised from the equation, the ordinary method of drawing an hyperbola might of course be adopted.

PROBLEM 180. *A and B are two fixed points and P a variable point, whose position is defined by the angles PAB ($= \theta$) and PBA ($= \phi$), what locus is represented by the equation*

$$a \cot (\theta - \alpha) + b \cot (\phi - \beta) = c,$$

where a, b, c, α, β are constants?

Equations of which the above is the general form frequently occur in statical problems, and therefore a knowledge of what it represents and how it is liable to modification may be useful (Fig. 183).

Draw AC, BC making with AB the angles $BAC = \alpha$ and $ABC = \beta$. The required locus is a conic circumscribing the tri-

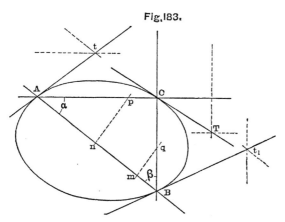

Fig. 183.

angle ABC, the tangents to which at those points are easily drawn.

The distance of any point T on the tangent at C from BC : its distance from AC produced :: $b \sin \alpha : a \sin \beta$.

If Ap on $AC = b$ and pn be drawn perpendicular to AB,

$$pn = b \sin a,$$

and if Bq on $BC = a$ and qm be drawn perpendicular to AB,

$$qm = a \sin \beta.$$

T can therefore be determined by drawing parallels to BC and AC at distances $= pn$ and qm respectively.

The tangent at A divides the exterior angle at A so that the distance of any point t from AC : distance from

$$AB :: a : (a \cot a + b \cot \beta + c) \sin a.$$

The length given by this last term is easily obtained, for if the angle mAB (fig. 184) $= a$, and Bm perpendicular to $Am = a$, $Am = a \cot a$, draw Bk parallel to Am and make $kBC = \beta$, and Ck perpendicular to $Bk = b$,

then $\qquad\qquad Bk$ or $mn = b \cot \beta$,

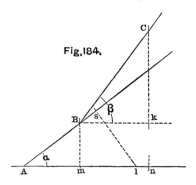

Fig.184.

make $nl = c$, l being taken on the same side of n as A if c is negative and on the opposite side if c is positive and the length $Al = a \cot a + b \cot \beta \pm c$: from l draw ls perpendicular to AB and $ls = Al \sin a$.

The tangent at A is determined by drawing parallels to AC, AB respectively at distances a and ls intersecting in t.

Similarly the tangent at B divides the exterior angle at B so that the distance of any point t_1 from BC : its distance from AB

$$:: b : (a \cot a + b \cot \beta + c) \sin \beta.$$

The conic is therefore completely determined.

E. $\qquad\qquad\qquad\qquad\qquad\qquad\qquad\qquad\qquad$ 24

$a \cos \theta + b \cos \phi = c$ and $k \cot \theta + l \cot \phi = m.$

If $a \cot a + b \cot \beta + c = 0$ the tangents at A and B evidently coincide with the line AB, and the locus becomes a straight line through C, identical with the tangent at C in the general case.

If a and β both equal zero, i.e. if the equation is
$$a \cot \theta + b \cot \phi = c,$$
the locus is a right line, which may be constructed as shewn in the next problem; for the point C is evidently in this case somewhere on the line AB, and the tangents at A and B again coincide with the line AB.

PROBLEM 181.   *To solve the equations*
$$a \cos \theta + b \cos \phi = c \dots\dots\dots\dots\dots\dots (1),$$
$$k \cot \theta + l \cot \phi = m \dots\dots\dots\dots\dots (2),$$
where a, b, c, k, l, m are constants (Fig. 185).

The second equation represents a right line which may be

Fig. 185.

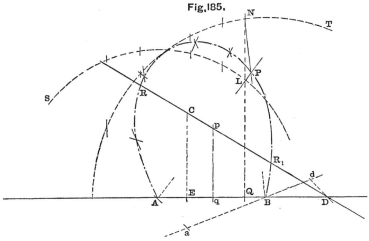

drawn as follows : Draw any straight line AB and produce it to D so that $AB : BD :: l - k : k$, and draw DC so that $\cot CDB = \dfrac{m}{l-k}$, i.e. if $DE = m$, $EC = l - k$.

[On any line through B make $Bd = k$, $da = l$, and draw dD parallel to Aa. This determines D. Make $DE = m$ and EC perpendicular to DE, $= aB$.

At any point p of the line we have, if $pAq = \theta$, $pBq = \phi$,

$$\cot \theta = \frac{Aq}{pq}, \quad \cot \phi = \frac{Bq}{pq},$$

and we want to shew therefore that

$$k \cdot Aq + l \cdot Bq = m \cdot pq \ldots\ldots\ldots\ldots\ldots\ldots\ldots (a);$$

but $$\frac{pq}{CE} = \frac{Dq}{DE}, \text{ or } pq = \frac{l-k}{m} \cdot Dq,$$

$\therefore$ (a) may be written $k\,(Aq + Dq) = l\,(Dq - Bq)$,

i.e. $k \cdot AD = l \cdot BD$,

which by construction it does.]

To find points on the locus represented by (1). With the points A and B as centres describe two circles S and T of radii $\frac{a}{c} \cdot AB$ and $\frac{b}{c} \cdot AB$ respectively. Draw any common ordinate NLQ, meeting S in L and T in N; then the lines AL and BN intersect in a point, P, on the required locus; for

$$AQ + QB = AB,$$

or $\quad AL \cos \theta + BN \cos \phi = AB$, if BAL is θ and ABN is ϕ,

or $\qquad \frac{a}{c} \cdot AB \cdot \cos \theta + \frac{b}{c} AB \cos \phi = AB,$

which is the given equation.

If the line DC meet the curve in R and R_1 the angles RAB, R_1AB are the required values of θ, and the angles RBA, R_1BA those of ϕ.

There is a precisely similar loop on the other side of AB.

In the particular case in which $a = b$ the locus is the *Magnetic Curve.* (Prob. 168.)

PROBLEM 182. *To find θ and ϕ from the equations*

$$\frac{a}{\sin \theta} + \frac{b}{\sin \phi} = c \ldots (1), \text{ and } \cos \theta = k \cos \phi \ldots (2),$$

where a, b, c, k are constants (Fig. 186).

$$\frac{a}{\sin\theta} + \frac{b}{\sin\phi} = c \quad \text{and} \quad \cos\theta = k\cos\phi.$$

Take two points A and B such that $AB = \overline{a + b}$; make $AO = a$, $OB = b$ and draw OD perpendicular to AB; with A as centre and

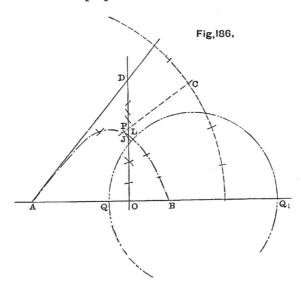

Fig. 186.

c as radius describe a circle, and draw any radius AC meeting OD in L; inflect $BJ = LC$ (J being on OD); then P, the point of intersection of AC and BJ is a point on the locus represented by (1), the angles θ and ϕ being ALO and BJO respectively.

There is a precisely similar loop on the other side of AB.

Again the equation $\cos\theta = k\cos\phi$ gives $\sin PAB = k \cdot \sin PBA$ or $PB = k \cdot PA$, i.e. P is the vertex of a triangle on a given base AB and with sides in a given ratio (Problem 17), i.e. the locus represented by the second equation is a circle whose diameter QQ_1 is the line joining the points which divide AB internally and externally in the ratio $1 : k$; i.e.

$$AQ : QB :: 1 : k :: AQ_1 : Q_1B.$$

The values of θ and ϕ which satisfy both equations are those belonging to the points of intersection of this circle and the previous curve.

EXAMPLES.

1. Solve the equation $\dfrac{\sin x}{x} = \dfrac{1}{2}$.

[Trace the loci $y = \sin x$ (harmonic curve) and $y = \dfrac{x}{2}$ (a straight line through the origin) : the values of x corresponding to their points of intersection are solutions.]

2. Solve the equation $\sin x = ax + b$.

[The intersections of the harmonic curve $y = \sin x$ and of the straight line $y = ax + b$ where a and b are constants.]

3. Solve the equation $2^\theta = 5 \sin \theta$.

[The intersections of the equiangular spiral $r = 2^\theta$ and of the circle $r = 5 \sin \theta$.]

4. Find θ and ϕ from the equations

$$\tan \phi = n \tan \theta \dots\dots\dots\dots\dots\dots\dots\dots(1),$$

$$a \cos \theta = b \cos \phi + c \dots\dots\dots\dots\dots\dots (2),$$

where a, b, c and n are given constants.

[The 2nd equation represents a locus identical with (1) of Problem 181, attention being paid to the usual conventions as to sign.

The 1st equation represents a right line perpendicular to AB (fig. 185), the base of this locus, and meeting it in D so that

$$AD = n \cdot BD.]$$

5. Find θ and ϕ from the equations

$$l \cos \theta + n \cos \phi = a - m \cos a,$$

$$l \sin \theta - n \sin \phi = m \sin a$$

where l, m, n, a and a are constants.

[Draw two lines AB, AC including an angle a, and make $AB = a$ and $AC = m$. With centres B and C and radii $= n$ and l

respectively describe arcs intersecting in D on the same side of BC as AB. Let CD meet AB in E. BED is the required value of θ and DBE that of ϕ.]

6. Determine θ from the equation

$$a \cos \lambda \cdot \cos (\lambda + 2\theta) = c \cdot \cos (\alpha + \theta)$$

where a, c, λ and α are given constants.

[The locus represented by the right-hand side of the above equation is a circle of radius c, the origin (O) being the extremity of a diameter, and the initial line making an angle α therewith.

To draw the locus represented by the left-hand side :—draw a line through the origin O making an angle λ with the initial line, and on it measure a length $OL = a$. Draw LN perpendicular to the initial line meeting it in N so that $ON = a \cos \lambda$. With centre O and radius ON describe a circle. From any point Q on this circle draw QM perpendicular to OL meeting it in M. Draw OP bisecting the angle NOQ and make $OP = OM$. P will be a point on the second locus, and any additional number of points may be similarly determined. Let the two loci intersect in X, and the angle between OX and the initial line is the required angle θ.]

This equation defines the position of equilibrium of a uniform rectangular board resting in a vertical plane against two equally rough pegs in a horizontal line.

THE END.

CAMBRIDGE: PRINTED BY C. J. CLAY, M.A. & SON, AT THE UNIVERSITY PRESS.

Recent Mathematical Publications.

Applied Mechanics: an Elementary General Introduction to the Theory of Structures and Machines. By JAMES H. COTTERILL, F.R.S., Associate Member of the Council of the Institution of Naval Architects, Associate Member of the Institution of Civil Engineers, Professor of Applied Mechanics in the Royal Naval College, Greenwich. Medium 8vo. 18s.

A Treatise on Differential Equations. By ANDREW RUSSELL FORSYTH, M.A., Fellow and Assistant Tutor of Trinity College, Cambridge. 8vo. 14s.

Integral Calculus, an Elementary Treatise on the; Founded on the Method of Rates or Fluxions. By WILLIAM WOOLSEY JOHNSON, Professor of Mathematics at the United States Naval Academy, Annopolis, Maryland. Demy 8vo. 8s.

Curve Tracing in Cartesian Co-ordinates. By the same Author. Crown 8vo. 4s. 6d.

Differential Calculus, an Elementary Treatise on the; Founded on the Method of Rates or Fluxions. By JOHN MINOT RICE, Professor of Mathematics in the United States Navy, and WILLIAM WOOLSEY JOHNSON, Professor of Mathematics at the United States Naval Academy. Third Edition, Revised and Corrected. Demy 8vo. 16s. Abridged Edition, 8s.

A Treatise on the Calculus of Variations. Arranged with the purpose of Introducing, as well as Illustrating, its Principles to the Reader by means of Problems, and Designed to present in all Important Particulars a Complete View of the Present State of the Science. By LEWIS BUFFETT CARLL, A.M. Demy 8vo. 21s.

A Treatise on the Dynamics of the System of Rigid Bodies. By EDWARD JOHN ROUTH, D.Sc., LL.D., F.R.S., Fellow of the University of London, Hon. Fellow of St Peter's College, Cambridge. With numerous Examples. Fourth and enlarged Edition. Two Vols. 8vo. Vol. I.—Elementary Parts. 14s. Vol. II.—The Advanced Parts. 14s.

A Text Book of the Method of Least Squares. By MANSFIELD MERRIMAN, Professor of Civil Engineering at Lehigh University, Member of the American Philosophical Society, American Association for the Advancement of Science, American Society of Civil Engineers' Club of Philadelphia, Deutschen Geometervereins, &c. Demy 8vo. 8s. 6d.

Differential and Integral Calculus. A Practical Treatise. By A. G. GREENHILL, M.A., Professor of Mathematics to the Senior Class of Artillery Officers, Woolwich, and Examiner in Mathematics at the University of London. Crown 8vo. 7s. 6d.

Weekly Problem Papers. With Notes intended for the use of students preparing for Mathematical Scholarships, and for the Junior Members of the Universities who are reading for Mathematical Honours. By the Rev. JOHN J. MILNE, M.A., Second Master of Heversham Grammar School. Pott 8vo. 4s. 6d.

MACMILLAN AND CO., LONDON.

Recent Mathematical Publications.

Solutions to Weekly Problem Papers. By the Rev. JOHN J. MILNE, M.A. Crown 8vo. 10s. 6d.

Constructive Geometry of Plane Curves. With numerous Examples. By T. H. EAGLES, M.A., Instructor in Geometrical Drawing, and Lecturer in Architecture at the Royal Indian Engineering College, Coopers Hill. Crown 8vo. 12s.

Elementary Algebra for Schools. By H. S. HALL, B.A., Master of the Military and Engineering Side, Clifton College; and S. R. KNIGHT, B.A., late Assistant Master at Marlborough College. In Globe 8vo., price 3s. 6d.; with Answers, 4s. 6d.

"This is, in our opinion, the best *Elementary* algebra for school use ... We confidently recommend it to mathematical teachers, who we feel sure will find it the best book of its kind for teaching purposes. Many subjects of interest are also treated of, and a vast collection of (3,500) examples will furnish ample exercise for the boys, and save the teacher the trouble of concocting illustrations of the best methods."—*Nature.*

Algebraical Exercises and Examination Papers. To accompany the above. By the same Authors. Globe 8vo.
[*In preparation.*

Higher Algebra for Schools. By the same Authors. Globe 8vo.
[*In preparation.*

Conic Sections. By CHARLES SMITH, M.A., Fellow and Tutor of Sidney Sussex College, Cambridge. Second Edition. Crown 8vo. 7s. 6d.

An Elementary Treatise on Solid Geometry. By the same Author. Crown 8vo. 9s. 6d.

Elementary Algebra. By the same Author. Crown 8vo.
[*Shortly.*

Elementary Geometry. Books I.—V. Containing the Subjects of Euclid's first Six Books. Following the Syllabus of the Geometrical Association. By the Rev. J. M. WILSON, M.A., Head Master of Clifton College. New Edition. Extra fcap. 8vo. 4s. 6d.

Euclid and his Modern Rivals. By CHARLES L. DODGSON, M.A., Student and late Mathematical Lecturer of Christ Church, Oxford. Second Edition. Crown 8vo. 6s.

Physical Arithmetic. By ALEXANDER MACFARLANE, M.A., D.Sc., F.R.S.E., Examiner in Mathematics to the University of Edinburgh. Crown 8vo. 7s. 6d.

Differential Calculus for Beginners. By ALEXANDER KNOX, B.A. 18mo. 3s. 6d.

Elementary Trigonometry. By Rev. J. B. LOCK, M.A., Senior Fellow, Assistant Tutor and Lecturer in Mathematics, of Gonville and Caius College, Cambridge; late Assistant Master at Eton. Globe 8vo. 4s. 6d.

Higher Trigonometry. By the same Author. Globe 8vo. 4s. 6d. Both Parts complete in One Volume. Globe 8vo. 7s. 6d.

MACMILLAN AND CO., LONDON.

210212